Happy b   y

Love f

5/8/10

The Scottish Nation: Identity and History

THE SCOTTISH NATION IDENTITY AND HISTORY

Essays in Honour of William Ferguson

Edited by
ALEXANDER MURDOCH

with the assistance of
EDWARD J. COWAN AND RICHARD J. FINLAY

First published in Great Britain in 2007 by
John Donald, an imprint of Birlinn Ltd

West Newington House
10 Newington Road
EdinburghEH9 1QS

www.birlinn.co.uk

ISBN 10: 1 904607 69 1
ISBN 13: 978 1 904607 69 4

The publishers gratefully acknowledge subsidy from the Scottish Historical
Trust and the Strathmartine Trust in the publication of this volume

British Library Cataloguing-in-Publication Data
A catalogue record for this book is available
on request from the British Library

Typeset by Vikki Reilly
Printed and bound in Britain by
Cromwell Press, Trowbridge, Wiltshire.

Contents

Foreword

It is now a commonplace to assert that the last three decades or so have seen a remarkable flourishing of Scottish historical studies. This has not simply been a matter of increased volume of published research, though that has indeed been a notable feature of the period. But, in addition, the number of postgraduate students is now greater than ever before and the national media shows an interest in the Scottish past to an extent that would have been surprising even a few years ago. Undeniably the strengthening of Scottish identity and the restoration of a parliament in Scotland after three centuries has powerfully influenced these positive developments.

Those scholars working in the field in 2007, however, would do well to remember and appreciate the pioneers of a previous generation whose outstanding contributions laid the firm foundations for the high-quality contemporary Scottish historiography which has sustained the renaissance. The historians of the 1950s to the 1970s were very few in number, but several were researchers of great ability and influence. That group included William Ferguson, whose eminence as a leading historian of Scotland is suitably and rightly honoured by the publication of this volume written by his former students and colleagues.

I was in my final honours year in 1968 when Bill Ferguson's pathbreaking *Scotland: 1689 to the Present* appeared as the fourth volume in The Edinburgh History of Scotland series. To that point Scottish History was imbalanced in its coverage, with the focus of most existing research effort on earlier times. Dr Ferguson therefore had almost to carve out a new intellectual territory, using for the most part original sources and the odd piece of published scholarship which had been written on the modern period. It is no exaggeration to say that this book provided the road map for a new generation of postgraduate students with an interest in the more recent Scottish past. As one of that cadre, I can say that we all owe Dr Ferguson a profound debt of gratitude for leading the way. It was not simply the new vistas revealed in this work and in his two later books, *Scotland's Relations with England* (1977) and the prize-winning *The Identity of the Scottish Nation* (1998) – deeper than those was the visible integrity of his scholarship: the importance of precision of expression; the vital connection between generalisation and evidence; the criticism, when warranted, of work which fell below his own high standards; and the scorn, as he himself put it, for 'fashionable present-day conceits'.

All those who have made this book possible are grateful to Bill Ferguson for all this and more. We hope he enjoys it.

T.M. Devine

Abbreviations

Ayrshire YU Fed Comm Mins	Ayrshire Young Unionists Federation Committee Minutes
BL	British Library
Bodl. Ms	Bodleian Manuscript
CACUA	Central Ayrshire Conservative & Unionist Association
CAYC Coun Mins	Central Ayrshire Young Conservatives Council Minutes
CAYC Ex Comm Mins	Central Ayrshire Young Conservatives Executive Committee Minutes
DNB	*Dictionary of National Biography*
EDC	Eastern District Council
Eglinton YC Mins	Eglinton Young Conservatives Minutes
EUL	Edinburgh University Library
EUNCL	Edinburgh University New College Library
Ex Comm Mins	Executive Committee Minutes
GCA	Glasgow City Archives
Glas YCRC Min	Glasgow Young Conservatives Regional Committee Minutes
Hist. Parlia.	The History of Parliament: *The House of Commons, 1790–1820*
HMC	Historical Manuscripts Commission
Kilwinning JU Mins	Kilwinning Junior Unionists Minutes
NAS	National Archives of Scotland

NLS	National Library of Scotland
NRA(S)	National Register of Archives (Scotland)
Oxford DNB	*Oxford Dictionary of National Biography*
OUP	Oxford University Press
SCUA	Scottish Conservative & Unionist Association
SHR	*Scottish Historical Review*
SJU Cen Coun Mins	Scottish Junior Unionists Central Council Minutes
SJUWA Comm Min	Scottish Junior Unionists Western Area Committee Minutes
STUC	Scottish Trades Union Congress
SYC Cen Coun Mins	Scottish Young Conservatives Central Council Minutes
TNA	The National Archives, Kew
WDA	Western Divisional Council
WDCOSJM Mins	Western Divisional Council Organising Secretaries Joint Meeting Minutes

A Bibliography of the Works of William Ferguson

THESIS

'Electoral Law and Procedure in Eighteenth and Early Nineteenth Century Scotland', University of Glasgow PhD thesis, 1957.

BOOKS

Scotland: 1689 to the Present, being volume IV of *The Edinburgh History of Scotland*, General Editor Gordon Donaldson (Edinburgh, 1968; paperback edition 1978)

Scotland's Relations with England: A Survey to 1707 (Edinburgh 1977, reissued in a new edition 1994)

The Identity of the Scottish Nation: An Historic Quest (Edinburgh, 1998)

ARTICLES

'The Urquharts of Cromarty', *The Scottish Genealogist*, vol. VI (1959), no. 2, 16–18, and no. 3, pp. 1–14

'Dingwall Burgh Politics and the Parliamentary Franchise in the Eighteenth Century', *Scottish Historical Review*, 38 (1959), pp. 89–108

'A Note on the Edinburgh University Library MS "Brian Fairfax's Account"', *The Bibliotheck, A Journal of Bibliographical Notes and Queries Mainly of Scottish Interest*, vol. 3, no. 2 (1960), pp. 71–2.

'The Making of the Treaty of Union of 1707', *Scottish Historical Review*, 43 (1964), pp. 89–110

'Carlyle as Historian', *The Carlyle Society of Edinburgh* (1966), pp. 1–13

'The Reform Act (Scotland) of 1832: Intention and Effect', *Scottish Historical Review*, 45 (1966), pp. 105–114

'The Problems of the Established Church in the West Highlands and Islands in the Eighteenth Century,' *Records of the Scottish Church History Society*, XVII (1972), pp. 15–31

'Imperial Crowns: A Neglected Facet of the Background to the Treaty of Union of 1707', *Scottish Historical Review*, 53 (1974), pp. 22–44

'Recent Interpretations of the Making of the Treaty of Union of 1707', *Scottish Tradition*, vii–viii (1977–8), pp. 95–114

'The Electoral System in the Scottish Counties before 1832', *Stair Society Miscellany 2* (1984), pp. 261–94

'George Buchanan and the Picts', *Scottish Tradition*, xvi (1990–1), pp. 8–32

'Introduction' to 'The Scots and Parliament', *Parliamentary History*, 15.1 (1996), pp. 1–10

'Ronald and Dorna, by a Highlander to his Mistress', a Literary Curiosity of the Early Eighteenth Century', *Scottish Historical Review*, 75 (1996), pp. 221–5

'Record Sources for the Electoral History of Scotland, 1707–1832', *Scottish Archives*, 4 (1998), pp. 21–31

'Samuel Johnson's Views on Scottish Gaelic culture', *Scottish Historical Review*, 77 (1998), pp. 183–98

'Christian Faith and Unbelief in Modern Scotland' in Stewart J. Brown and George Newlands (eds), *Scottish Christianity in the Modern World: Essays in Honour of Professor A.C. Cheyne* (2001), pp. 53–89

'On Patriotism' in Paul Henderson Scott (ed.), *The Saltoun Papers: Reflections on Andrew Fletcher* (2003), pp. 91–105

'A Reply to Professor Colin Kidd on Lord Dacre's Contribution to the Study of Scottish History and the Scottish Enlightenment', *Scottish Historical Review*, 86 (2007), pp. 96–107

Editions

'A Renfrewshire Election Account, 1832', *Miscellany 10 of the Scottish History Society* (1965), pp. 213–28

'James Anderson's Historical Essay on the Crown of Scotland, 1705', *Stair Society Miscellany 3* (1992), pp. 1–130

Reviews

A wide variety of reviews in *History* (the journal of the Historical Association of the UK), *The Expository Times* (published by T & T Clark of Edinburgh) and *The Scottish Historical Review*.

Introduction

ALEXANDER MURDOCH

The title of this volume has been chosen to reflect that of Dr William Ferguson's last book, *The Identity of the Scottish Nation: An Historic Quest*, published by Edinburgh University Press in 1998, winner of the Saltire Society History Book of the Year Award. This was one of three major books on Scottish history published by Dr Ferguson during his scholarly career. In 1968, *Scotland: 1689 to the Present* was published as volume 4 of the Edinburgh History of Scotland by Oliver & Boyd of Edinburgh (paperback edition 1978), and in 1977 *Scotland's Relations with England: A Survey to 1707* appeared, reissued in paperback by the Saltire Society in 1994. All three of these books remain widely cited and have been very influential, as well as controversial, since their publication. A native of Muirkirk in Ayrshire and a graduate twice of the University of Glasgow, and BA of Oxford University (Balliol College), from 1954 until his retirement as Reader in Scottish History in 1989, Dr Ferguson taught in what was then the Department of Scottish History at the University of Edinburgh, and since his retirement he has continued to hold the status of Honorary Fellow in Scottish History at the university. On my appointment to the same department as a lecturer in 1995, I was determined to publish a volume of essays by former colleagues and students of Dr Ferguson's to mark his achievement as a pioneering historian of modern Scotland whose interests also included the totality of the country's history. Dr Ferguson was not a modernist who viewed the early history of Scotland as irrelevant to its modern history, and this has imparted a distinctive if not unique quality to his work. I am very grateful to former colleagues and students of Dr Ferguson, Professor Edward J. Cowan and Professor Richard J. Finlay, for their help in bringing this project to a successful conclusion after so many years. Mrs Doris Williamson, formerly secretary of the Department of Scottish History at the University of Edinburgh for over twenty years, has prepared the text for publication, having in the past helped many a doctoral student, including some contributors to this volume, finalise the text of their PhD theses. That this project has been brought to fruition is a tribute to Dr Ferguson's eminence as a historian of Scotland who never shirked controversy and never wavered in his fascination for the subject, or in his desire to promote it in the country of his birth and beyond.

This achievement has been recognised by grants to make the publication of this book possible from the Scottish Historical Review Trust and The Strathmartine Trust (for those unaware of this trust, its primary objective is to support research and education in Scottish history). My colleagues and I are very grateful to Hugh Andrew of Birlinn Limited, publishers, for his support, which included meeting with prospective contributors after many of them presented papers to the Scottish history seminar at the University of Edinburgh in 2003. Two of our contributors have passed away since this project was first conceived. Professor Ronald M. Sunter died in 2005. He was the first contributor to send me an essay, and for years I wrote to him annually to reassure him that I had not given up on the project, that it did have support, and that somehow it would be brought to a successful conclusion. Readers should bear in mind that Professor Sunter's essay was submitted to me in 1997 and that he was denied the opportunity of further revision before publication. The archival research on which it is based, however, reflects the high standards Dr Ferguson demanded of his students, of whom Professor Sunter was one. His book, *Patronage and Politics in Scotland, 1707–1832*, published by John Donald publishers of Edinburgh in 1986 and recently reissued, was based in part on his University of Edinburgh PhD thesis completed under the supervision of Dr Ferguson in 1971, 'Stirlingshire Politics, 1707–1832'. Iain Maciver died in March 2007. His University of Edinburgh MLitt thesis of 1977, 'The General Assembly of the Church, the State, and Society in Scotland 1815–1843' was completed under Dr Ferguson's supervision after Iain joined the manuscripts department of the National Library of Scotland, where he spent his entire career. Author of numerous publications despite his extensive commitments as a curator, he was an unwavering supporter of this project and had looked forward to its completion. It is a matter of great sadness to those of us who have contributed to the book that he was not able to see its publication.

The rest of the contributions to this volume further reflect the full range of William Ferguson's interests in Scottish history and his influence on the development of the subject, in particular in regard to the connection between Scottish history and Scottish national identity reflected in the title of his last book as well as this volume of essays, and in the study of Scottish political history, comparatively neglected in modern Scottish history. Professor Cowan, a former student as well as colleague of Dr Ferguson until he took up the chair of Scottish Studies at the University of Guelph in Ontario that reunited him with Professor Sunter, returned to Scotland in 1993. His study of 'John the Commonweal' reflects William Ferguson's suspicion of elites and belief in the integrity of the Scottish people. Dr Tristram Clarke, a former doctoral student with Dr Ferguson ('The Scottish Episcopalians 1688–1720', 1987), has contributed an essay on Scottish biographical compilations that reflects the recent experience of several of those involved in this volume in contributing to the creation of the *Oxford Dictionary of National* [British] *Biography* published in 2004 and still in development as an online publication.

The remaining contributions reflect William Ferguson's interests in political history, including my own essay on the Revolution of 1689 in Scotland, which Dr Ferguson made the point of departure for his first book. The essays on Scottish politics in the second half of the twentieth century by Dr Iain Hutchison and Professor Richard Finlay, both of whose University of Edinburgh doctoral theses were supervised by Dr Ferguson, address the neglect of twentieth-century Scottish history until recent times. For the eighteenth and nineteenth centuries, in addition to the essays by Iain Maciver and Ronald Sunter already mentioned, Dr Ken Logue, who studied with Dr Ferguson at the University of Edinburgh as an undergraduate and postgraduate, returns to pioneering research he carried out in the 1970s in his essay on the Porteous riots of 1737 in Edinburgh. His monograph published by John Donald of Edinburgh in 1979, *Popular Disturbances in Scotland 1780–1815*, has been reissued in recent years (and in 1991 was discussed at some length in E.P. Thompson's last book, *Customs in Common*, pp. 306 and 313). Dr David Brown, whose University of Edinburgh doctorate, 'Henry Dundas and the Government of Scotland', was supervised by Dr Ferguson, completes the collection with an elegant essay on a neglected episode in nineteenth-century Scottish political history, the Scottish policy of the so-called 'Ministry of all the Talents', a government famously dismissed by Dr Ferguson in *Scotland 1689 to the Present* (p. 269) as 'in fact narrowly based and not particularly talented'.

In the years since Dr Ferguson retired from teaching, more and more new historical scholarship on all aspects of Scottish history has been published both in Scotland and beyond, as Professor Tom Devine notes in his foreword to this collection. All Scottish universities with an interest in history as a discipline now teach Scottish history, and there has been a marked increase in postgraduate research in Scottish history in all periods. Dr Ferguson was one of the pioneers who made this possible, and the contributors to this book felt that it was important that his contribution be recognised. He continues to carry out research, publish and engage in vigorous debate; most recently, as so frequently in the past, in the pages of the *Scottish Historical Review*. His passionate commitment to the subject has benefited all with an interest in the history of Scotland, whether they agree with all of Dr Ferguson's views on the subject or not. It has been a privilege to work with colleagues to endeavour to present him with a collection of studies that pay tribute to his achievements as a teacher, supervisor, colleague and scholar.

Bill Ferguson: An Appreciation

Editor's Note
A former colleague of Dr Ferguson's who wished this project well was John M. Simpson, who taught in the former Department of Scottish History at the University of Edinburgh from 1964 to his retirement in 1995, when the editor of this volume had the honour to succeed him, in addition to the honour of having been one of his former students. In 2004, at the editor's request, he submitted the following memoir for inclusion in this book. John's death in 2005 meant that, having supported this project for so long, he was unable to witness its completion.

I'm mindful of the fact that Bill Ferguson, my friend and colleague with whom I took morning coffee over so many years, is also a major historian. The sixteenth-century humanist, Polydore Vergil, told Bishop Gavin Douglas that history 'showld nether abhorre the discoveringe of falsehoode, neither in anie case allowe the undermining of veritee'. Bill Ferguson has excelled at both of these duties. And if he has by temperament seemed especially zestful in discovering falsehood, it should be remembered that it is only once the old myths have been expunged that, as in the case of his superb book, *The Identity of the Scottish Nation: An Historic Quest* (1998), a new and truer account can be substituted.

Bill's writings exemplify unfamiliar virtues. Several acclaimed recent books are seamless, generalised and almost bland in style, as if to say: this is the last word (for the moment). Bill's writings tend to be more concrete, each page with its quota of proper and placenames. He pays his readers the compliment of believing that their curiosity is as keen as his own, and that they will want to check out some of the people and places for themselves.

Other things being equal, a small university department stands a good chance of being a harmonious one, and so it was with the Department of Scottish History at Edinburgh. I have been fortunate in all my colleagues, but since Bill and I shared the teaching of the modern period, it was to him that I often turned in times of personal or professional crisis. What he always provided me with was not just practical help but also a kindly sympathy which affected me deeply.

Bill Ferguson is by birth and early upbringing an Ayrshireman. I hope it's not unduly fanciful to see in him some abiding characteristics of the folk of the south-west. In 1978, Bill's attitude reminded me forcibly of the reaction of some of the covenanters to their defeat at Dunbar in 1650. 'I am absolutely satisfied,' wrote Samuel Rutherford, 'that our army, through the sinful miscarriage of men, hath fallen.' In other words, God chastised us because He loved us, and it was for our own good. In 1978, as our national football team left for Argentina amid a mood of national euphoria, Bill explained mordantly and at length why, with such a team and such a manager as we had, we were bound to be humiliated. After we had been duly humiliated, it wasn't necessary for Bill to say anything; and as far as I recall he didn't.

Then there were the Ayrshire miners and their families. I am sure that Bill Ferguson would adhere to the belief which, as expressed by Bill Shankly's mother, is the most life-affirming that I know: 'Every day that you have the health and strength to get out of your bed you should regard as a holiday.'

John M. Simpson

1

Scotching the Beggars: John the Commonweal and Scottish History

EDWARD J. COWAN

Quhen the corruptit flesche is consumit fra the
banis no man can put defferens betuix ane prince
and ane begger.[1]

There is a significant streak of anti-authoritarianism in most Ayrshire folk, a dour, even grudging, suspicion of rulers, administrators and posers in presumed positions of power. Acquaintances and friends will recognise some of these characteristics in Bill Ferguson. Bill has always shared Robert Burns' sense of scepticism and his contempt for ridiculous posturing, while manifesting a notable care and concern for the plight of disadvantaged humanity. Although he will always be best remembered as a distinguished and pioneering historian of modern Scotland, his panoramic surveys of Anglo-Scottish relations and Scottish identity reveal an intimate knowledge of the totality of his nation's past. One for whom he has always had considerable regard and whose raucous, often scurrilous, wit has afforded him much amusement, is Sir David Lindsay of the Mount, the registrar par excellence of Scottish sixteenth-century public opinion, whose famous drama seems to encapsulate, as it heralds, the defining event of sixteenth-century Scotland. Indeed Bill has quoted with approval T.G. Law's observation that before the Reformation, 'it was the play, the ballad and the popular song which were doing the real mischief to the established system, and were preparing the ground for the coming revolution'.[2]

In Lindsay's remarkable play, *Ane Satyre of the Thrie Estaitis*,[3] performed in Fife in 1552 and at Edinburgh two years later, there appears the memorable character, John the Commonweal. The play is in the medieval morality tradition and concerns corruption at the court of the young king of Scots, irresistibly recalling – though the identification has been challenged[4] – that of James V (1513–42), whom Lindsay personally served as usher, mentor, herald and diplomat. As is well known, the action involves the reform of the court and secondly the reformation of the parliamentary estates, followed by the salvation of the commonweal, or commonwealth, of Scotland – the people at large – as they are rescued from the twin oppressions of state and church. At the beginning of the play, Justice has been banished the kingdom resulting in the suppression of the poor. Rulers and churchmen have failed to honour their responsibility for good order without which the 'puir opprest' will cry vengeance 'up to the hevin' (lines 1049–50). At this court Chastitie is a beggar at the bar (1402), as is Gude Counsall (1640). Towards the end of Part 1 Pauper, or the Pure Man, invades the allegorical world as a blast from the present, the voice of contemporary reality. Described as 'ane wilde begger carle' (1941) and a 'begger bogill' (1962), his appearance almost causes the cancellation of the play. In a famous speech Pauper explains how he has become impoverished to the point of total destitution through the death duties appropriated by the church. On being informed that churchmen operated according to consuetude or custom he retorts that 'ane consuetude against the common weill sould be na law' (2022–3). When the reformed king invites pleas and petitions or complaints, John rushes forward to protest that his rapacious oppressors have literally taken the clothes off his back, forcing him to consider the possibility of begging 'on the bordour' (2465).

John is both a spokesman for the Pauper and a symbol of the commons of Scotland at large, as well as the defender of the well-being of the community as a whole. It is of the greatest significance that John lacks clothes; so desperate is he that he is prepared to beg on the Border (2465), a point not glossed by any of the play's editors but which implies at least two menacing threats born of the last resort. He is so hard-pressed that he will take his chances with the reivers, thieves and caterans of the volatile Border country between Scotland and England (contemptuously mentioned elsewhere in the play (2587–97)), or he will solicit a remedy for his predicament from the English authorities, so pathetic and uncaring are those in Scotland; to live in chaos or in exile are preferable alternatives. Others agree. The king is told:

> Without ye mak sum better diligence,
> The Common-weill mon uther wayis be styllit,
> Or, be my faith, the King wilbe begyllit.
> Thir pure commouns daylie, as ye may se,
> Declinis doun till extreme povertie (2569–73).

John, on stage, is a vital and memorable character. Usually depicted as a kind of archetypal Scottish male – tall, shaggy, menacing, potentially violent and semi-naked – he bears all the characteristics of his people remarked upon by authorities as disparate as Greek and Roman writers all the way down to modern American historians describing the Scotch–Irish.[5] He appears elsewhere in Lindsay's work as Jock Uppaland, or John Upon-the-Land, and there is even a reference to Uppaland's wife (4071). He is literally the salt of the earth. Later in the century his name appeared on at least one petitionary placard addressed to the authorities, suggesting that he was also seen as a figure of dissidence and possible subversion. John's antecedents, it will be argued, stretch back to the Wars of Independence in the thirteenth and fourteenth centuries. It is my contention that he stalks the sixteenth century as an ever-present threat to the authorities, the personification of the Scottish common man whom monarchy ignores at its peril. As such he is a creation that would, in future centuries, bolster the Scottish self-myth of democratic patriotism and honest, steadfast commonalty, to be found, for example, in the works of Robert Burns. When Jock first appears in Lindsay's *Ane Satyre* he is, without a shadow of doubt, depicted as a beggar, if one who had once been a man of some status. He is, above all, in both literary and historical terms a most powerful metaphor at a critical juncture in Scottish history. Within eight years of the play being performed at Cupar in Fife, the Scottish Reformation had come about, and in that process, as I shall argue, the image of the beggar played a central role, notably in the propagandist but surprisingly little investigated 'Beggars' Summons' of 1559.

The poor, of course, were ever present, though not all poor were beggars, nor all beggars poor. There was something of an obsession with beggary in sixteenth-century Scotland and then, as now, beggars generated such antithetical responses as concern and condemnation, embarrassment and exploitation. Beggars were banished from the streets during the grand entry of Mary of Guise, Queen of Scots, to Edinburgh in 1538,[6] yet twenty years later their plight was invoked to inspire revolutionary action. In Scottish terms they first received favourable legislation in the reign of David I (1124–53). The word 'beggar' occurred for the first time in legislation of 1424 and was thereafter oft repeated. No-one between the ages of fourteen and seventy was to be permitted to beg unless they were unable to gain a living by any other means. In 1449 masterful beggars with horses and hounds, as well as feigned fools and bards, were to be punished with forfeiture and imprisonment, or by having their ears nailed to the Tron and banished. Thirty years later there was reinforcement of laws concerning stark or sturdy beggars.

In the reign of James IV (1488–1513), parliament defined legitimate beggars as the impotent, the blind and the weak. Parliamentary legislation of James V in 1535 stipulated that the destitute could only beg in their native parishes, and then with a token so that, as Rod Lyall correctly points out, the Pauper of Lindsay's play was technically a criminal.[7] By 1540 it was reported that 'ane multitude of vyle, unhonest and miserable creatures' gathered daily at the Edinburgh meal market for support. Legislation of 1574 demonstrates that the reformers fared no better in tackling the problem, but it drew its inspiration from previous enactments and, it might be thought, from *Ane Satyre of the Thrie Estaitis*; it is seldom that playwrights inspire laws, but some of the language employed in 1574, fortuitously or otherwise, inescapably recalls the sentiments of John the Commonweal. The material concerned with beggars follows immediately upon legislation about the provision of stocks and irons (of the branding as well as the restrictive variety) and the building and repair of common prisons. Parliament aimed at 'the stanching of maisterfull ydill beggaris, awayputting of sorners and provisioun for the puyr'. Street entertainers, bards and 'utheris siclyke rynnaris about' were to be imprisoned if they could pay for their own accommodation; otherwise their ears were to be nailed to the Tron or a tree before they were cut off and their owners banished; a second offence was to be punished by hanging. None were to be suffered to beg except 'cruikit folk, seik folk, impotent folk and waik folk', who were confined to their native parishes. Since strong, idle beggars were 'outrageous enemies to the commonweal' all those between the ages of fourteen and seventy were to be apprehended and examined. Upon conviction, if they could not find a cautioner, they were to be scourged and 'burnt throw the girssill of the rycht eare with ane het irne of the compasse of ane inch about'. Anyone interfering with the punishment of beggars was to receive the same treatment; those who offered money, hospitality or lodging to sturdy beggars were to be fined a maximum of £6, although it was perfectly charitable to assist genuine cases 'that thay sould not neid heireftir to beg or wander about to the sklander of a cristiane commoun welth that hes ressavit the evangell'. Registers were to be kept of the deserving poor. Beggars' children between the ages of five and fourteen could be forcibly taken into service: females until they were eighteen, males up to the age of twenty-four.

The definition of idle and strong beggars and vagabonds included those persons 'using subtle, crafty and unlawful plays such as jugglery fast and loose'. Listed also were 'Egyptians' or gypsies, and any others who pretended to have knowledge of 'physnomie, palmestre or utheris abused sciencis quhairby thay perswade the people that thay can tell thair weardis, deathis and fortunes and sic uther fantasticall ymaginatiounis'. The savage persecution of gypsies verged upon genocide; as late as 1609 they were condemned to expulsion or execution. Another interesting category of persons describes those who claim 'to have bene hereit in the sowthland brint in the late troubles', in other words incapacitated through warfare, which seems to have been a common claim reflected in John the Commonweal's statement, 'In to the south, allace, I was neir slane'.[8] Folk who were also deemed to be beggars were those who could give no account of how they lawfully made their living, namely all minstrels, songsters and tale-tellers lacking patrons; all common labourers 'living idly and fleeing labour'; all counterfeiters of licences to beg or those knowingly using the same; all vagabond scholars of the universities not licensed to ask alms; and ship-broken mariners travelling without testimonials. Finally, no Irish and Highland bards or beggars were to be brought to, or received in, the Lowlands by means of boats or otherwise under penalty of a fine of £20 to 'the bringaris'. In retrospect the legislation appears relentless. By the end of the sixteenth century masters of coal mines and salt pans were allowed to apprehend and put to labour all vagabonds and sturdy beggars. Such unfortunates were being transported to the West Indies in the Cromwellian period, and by the 1690s idle, loose and vagabond persons could be compelled to serve as soldiers.[9]

There was a rich lexis to describe beggars; all of the following occur in Lindsay's play – bummilbaty, swyngeour, sleutcher, blaitiebum, vager, liddir and brybour. One refinement was represented by the thigger, often associated, though not exclusively, with the Gaelic-speaking population; to 'thig' was to beg with violence. The role of the beggar was thus of central concern in the period, while the culture of beggary was remarkably inclusive.

The ballads furnish further details about beggary and its practitioners. For example, they were considered promiscuous or randy, enjoying the same sort of reputation as milkmen or window cleaners at a later date. According to ballad-lore, folk often pretended to be beggars, the idea being that begging was not a steady-state occupation. In *The Jolly Beggar* (Child[10] 279), which has many variants, the eponym liked his home comforts, preferring the fire of the hall to barn or byre. Of course he seduced the daughter of the house and then questioned his lover as to the whereabouts of the town's dogs so that he could avoid those potential shredders of his meal-pokes. 'Then she took up the mealpokes and flang them o'er the wa / The deil gae wi' the mealpokes my maidenhead an a.' Needless to say he turned out to have been a gentlemen – of a kind – all along. The meal-pokes are also mentioned in *The Beggar-Laddie* (Child 280) in which a girl followed her lad to the begging, an experience she found embarrassing before he revealed that he was a knight.

These pokes are the same as the wallets of the Gaberlunzie man; indeed in English the origin of the word 'wallet' was a beggar's pack. Wallets should be thought of as detached pokes or pockets strung in different parts of the beggar's clothing, beneath his long cloak or gaberdine. The *gaber* of 'gaberdine' and 'Gaberlunzie' must be connected and seems to designate 'beggar', although the dictionaries claim that gaberlunzie is of unknown origin. At any rate it should be understood that each poke had a specialised function – one for meal, one for dried meat, one for fish, and so on. Thus the beggar became something of a magical creature, a kind of human cabinet or cupboard. When he carried other items for purposes of utility or trade, then he was almost like a mobile shop since in pre-pram or shopping trolley days he carried everything on his own person. That is why the naked beggar, such as Jock o the Commonweal is depicted, would have seemed such a shocking image to the play's audience, for he is the poorest of the poor, the absolute bottom of the begging heap.

By the time of Allan Ramsay's *The Gaberlunzie Man* in his *Tea-Table Miscellany* (1724),[11] the beggar had become a licensed professional who nonetheless was prepared to indulge in real work from time to time as a maker of spindles and whorls, or as a kind of tinker, fixing pots and other metal objects or sharpening knives and tools. He was also something of an actor in fulfilling his role at the begging; overall a character of considerable literary and metaphorical potential.

In the play the idea is clearly enunciated by both John the Commonweal and the Pauper that the true poor, those who had once been able to sustain themselves but who had been driven into destitution by their social superiors, were being ignored in favour of the idle beggars so frequently mentioned in the legislation. John clearly has no starry-eyed, romantic vision of beggary.

I compleine upon the idill men.
For quhy, Sir, it is Gods awin bidding
All Christian men to wirk for thair living.
Qui non laborat non manducet.
This is in Inglische toung or leit:
Quha labouris nocht, he sall not eit.
This bene against the strang beggers,
Fidlers, pypers and pardoners;
Thir jugglars, jestars and idle cuitchours *gamblers*;
Thir carriers and thir quintacensours *alchemists*;
Thir babel-beirers *fools* and thir bairds *bards*;
Thir sweir swyngeours *scoundrels* with lords and lairds
Ma then thair rentis may sustaine,
Or to thair profeit neidfull bene,
Quhilk bene ay blythest of discords
And deidly feid amang thar lords (2599–617).

He lambasts the fat-cat clergy, 'lyand in dennis lyke idill doggis / I them compair to weil-fed hoggis', and upon being invited to tender further complaints he obliges with relish.

The pure peopill cryis with cairis
The infetching of the Justice Airis,
Exercit mair for covetice
Then for the punisching of vyce.
Ane peggrell *paltry* theif that steillis ane kow
Is hangit, bot he that steillis ane bow *herd*
With als meikle geir as he may turs *carry off*,
That theif is hangit be the purs.
Sic pykand peggrall theifis ar hangit,
Bot he that all the warld hes wrangit,
Ane cruell tyrane, ane strang transgressour,
Ane common publick plaine oppressour,
By buds *bribes* may he obteine favours
Of tresurers and compositours;
Thocht he serve greit punitioun,

The common peopill ar put sa under.
Thocht thay be puir, it is na wonder (2654–73).

John had earlier appeared in Lindsay's poem 'The Dreme', possibly composed in 1526, in which he was made to present 'The Compleynt of the Comoun Weill of Scotland', a piece rather similar in tone and sentiment to his speeches in the play. His plight was signified by his raiment, 'all raggit, revin, and rent'. Justice had been overtaken by disloyalty and treason; warfare wracked the south of Scotland, while theft, murder, poverty and strife were endemic in both the Borders and the Highlands and Islands. Lawyers and covetous clergy had conspired in John's demise. Furthermore:

Oure gentyll men ar all degenerate;
Liberalitie and Lawte *Loyalty*, boith, ar loste;
And Cowardyce with Lordis is laureate *crowned*
And knychtlie curage tumit *emptied* in brag and boste b*oasting*;
The Civele weir misgydis everilk oist.
Thare is nocht ellis bot ilk man for hym self,
That garris me go, thus baneist lyke ane elf. (988–94)[12]

And go he does, quitting Scotland altogether until the country should once again be guided by the wisdom of 'ane gude auld prudent kyng', the creation of whom is, of course, one of the major themes of *Ane Satyre*; wherein, however, although the Commonweal still threatens defection, he must remain to resolve the crisis in the kingdom.

Jock's earliest appearance was in an anonymous poem broadly dated to the minority of James V, 1513–28. *Jok Up-a-lands Complaint against the Court in the Kings Nonaige* was printed for the first time, so far as is known, in the incomparable Allan Ramsay's invaluable *The Ever Green.*[13] However the poem, or part of it, was probably either written or recycled by David Lindsay, for there are close parallels between its language and Jock's speeches in the play. The *Complaint* protests that the poor commons are plundered by their social superiors who allow the land to lie untilled. 'Wer I king,' says Jock, the lords and barons would be hoisted on the gallows, these men who have wrongfully usurped the king's powers during his minority. He knows that the laws that govern him are not sound and he curses those who made them, calling upon Christ to ensure that they are 'dinged doon'; 'thus said Johnne uponland'. The poem certainly fits well with a perceived Scottish tradition of popular intervention occasioned and necessitated by monarchical failure.

Robert Sempill ensured that the ballad remained as effective a tool of propagandist derision of the establishment after the Reformation as it had been before. Johne Upaland is invoked in his *Ane Exhortation derect to my Lord Regent and to the Rest of the Lordis accomplisis* of 1567, which accuses the Protestant lords of proving no better than their Papist predecessors. Indeed his poem stresses the notion of *plus ça change, plus c'est la même chose* when criticising in Lindsay-like language,

> the greit penuritie
> Off laubouraris, and of your tennentis pure,
> Quha sair opprest hes bene in this cuntrie,
> This mony yeir, by the Nobilitie.

Jak, it seems, 'will never do good' (that is to say prevail) in either a Protestant or a Catholic Scotland.[14] Sempill returns to the theme following the assassination of the Regent Moray in 1570, a traumatic moment in the Scottish Protestant experience which has so far failed to receive proper historical analysis, in a ballad with the rather unoriginal title of *The Cruikit liedis the blinde.*

> This warld it waggis I wat not how,
> And na man may ane uther trow;
> And everie man dois pluke and pow,
> And that the pure may finde,
> Our Court it is decayit now
> The cruikit leidis the blinde.

Maitland of Lethington now dominated the political scene, a man so accomplished that he could whistle and chatter with his mouth full of oatmeal and who was so cunning that he could 'begyle ane Landwart Jock'.[15]

Jock's final appearance was in a tract of 1597, *To the late Commissioners of the Kirk, chosin by his Majestie for disordering things ecclesiasticall, Jockupaland, in the name of the Commons, wisheth greater grace, and less witt.* It appeared towards the end of a particularly fraught decade during which the crown appeared to gain the upper hand over the kirk against a background of noble strife, assassination, Catholic conspiracy and witch-hunting. The tract, described as a 'rustical letter', purported to have been written by 'a man of meane estat and calling, yea, of the meanest and poorest estat of all the countrie, one of the commouns' on behalf of 'the poor laicks and commouns of this countrie'. It protests that James VI, like his grandfather, has been misled by evil counsel, but what is novel is the assertion that the poor commons have been betrayed by the Protestant ministers who have feebly succumbed to the king. The letter appears to threaten remedial violence: 'Before we traterouslie suffer his Majestie thus to be abused by the devil and his instrumentis in this land, we sall, God willing, withstand the same by all meanes possible,' More intriguingly, Jockupaland asserts that bad counsellors have turned James against God, 'and so alienat his subjects' hearts from him, without which he cannot be a king'.[16] Herein the possibility of popular revolt is made explicit, that when the king fails in his duty the poor commons will intervene. It is noteworthy that in Lindsay's play both John (2592, 2846) and Pauper (2962) use the phrase 'war I ane King', which could be construed as conveying an implied threat (albeit in fact a remote one) that monarchy must honour its obligations lest its powers be usurped by others, an idea which informs George Buchanan's influential tract *De Jure Regni Apud Scottos*,[17] but one which was central to the career, and later the legend, of one of Scotland's greatest heroes.

As is well known, William Wallace emerged in 1297 to lead his people against the tyrannous ambition of Edward I of England. He was the younger son of a knight in the south-west of Scotland who, with others, led the resistance to English occupation, won a great victory at Stirling Bridge (1297), was defeated the following year at Falkirk, was involved in diplomatic embassies to the king of France and the Papacy and who was betrayed, captured and suffered a hideous execution as a 'traitor' to the English king in 1305. He was first mentioned as a thief and outlaw in Ettrick Forest, and though he was never portrayed as a beggar he enjoyed a similar register of baseness, as the outsider or the other. In the eyes of English chroniclers he was regarded as an unnatural being, mainly on account of his supposed low-born status, which dictated that he had no business or entitlement to usurp the command of the national army in order to defy the might of Edward I. Wallace was the kind of man who could potentially shatter the 'Great Chain of Being' or turn the world upside down.

The earliest Scottish chronicler to notice the deeds of Wallace was John of Fordun in his *Chronica Gentis Scotorum*, which was compiled in the 1360s. Fordun's account contains the startling information that Wallace lost the battle of Falkirk due to the treachery of Robert Bruce, future king of Scots, an assertion repeated in Andrew of Wyntoun's vernacular *Orygynale Cronykil* composed circa 1420. Supported by the 'lele comownys off Scotland' William lived simply as an outlaw before his untimely end. That there were already stories or ballads in circulation about the hero is implied by Wyntoun's remark: 'Off his gud dedis and manhad / Gret Gestis, I hard say, are made.'[18] In Walter Bower's *Scotichronicon*, written in the 1440s, Wallace and Bruce are made to have a discussion across 'an impassably deep valley' following the disaster at Falkirk. Bruce asked his opponent the source of his arrogance and rashness in opposing not only the might of Edward I but also the wishes of the Scottish nobility, to be told that it was his own inactivity and cowardice that had inspired Wallace to attempt to free his native land.[19] The altercation on the banks of the River Carron became absolutely central to Scottish historiography dealing with the Wars of Independence right down to the end of the nineteenth century. It was mentioned by virtually every single authority or commentator, most of whom did not hesitate to add a little embroidery to the versions of their predecessors.

Wallace's sentiments were perhaps best expressed by George Buchanan in his *Historia* of 1582:

> You, to whom ignominious slavery with security is dearer than honourable liberty with danger, embrace the fortune you so much admire. I, in the country which I have so often defended, shall live free or freely die; nor shall my affection leave me, but with my last breath.[20]

The legend of Wallace, which over time seems to have absorbed elements of Robin Hood, received further elaboration in Blind Harry's lengthy poem, which appeared around 1478, a patriotic epic that was one of the earliest publications to be issued from the press of Scotland's first printers, Chepman and Myllar, in the first decade of the sixteenth century. Thereafter it remained one of the most popular books in Scottish publishing history.[21] It is not without interest that Harry, who was almost certainly not blind and whose name may not even have been Harry, wrote in the same decade that witnessed the refinement of the legend of William Tell as well as William Caxton's publication of Malory's *Le Morte D'Arthur*;[22] historiography often cannibalises historical heroes for purposes of the present.[23]

What is significant is that in the fully developed legend of William Wallace he came to be regarded as the man from nowhere, the commoner who came to the fore in his country's hour of need, in the absence of the kingdom's natural leaders, the nobility. Each time listeners or readers encountered the exchange between Bruce and Wallace after Falkirk they experienced a reinforcement of the idea that a quisling aristocrat (and future king) was confronted by a kind of proletarian worth. Wallace served to remind future monarchs that if they failed in their duties, the commons of Scotland would step in. It is thus not difficult to see Wallace as the spiritual or ideological ancestor of John the Commonweal.

Subsequent developments during the Wars of Independence tended to nurture the same powerful myth. After Robert Bruce made himself king in 1306 he created a resilient propaganda department to argue the righteousness of his cause, built around the concept of freedom. Wallace was something of an embarrassment to Bruce, but it was, in part, due to his memory that the community of the realm of Scotland, addressing a famous letter to the Pope in 1320, enunciated the idea of the contractual theory of monarchy, to be followed by the ringing declaration that 'it is not for glory, nor riches, nor honours that we fight, but for freedom, which no honest man will lose but with life itself'.[24] It has been suggested that serfdom disappeared from Scotland as a result of the independence struggle.[25] In terms of the contract, both Robert II and Robert III were set aside as unfit rulers as John Balliol had been 100 years earlier. John Barbour famously eulogised freedom in his great poem 'The Bruce', later to provide the main inspiration for Harry's 'Wallace'.

A! fredome is a noble thing,
Fredome mays man to haiff liking,
Fredome all solace to man giffis,
He levys at es that fely levys.
A noble hart may haiff nane es
Na ellys nocht that may him ples
Gyff fredome failye, for fre liking
Is yharnyt our all other thing.
Na he that ay has levyt fre
May nocht knaw weill the propyrte
The angyr na the wrechyt dome
That is couplyt to foule thyldome,
Bot gif he had assayit it.[26]

James I (1424–37) appointed a poor man's advocate, and thus established the principle of the right to a legal defence irrespective of status or wealth. He attempted to place restraints on the tyrannous behaviour of his nobility though, ironically, according to some he was himself the tyrant who had to be assassinated in 1437.[27] The rhetoric of tyranny which pervaded the pronouncements of the period 1290–1320 survived into the sixteenth century: 'Na peopill (may) have prosperitie, / Quhair ignorance hes the dominioun, / And Common-weil be tirants trampit doun' (3814–16).

It is beyond the scope of this essay to trace in detail the constancy of the idea of freedom in Scottish history, or for that matter Scottish literature. It was well established in tract after tract that good governance demanded that the poor be treated well, but there was another side to the coin – namely, that the obsession with the idea of freedom generated something of a contempt for those who failed, themselves, to be free.

Some insight into contemporary perceptions is provided by *The Complaynt of Scotland* (1550), attributed to Robert Wedderburn, in which Dame Scotia appeals to the Three Estates to cooperate with one another because the friction between them is destroying the kingdom and leaving it wide open to attack by the English. The noble, the clergyman and the poor labourer are depicted as the three sons of Dame Scotia, and each of them is allowed to say his piece. The Labourer claims that he is so oppressed by his elder brothers – 'I am be cum ane begger' – that no-one can be surprised if he prefers rule under the English, 'my tua brothir Nobilis and Clergie, quhilk suld defend me, tha ar mair cruel contrar me nor is my ald enemes of Ingland'. Although the Labourer is always referred to as the youngest brother, in fact he is the oldest; 'the begynnyng of

Nobillis and Spiritualite hed bot pure lauboraris to there predecessouris', but of course, 'thai vil nocht consider that al there gentreis hes procedit and descendit fra me'. The other brothers are always accusing their lesser sibling of treason, but they should know that treason is never engendered or invented in the hearts of the poor commons. While the ignorance of the latter might lead them to conceive a deep-seated malice towards a king who has perpetrated exactions upon his people, they have neither the knowledge nor the prudence to take matters further, though the point is explicit that there is some potential on the part of the commons for revolt.

Dame Scotia shows herself, not surprisingly, to be an unrepentant aristocrat who has little or no sympathy for the plight of the commons.

> For as sune as ye that are comont pepil ar unbridilit and furtht of subiectione, your ignorance, inconstance and incivilite, pulcis *drives* you to perpetrat intollerabil exactiouns. For al the insurrectionis that evyr occurrit in ony realme contrar the prince and the public veil *weal*, hes procedit of the ignorance and obstinaitone of the comount pepil. There for none of ly dantit and haldin in subjectione, be cause that your hartis is ful of maleis, ignorance, variance and inconstance.

She is something of a tartar, this dame; if her eldest son is feeling somewhat self-righteous he is rapidly disabused of that notion. He is even worse than the Labourer, because he should know better. 'Ane man is nocht reput for ane gentil man in Scotland bot gyf he mak mair expensis on his horse and his doggis nor he dois on his vyfe and bayrnis.' Needless to say Spirituality receives a blistering as well. She concludes by asserting that her three sons have done her more damage than the English army ever did, conspiring as they have in the demolition of the commonweal.[28]

It is something of an irony that James V, who was the object of so much contemporary advice and criticism, should have been remembered as the poor man's king, John Leslie's *Rex plebeiorum*, 'for the pure, opprest with the potent, he helpet ay, and the potent nocht spairing the indigence of the pure and nedie, he ouirthrew, and that with gret severitie'.[29] Buchanan also commended his accessibility to the poor.[30] However, John Knox was probably the earliest commentator to refer to James as 'a good poor man's king'.[31] James V's harsh policies towards the inhabitants of the Borders and the Highlands would have been applauded by John the Commonweal, while the king's personal request in 1535 that the lords of council appoint an *advocatus pauperum*,[32] thus reviving legislation of James I, can definitely be seen to favour the disadvantaged of his kingdom. The idea that 'he certainly mixed freely with subjects of low degree'[33] – whatever that may mean – seems to owe more to the imagination of Sir Walter Scott than to any contemporary source. On one occasion James reportedly disguised himself as a servant in order to view a prospective bride,[34] an anecdote out of which Scott apparently manufactured the entire legend of the Gudeman of Ballengeich:

> James V, like his father James IV, had a custom of going about the country disguised as a private person, in order that he might hear complaints which might not otherwise reach his ears, and perhaps, that he might enjoy amusements which he could not have partaken of in his avowed royal character.[35]

A goodman is a tenant farmer, far removed from the designation of 'beggar', yet due to the invincible authority of the great fabricator, Scott, the popular image of the beggar-king persists even at the present day. The popularity of Lindsay's works during the first century of Reformation, during which he was given the status of honorary reformer,[36] may have helped to foster the legend of Rex Humanitas or Rex Sapiens, who eventually is made to realise that he must tend the needs of the poor; his works also served to effectively place the word 'commonweal' in the national vocabulary.

It is just possible also that the figure of John the Commonweal himself may have received some reinforcement, in terms of popular culture, from the bizarre case of John Scot, a bankrupt who, in 1531, sought refuge in the sanctuary of Holyrood Abbey and who came to the attention of the king when he allegedly fasted for days on end. James had him change his clothes and then shut him up in the David Tower of Edinburgh Castle where, under observation, he survived a fast of thirty days, after which he was exhibited to the populace naked. He claimed that he received his powers from the Virgin Mary, and in a further bid for sainthood he journeyed to Rome, Venice and Jerusalem, returning via London to Edinburgh where he set up a shrine featuring his own daughter as the Virgin. Buchanan dismissed his claims as 'preposterous', condemning his 'genius for inventing impiety' but the Catholic John Leslie was a believer.

> Mekle speikeng with mony is hard of this fasteng, sum wounderis and esteimes it to proceid of singular halynes, utheris lauch and skorne thinking it cam of phrenesie: bot how ever it be, albeit wicked persounes speik wickedlie to discommend that haly man, and to diminise and pare his prais, mony gude men nochtwithstandeng constantlie affirme that he was inspiret with the spirit of prophesie from hevin.[37]

That he was allowed to proceed to the continent suggests that the king kept an open mind, but in the hothouse atmosphere of pre-Reformation Scotland many of the poor commons must have believed that John Scot's powers were truly miraculous. The ragged and near-naked John the Commonweal was not depicted as a prophet, but his words, unheeded, contained the seeds of prophecy, while his creator, as Carol Edington has shown, was keenly interested in matters apocalyptic.[38]

In Lindsay's play all ends well because John's words are taken seriously. Before Correctioun exits the stage he is besought by Gude Counsall.

> Gif Johne the Common-weill ane gay garmoun;
> Becaus the Common-weill hes bene overluikit,
> That is the caus that Common-weill is cruikit,
> With singular profeit he hes bene sa supprysit,
> That he is baith cauld, naikit and disgysit (3794–8).

John is given not only 'ane new abuilyement' of gorgeous materials but also a seat in the parliament, and so is rescued from beggary. But that the concern about beggars was no mere abstruse literary conceit or whimsy is convincingly demonstrated by subsequent developments.

John Knox, for good or ill the father of the Scottish Reformation, believed in his heart of hearts that reform should be imposed by the monarchy. Since that option did not exist under the regency of Mary of Guise while her daughter was removed to France, Knox appealed to the nobility to bring about 'perfect reformation'. They too failed to heed his pleas and so, in 1558, he penned a 'Letter to the Commonalty of Scotland', in which, as a last resort, he pleaded with them to assume the responsibilities that their social superiors had shirked.

> Albeit God hath put and ordained distinction and difference betwixt the king and subjects, betwixt rulers and common people, in the regiment and administration of civil policies, yet in the hope of the life to come he hath made all equal . . . to you it doth no less appertain, than to your king or princes, to provide that Christ Jesus be truly preached amongst you, seeing that without his true knowledge can neither of you attain to salvation. And this is the point wherein, I say, all men is equal.[39]

Knox's sentiments were, of course, not greatly original, but in the Scotland of the 1550s they were revolutionary.

His tactics in pursuit of his ultimate goal included the production and circulation on 1 January 1559 of the remarkable document known as 'The Beggars' Summons'. On that date 'there wes ticketts of warning, at the instance of the whole poore people of this realme, affixt upon the doores of everie place of Friers within this countrey'.[40] The friars were targeted for the good reason that during the first half of the sixteenth century many of the endowments of almshouses and hospitals, upon which the beggarly poor relied for their sustenance, had been transferred to them. In 1548 James Harrison in his 'Godly and Golden Book' had demanded the restoration of these charitable buildings which evil churchmen had pulled down 'for their lucre and profit'.[41] Also, the friaries were conspicuous in a way that monasteries were not, because most of their properties were situated in cities and towns. The document, which is couched in the terminology of a summons of removal, is addressed by the blind, the crooked, the bed-ridden, by widows and orphans and all other poor who cannot work, to all the friars in the realm, demanding restitution for bypast wrongs, and Reformation in time coming. They claimed that the friars themselves were aware, as was the whole world, that the benignity, or alms, of all Christian people pertained to the poor alone. These had been stolen by those who were strong in body and able to work, under the pretence of poverty (though in reality enjoying abundance of everything), false simplicity and feigned holiness, which were now declared superstition and idolatry. The friars had also, by false doctrine and dishonest manipulation of God's holy word (learned from their father, Satan), convinced the whole people that the clothing, feeding and nourishing of themselves were the most acceptable type of alms, and that the giving of a penny or a piece of bread once a week was sufficient for the poor.

Furthermore, they had persuaded the charitable to build them large hospitals in which to maintain themselves, although originally endowed for the indigent 'of whois number ye are not, nor can be repute, nether be the law of God, nor yit be na uther law proceding of nature, reasoun or civile policie'. The number of the destitute was so great, and so oppressed were they by the clergy, that nobody was concerned about their misery; it was thus better to provide for the impotent by outright opposition, rather than to observe the friars stealing their lodgings while they perished for lack of same. 'We have thocht gude therfore, or we enter with yow in conflict, to warne yow, in the name of the grit God, be this publick wryting, affixt on your yetts quhair ye now dwell' that they remove before Whitsunday next.

> Certifying yow, gif ye failye, we will at the said terme, in hale nummer (with the help of God, and assistance of his sanctis in erthe, of quhais reddie support we dout not), enter and tak posession of our saide patrimony, and eject yow utterlie fourth of the same. *Lat hym therfore that before hes stollin, steill na mare; but rather lat him wyrk wyth his handes, that he may be helpefull to the pure.*[42]

The 'Summons', which survives in an unique cropped copy in Edinburgh University library, has received remarkably little critical attention. What is significant is that on the eve of Reformation the beggars became a revolutionary icon, yet, as in most revolutions, when the last banner had been furled and the final drumbeat faded, the lot of the poor remained much as it had always been. Scotland was still 'a land of poverty and beggars',[43] but such were the expectations raised by John Knox rather than John the Commonweal that beggars remained firmly on the agenda of the reformed church and were the subject of much church and state legislation.

It may be thought that the entire drift of this article has been to present Jock o the Commonweal or Jock Uppaland as somehow quintessentially Scottish. It is thus with some diffidence that it must be admitted that Jock was originally English. Jak Upland appeared in English manuscripts of around 1420, subsequently printed in black-letter, in 1536. Jack the Countryman adapts Lollard criticism of the friars in a prose tract, making many hard-hitting and contemptuous remarks of a type that were fairly widespread. Above all he asks them to justify their fondness for begging when they already inhabit palatial accommodation. Like beggars, friars wear a special uniform; like beggars, friars are supposed to be notorious stealers of children.[44] In the second tract, Friar Daw responds in what appears to be blank verse, patronisingly repeating Jak's name and objecting that laymen do not know enough to make an effective argument. He, of course, denies Jak's accusations, but not that friars depend upon charity; friars, however, are not direct competitors – there is no honour in begging from beggars. In the third English tract Upland is permitted a rejoinder, which is basically more of the same material that had appeared in the first, belonging to the well-defined medieval genre of critical hostility visited upon the friars. The debate was widespread. Walter Bower, for example, was vehemently opposed to the Lollards, but he also shared many of their suspicions of the friars.[45] So too did David Lindsay, and there can be little doubt that his debt to Jak Upland was substantial or, indeed, that he transferred some of Upland's sentiments to Jock Uppaland and Jock o the Commonweal.[46] Such English medieval Lollard tracts must have had a greater influence upon Scottish thinking than severe Presbyterian critics have traditionally allowed. The editor of one such, *The examinacion of Master Thorpe*, published in 1530, having noted that he put forth the work in the English then current in England, announced that he also intended to publish a version in old English, which would serve for readers in northern England 'and the faythfull brothern of scotlande'. We might suspect that another English Lollard tract, *The praier and complaynte of the ploweman unto Christe* (1532), would have found a certain resonance among Scots of Lindsay's ilk.[47] Nor is it unlikely that such tracts[48] informed the 'Beggars' Summons'.

The metaphor at the heart of Lindsay's play thus had a much wider application than is usually allowed; in Scotland, at least, a popular literary genre had a measurable impact upon the historical process. In the final submission, John the Commonweal is not only a remarkable literary and dramatic creation but also, in the context of beggary, he represents an accurate reflection of contemporary concerns. Furthermore, for one brief moment on 1 January 1559 the culture of the Scottish undermass was placed at centre stage as soothsayers, bards, prophets, jugglers, balladeers, the halt, the lame, the indigent, destitute Gaels and impoverished students – in short, beggars of all descriptions – were involved in a revolutionary process of bringing about the Scottish Reformation. It is a cruel irony that the Reformers from the 1560s onwards were to become so vehemently opposed to the very culture and the colourful folk who were its practitioners, so fulsomely invoked by them in 1559.

2

Paper Monuments: Collecting the Lives of Scots

TRISTRAM CLARKE

If history is 'a family of genres', then collective biography is, historiographically speaking, the poor relation who is commonly taken for granted as a useful servant. The collected lives of Scots have yet to be studied even to the limited extent to which compilations of English or British lives have been discussed.[1] As a contribution towards understanding the genre, the following account attempts to trace the development and significance of collective biographies of Scots. The creation of a 'biographia Scotica', or Scottish national biography, was for long a goal towards which writers struggled, with mixed success. Now that the *Oxford Dictionary of National Biography* (*Oxford DNB*) (2004) has reinforced the scope of the British national biography defined by its Victorian predecessor, the *Dictionary of National Biography* (*DNB*), it is worth examining the attempts to construct a distinct national biography that commemorated Scottish worthies and embodied aspects of the historic identity of Scotland. In following the fitful history of this genre, most attention will be paid to the period from the eighteenth until the mid-nineteenth century, before examining more recent developments. Brief consideration will be given to the reputations of Scottish historical figures, which have become a matter of academic interest, as well as being a favourite press topic.[2] However, this survey can only pay limited attention to the complex composition of Scotland's multiple identities. It approaches the subject from a different angle than discussions of the history, images, perceptions and representations of those identities.[3]

Although biographical dictionaries in their different forms stem from one of the classic forms of historical writing, the collected lives of the eminent or the exemplary (the best-known of which was Plutarch's *Lives*), as a sub-genre of biography they have scarcely caught the attention of students of historiography.[4] The uneasy relationship between biography and history has contributed to the neglect of collective biography as a historiographical genre, for good biographers and good historians are rarely the same people, and biography has not always been accepted as a valid form of historical investigation and analysis.[5] This has not prevented the periodic flourishing of collected lives down to the present day, whether as a means of moral instruction, an enshrining of a nation's greatest and best figures, a form of historical and literary biography, or a reference tool for historical investigation. The sheer variety of the forms taken by collective biography has perhaps also hindered study of the genre, although recent investigations of the history of the book, and especially of the antecedents of the *DNB*, have begun to supply the gaps in our knowledge.[6] In part this signals the engagement of academic scholars with a genre which was largely the domain of professional and amateur authors.

Keith Thomas has lucidly classified the different strands of collective biography which contributed to the development of the *DNB*.[7] At the supra-national level, universal biography ignores national boundaries and records the lives of worthy subjects of all periods, usually in the form of encyclopaedic dictionaries. This genre emerged in the seventeenth century and reached its apogee in the multi-volume works of the nineteenth century. Group biography has concerned itself with members of institutions or other bodies of men and women, often professionals such as judges or ministers of various denominations, the alumni of universities and schools, and politicians. It could play an important role in reflecting historic identity by furnishing certain strands of a national biography. Group biographies of eminent figures in several important areas of Scottish life, literature, the church, government and the law will be examined below.

Drawing on universal and group biography, the genre of national biography 'was closely related to the emergence of nationalist sentiment'.[8] Typically developed from commemoration of canonical literary figures, it could combine bibliographical with biographical information. The first extensive British work to achieve this national status after the Union was the *Biographia Britannica* (1747–66), which held the field until the arrival of the *DNB*. During the mid-nineteenth century other nations compiled national biographies. Sweden was the first to publish on a large scale, commencing a series of twenty-three volumes in 1835.[9] Also published that year were the comparatively modest four octavo volumes of Robert Chambers' *Lives of Illustrious and Distinguished Scotsmen*. This pioneering Scottish national biography was not part of the conscious efforts at nation-building being undertaken on the continent, but was rather an attempt to rescue national identity from historical neglect, and to celebrate national characteristics such as presbyterian Protestantism and native genius. Inevitably, attempts to write a national biography reflected facets of historic identity, and Scotland was no exception. Its character by the early nineteenth century could broadly be described as presbyterian, independent-minded but loyal, enterprising, educated and, if construed in negative terms, not English and not Roman Catholic.[10] Scots shared some of these attributes with the English, but apart from the formative influence of the Scots' ethnic origins, the Wars of Independence, the Reformation, the Covenant and the Union, they were all regarded as defining the Scottish character and experience.

In 1834 Chambers noted that a biographical dictionary dedicated to Scots had been 'a desideratum in our national literature for the greater part of a century'.[11] In fact it is to the scholarly circles of seventeenth-century Scotland that it is possible to trace the first attempts at writing a broad-ranging collective or national biography in Scotland. Literature first attracted the attention of the compilers of collected lives, as part of the antiquarians' enquiries into history, geography, natural history and literature. In 1623 Thomas Dempster published *De Historia Ecclesiastica Gentis Scotorum*, which, although not a dictionary, contained biographical and bibliographical accounts of about 1,300 Scottish clergy, authors and saints. It became the standard reference work for over a century, despite its Roman Catholic bias and anti-Protestant abuse. One reason may have been Dempster's patriotic stance, even though his desire to reclaim Scots figures for Scotland led him, for example, to elide distinctions between *Hiberni* and *Scoti*, to inflate his number considerably and to appropriate men such as St Boniface from the English. Among his faults were over-reliance on unreliable sources and false linguistic inferences, which led him to make spurious claims in his determined search for Scots. Despite its flaws, Dempster's *Historia* has been described as a new departure in Scottish historical writing: an independent Scottish work (although published in Bologna) written neither from an English nor a British viewpoint, which stands at the beginning of a historiographical tradition that would lead ultimately to a national biography.[12]

Dempster's work showed that one of the main components in such a project was the gathering of the lives of a nation's learned men and writers, for as Keith Thomas has remarked, every nation needs a literary canon in addition to its great men.[13] In the years immediately before the Union of 1707, several studious Scots were contemplating writing an account of the nation's scholars or compiling a bibliography of their works. A general impetus for celebrating national worthies was provided by the controversies about Scottish sovereignty and the independence of its church, which had brought into question aspects of Scotland's national identity during the late seventeenth and early eighteenth centuries. The antiquarian Sir Robert Sibbald drafted a defence of the Scottish king lists,[14] and also planned a 'Bibliotheca Scotica or Ane account of thes Scotish authors who by their writings have improved all sort of Learning from the year 1500 to the present year 1700. To which is added all the Eloges [eulogies] or censures Learned men have given of them.' His aim was a critical bibliography for the use of scholars, divided by subject and amplified with notes about the writers: 'The tyme they flourished, the language they wrotte in, the purity or rudeness of their style and the Quality of their Work.'[15] Sibbald scorned Dempster for being driven to conjecture rather than fact by his 'too great affection to his Country, togither with his bilious and haughty humour'.[16]

Sibbald himself escaped similar censure by never completing his scheme for the 'bibliotheca', though he inserted a life and a likeness of the poet Mark Alexander Boyd in his *Scotia Illustrata*.[17] His friend Walter Paterson, parish minister of Bolton, also worked on Scottish writers and drafted a list of those whose works he had seen or of which he had got certain information. Unfortunately this 'judicious and diligent man' died in 1692 before he could get any further.[18] He had been helped by a fellow minister and former professor of divinity, Laurence Charteris, who penned his own 'short account of Scots divines', 1500–1700, likewise unpublished.[19] At about this date the English nonjuring antiquary Dr Thomas Smith told a Scottish scholar, James Gray, that it was 'very much wanting to the honour of your country in not publishing in Latine an account of the many learned men Scotland has produced in these 3 last Centuryes'. He drafted a scheme for such an account. Later, in 1707, on being shown a specimen of the proposed work, Smith commented tellingly on the difficulties common to all endeavours to collect lives: 'I easily grant that such a various work can not be made perfect & finished of a suddaine and all at once – it being capable of such vast improvement and additions, by continuall discoveryes and new notices of things either from manuscripts memoires or printed books.'[20] Whether or not these considerations hindered the compilation of a 'bibliotheca Scotica', no substantial work appeared, nor any lives to match the idiosyncracies of John Aubrey and Anthony à Wood.[21]

Although Sibbald, Paterson, Charteris and other episcopalian scholars all failed to make more than limited progress, an ambitious scheme for a 'bibliotheca Scotica' by an Edinburgh physician, Dr George Mackenzie, did come to fruition between 1708 and 1722. His work was a response to Bishop Nicholson's observation that it was 'strange and unaccountable' that the learned Scots, many of whom had shone in European universities and were 'mighty Hero's in Learning, to whom the Old Romans and Athenians would have erected Altars, should want even the cheap Acknowledgment of a Paper-Monument'.[22] Mackenzie constructed a veritable mausoleum in three folio volumes, presenting in elaborate detail his lives of the writers, catalogues of their works and critics' opinions of them, as well as accounts of controversies, of which there were plenty since most of his subjects were sixteenth-century divines. He used Dempster critically, as he was 'Naturally Credulous and Inclin'd to believe Monkish Stories and Miracles', and helpfully listed those writers included by Dempster but whom he omitted for various reasons.[23] However, despite all the show of learning it was said that Mackenzie was 'a great pretender to things he understood not; as a physician, he knew nothing of his own business'. Mackenzie's drinking partner, the Jacobite satirist Dr Archibald Pitcairne, 'at first commended his lives to every body, but when he had read some of them, he declared they were not worth a button'.[24] About a century passed before the next work of collected lives of literary figures was published.[25]

There had been improving and exemplary lives of saints and medieval bishops, but the first major attempt at gathering the lives of post-Reformation churchmen seems to have occurred in the early eighteenth century. In 1717 Robert Wodrow, parish minister and antiquarian, began work on a collective biography of the reformed church and was pursuing it after publishing his *History of the Sufferings of the Church of Scotland* in 1721–2.[26] He was interested in the spiritual lives of his presbyterian subjects, who included many minor figures besides the leading reformers. Drawing on original sermons, diaries and stories concerning the travails of presbyterians, especially during the Restoration episcopate, but also going back into the sixteenth century, he wrote some biographies, though fewer than he intended. His model was probably Calamy's work on the English presbyterian clergy ejected after the Restoration.[27] Wodrow's work remained unpublished until massive nineteenth-century editions transformed it into accessible source material from which many later biographical writers drew.[28] Wodrow, like other contemporary antiquarians and historians, was an avid collector of historical evidence, even though occasionally credulous, and he saw value in gathering biographies together, albeit for a confessional purpose. In this respect he was working in the long tradition of writing lives as moral exemplars.

The pre-eminent presbyterian hagiography was John Howie's *Biographia Scoticana* (1775), apparently inspired by Foxe's martyrology. It was very popular from the outset and for over a century was republished in many editions as *Scots Worthies*. It addressed an audience largely attuned to the values contained in its 'useful, holy and exemplary lives' of presbyterians.[29] In celebrating the presbyterian tradition as an essential part of Scotland's post-Reformation identity, the *Scots Worthies* represented a major strand of the national biography. Later, the defining moment of the Disruption in 1843 was first commemorated in two group biographies, then as a part of a history of the Free Church.[30] All major Scottish denominations are now served by collective biographies, but the parish clergy were late in becoming the subject of a group biography. Any enterprise to commemorate the ministers of the national church had to overcome the difficulties thrown up by fierce historical divisions, and the sheer difficulty of writing about the clergy in some 1,000 parishes. However, the historical insignificance of the majority of the clergy as individuals meant that any work would necessarily mainly consist of a factual work of reference rather than gathered biographies. The lives of the parish clergy in Hew Scott's *Fasti Ecclesiae Scoticanae* (1866–71), arranged by synod, presbytery and parish, were written in fairly concise prose, which was later abbreviated.[31] This monument of Victorian scholarship attests to the commitment and stamina that was required to complete a group biography successfully. For about thirty-five years Scott, a parish minister, trawled a huge quantity of original records and secondary sources to draw up the lives of the ministers, which he meticulously entered on the backs of letters and envelopes saved for the purpose. During his lengthy research he did not enjoy great encouragement, so he must have valued the words of Thomas Chalmers: 'Go on, Mr Scott, go on; the unborn will bless you, sir.'[32]

By contrast, George Crawfurd claimed only the secular aim of the honour of his country in writing his work, *The Peerage of Scotland* (1716).[33] In 1710 he had published an account of the royal house of Stewart, a cross between a group biography, royal and aristocratic family history, and glorified king list.[34] Crawfurd's pioneering genealogies of the Scottish aristocracy were the forerunners of more comprehensive works, and emerged from the aristocratic craze for pedigree during the seventeenth century. Genealogies provided a record of the status and marriage connections of families or clans, and were a potent tool for providing 'identity, unity and historical legitimation'.[35] The impulse behind such image-making seems to have contributed to the upholding of the honour and antiquity of Scots noble lineage as a whole, which was expressed in the national interconnections of family and kinship networks in Crawfurd's *Peerage*. However, the schematic outlines of aristocratic lives disqualify the *Peerage* as group biography, and Crawford only occasionally observed a character trait, hinting at the person behind the facts.

His next work, *The Lives and Characters of the Officers of the Crown, and of the State in Scotland* (1726), was a group biography arranged by the office which the subject held, enlivened with some recent biographical details drawn from oral evidence. In taking as his terminal point the Union of 1707, when many of the offices ceased to exist, Crawford recorded a milestone in Scotland's history through the medium of collected lives. At this period a more sophisticated historiographical approach was evident as research in primary sources began to transform historical understanding, for example in Fr Thomas Innes' *Critical Essay on the Ancient Inhabitants of Scotland* (1729), which demolished the mythical dynasties of Scottish kings. The critical and document-based approach was evident also in the work of Bishop Robert Keith,[36] whose careful research in difficult sources yielded a group biography from the episcopalian perspective, *Catalogue of the Bishops of Scotland Down to the Year 1688* (1755).[37]

During the eighteenth century the investigation of primary sources spread to other historical subjects, including the law, which has long formed another cornerstone of Scottish identity. The compilation of the lives and careers of judges and lawyers formed an important theme in the development of the collective biography in Scotland. David Dalrymple, Lord Hailes, better known for his pioneering examination of the middle ages, *Annals of Scotland* (1776–9), published *A Catalogue of the Lords of Session from the Institution of the College of Justice, in the year 1532* (1767). He listed every judge from Alexander Milne, abbot of Cambuskenneth and president of the court in 1532, to James Burnett, created Lord Monboddo in 1767. Hailes requested notice of any additions or corrections, because 'a first sketch of this nature must be imperfect'. The chronological list of judges was supplemented by historical notes, which he scrupulously omitted for living or recent judges.[38] However, Sir James Foulis of Colinton was so outraged by a description of the inferior status of a sixteenth-century ancestor that Hailes was obliged to suppress the book.[39] Difficulties of giving offence attend the publication of what a biographical writer believes are matters of fact. Wariness, tact or deference help explain why writers of peerage works, for example, have tended to omit uncomfortable facts, such as death by suicide.[40]

When the usefulness of Hailes' *Catalogue* was recognised by an updated edition in 1798, another writer was becoming interested in extending its scope to cover other important figures in the Scottish judiciary, government and administration, and the bar. John Philp Wood, auditor of the Scottish excise, is credited with writing the first Scottish parochial history in 1794.[41] Notes on the Scottish gentry occupied him in the mid-1790s, and his later work on the post-Union peerage of Scotland led him to revise Douglas' *Peerage* of 1764 in two volumes in 1813. After gathering information from printed and manuscript sources on the lords of session, law officers, barons of exchequer and advocates, between about 1812 and 1818 Wood drafted brief lives of men in all these categories in ten folio volumes.[42] He included some genealogical details and outlined the subject's career, but the occasional quotations from original documents added little insight.

Wood intended to publish his lives of the judges and advocates,[43] and in 1817 sought the advice of the great record scholar, Thomas Thomson, the deputy clerk register. Instead of 'regular and formal lives', Thomson saw the value of brief notices of professional and official careers for 'easy and useful reference' by lawyers and others. Only eminent judges should be included: 'The Lords of Session of the last three centuries are a numerous body, including a large proportion of insignificant or contemptible individuals. Why should such poor creatures be immortalized merely because they had the misfortune to be advanced to a station for which they were unfit.' He approved of Wood's biographical notes on the advocates as a useful addition to Hailes' *Catalogue*, but the same reservations would apply 'still more forcibly' to his fellow advocates: 'Lawyers are an ephemeral race of beings, who must be left to their natural oblivion unless they have done something for which they ought not to be forgotten.'[44] Thomson's acceptance of the value of a proper biographical reference work of 'brief notices' did not extend to Wood's comprehensive and inclusive approach, and instead he advocated selectivity on the grounds of historical significance. Whatever effect Thomson's critique had, Wood never published his legal lives, although he updated his notes until near the end of his life in 1838.

In 1830 John Hill Burton, then a young lawyer recently arrived from Aberdeen, considered an approach to the publisher Constable concerning a biographical publication on Scottish lawyers and statesmen.[45] Although his scheme came to nothing, in 1836 Hailes' *Catalogue* was definitively superseded as the standard work of legal biographical reference by *An Historical Account of the Senators of the College of Justice*. George Brunton, an Edinburgh solicitor and journalist, and David Haig, assistant librarian to the faculty of advocates, listed the chancellors, presidents and other lords of session chronologically, with a biography of varying length for each subject. For the early period they gave more detail, but nearer their own day they became more reticent. Their 'utmost conciseness of narration, as well as brevity of diction'[46] contrasts with Wood's looser and uneven style, and marks their book as a recognisable forerunner of modern biographical reference works.

Wood's unpublished notes were later quarried by Sir Francis Grant for his biographies of the advocates, which summarised their legal careers but excluded family and other information.[47] From a prosopographical perspective, the writers to the signet, who trace their history to the sixteenth century, have been better served in the standard history of their society, which provided details of each writer's parentage, marriage and death in addition to his legal career.[48] Of all the Scottish professions, elite groups of lawyers have attracted most biographical attention from writers who thereby commemorated, albeit without overt expressions of patriotism, the most eminent national body surviving from the pre-Union kingdom. Similar treatment has not been accorded to the internationally famed Scottish medical profession, for which there is little published biographical information.[49]

None of the genres of group biography, which have been traced as far as the nineteenth century, constituted a Scottish national biography, so the emergence of the 'biographica Scotica' needs also to be understood in the context of the evolution of the European encyclopaedia and the universal biographical dictionary. As repositories of biographical knowledge, they laid the foundations of British national biography during the seventeenth century. Universal biography formed part of Moréri's *Grand Dictionnaire Historique* (1673). The first such work to be arranged biographically was Pierre Bayle's *Dictionnaire Historique et Critique* (1697),[50] which included lives of George Buchanan, John Knox and about ten other Scots, mostly scholars with a European connection. The superior English version of Bayle's work, *A Biographical Dictionary, Historical and Critical* (1734–41), incorporated 889 new British lives, of whom about 25 were Scots. Almost all were divines and authors, but recent Scottish scientific and mathematical achievement was acknowledged in the articles on David, James and John Gregory, and James and John Keill.[51] Bayle's group entries on the Drummond and Lesley families were omitted.

The most significant work to commemorate Scots worthies in this period was the first British national biographical dictionary, the *Biographia Britannica* (1747–66). Its six volumes contained lives of statesmen, prelates, patriots, lawyers and divines of distinction in Britain and Ireland. In the manner of Bayle's dictionary, the text ran above a solid foundation of references, the subject's bibliography, and extensive critical commentary and quotation. Avowedly a celebration of British national achievement, the dictionary has been described as 'the literary counterpart to the emerging national pantheon in Westminster Abbey'.[52] This claim to inclusivity is supported by the presence of Scottish figures, some of whom were accorded generous space. Cardinal David Beaton (1494–1546), for example, enjoyed about eighteen pages, compared to twelve given to his English contemporary, Cardinal Pole (1500–58).[53] However, there were fewer than thirty Scots in the main body of the text, and eight in the Supplement, out of several hundred subjects. The promising proportion of seven Scots lives out of the 117 under 'A' in the first volume was not sustained in the rest of the *Biographia.*[54]

The omissions illustrate the perspectives of this product of metropolitan culture. As in Westminster Abbey, space could not be found for every Briton of note. The reader vainly searches the metaphorical Poets' Corner for the makar William Dunbar; nor was William Drummond of Hawthornden accorded a niche between his friend Michael Drayton and John Dryden.[55] Such omissions were presumably due partly to the vagaries of literary and critical fashion, and partly to editorial anglocentricity, accentuated by more readily available sources for English lives. Whether historical and religious bias also affected the selection might be determined by investigation of the extent to which the compilers were swayed by, for example, Anglican or dissenting prejudices.[56] The unevenness of coverage is also evident in the treatment of leading landed families. There are entries on the Campbells and Grants,[57] but none for the Drummonds (who had featured in Bayle's *General Dictionary*), nor the Camerons, Forbes or Gordons, nor indeed on any individuals bearing those surnames. In truth, the shortcomings of the family entries were widespread, and the general under-representation of subjects also applied to the Welsh and Irish. Yet the question of the national identities embodied in the *Biographia Britannica* and other purportedly British biographical dictionaries has still to be addressed.[58]

While the structure of the *Biographia Britannica* was indebted to Bayle's universal biographical dictionary, during the seventeenth and eighteenth centuries knowledge in the arts and sciences was being incorporated into increasingly sophisticated encyclopaedias, most famously in Diderot's *Encyclopédie* of 1750. The first eighteenth-century British dictionary of arts and sciences to call itself an encyclopaedia, and ultimately the most successful work, was founded in Edinburgh in 1768 as the *Encyclopaedia Britannica.* Like Diderot's work it contained no biographies at all, because the scheme of knowledge on which it was based did not incorporate history. It was only with the second edition of 1777–83 that the publishers included biography and history. Much of this edition was hastily written and assembled.[59] Its biographical content was essentially that of a compact universal biography. Primacy still rested with men of learning, but hitherto neglected monarchs and patriots, such as Robert I and William Wallace, were included.[60]

It is possible that the quality of these biographies stirred up Lord Hailes, who was actively pursuing his scheme for a 'biographia Scotica' by the time of the last part of *Britannica*'s second edition in 1783. Certainly his efforts should be seen in the context of the encyclopaedia tradition as well as of the developing national dictionary. His inquisitive historical mind, and his enthusiasm for what we know as 'research projects',[61] led him to consider the need for biographies of Scots. The result was a series of five brief lives which he published at his own expense from about 1784 to 1787. His subjects were sixteenth- and early seventeenth-century divines and scholars, including the poet Mark Alexander Boyd, and a soldier, Sir James Ramsay, a senior commander under Gustavus Adolphus.[62] He chose obscure and less interesting figures[63] as a challenge to discover sufficient information to show how the 'biographia' could be achieved. As he explained: 'Other Lives of more celebrity might have been composed with less pains.'[64] His subjects had in common that they had spent some time on the continent, and Hailes delighted in tracing their paths through obscure books and in polishing his prose, expressive of enlightened detachment.[65]

His sketches contained a chronological account, mostly followed by an assessment of the subject's writings, and were carefully notated with sources and further editorial comment. Patriotically, he hoped that each life would stimulate Scots scholars to take up their pens for a 'biographia Scotica'. 'Such a work,' he wrote, 'however imperfectly executed, would be amusing, and, if well executed, useful.' He claimed to know twenty men who might further the project 'with honour to themselves and to their native country', and that many other learned gentlemen were qualified to do so. Instead of writing pamphlets, men of letters could profitably write a biographical article or two. Biography was, he argued, a proper function of the Society of Antiquaries of Scotland, who might produce 'literary' lives, and likewise the public might naturally expect the Royal Society of Edinburgh to honour mathematicians and men of science. As he demonstrated, 'want of leisure and want of materials' were vain excuses, and single lives in small impressions would cover the publisher's costs.[66]

His scholarly friends among the English bishops approved of his project. In 1784 the Bishop of Worcester congratulated him on his life of John Hamilton, which was

> composed with your usual Care and exactness. And if your setting this example of Scotch Biography should induce your literati to write the lives of their illustrious Countrymen, instead of bewildering themselves or their Readers in modern or antient Metaphysics, your pains would be employed to good purpose.[67]

How did the Scots literati respond to Hailes' proposals? In apparently the only surviving response, the author Gilbert Stuart excused himself because his work obliged him to live in London.[68] Hailes' project held most significance for the earl of Buchan, who in 1787 claimed to have conceived his own wish to create a *Biographia Scotica* about twenty years earlier. This dates his inspiration to the time of Hailes' *Catalogue* (1767), and indeed he admitted that Hailes had encouraged him to prosecute his biographical research. In 1787 Buchan described Hailes as his 'respectable coadjutor', who in his recent biographies had generously offered 'to forward the undertaking I wish to prosecute'. He shared Hailes' optimism that scholars would easily be found to write lives from their expert knowledge, as well as his disappointment at their failure to do so. His conception was of a series of independently written lives that would be absorbed, in corrected form, into later editions of the *Biographia Britannica*. In order to rectify an omission from the dictionary and provide a model biography, in 1787 Buchan collaborated with a specialist to produce the life of the inventor of logarithms, John Napier of Merchiston.[69]

Buchan later wrote four brief lives for the liberal periodical *The Bee, or Literary Weekly Intelligencer*,[70] and an account of Fletcher of Saltoun and James Thomson, in the tradition of Whiggish patriotism.[71] However, his biographical energies were diffused into other patriotic projects to honour Thomson and Burns, to collect and commission portraits of Scots worthies,[72] and to found the Society of Antiquaries of Scotland. In the antiquaries' first volume of *Transactions* (1792) two brief biographies appeared, one by Buchan himself. This was a scant response to Hailes' call for biographies, and later volumes did no better.[73] After 1793 the Royal Society of Edinburgh provided a more sympathetic milieu for the commemoration of outstanding Scots of the recent past. Adam Smith, Thomas Reid, William Robertson, James Hutton and Joseph Black were all commemorated in papers read to the Society, in published accounts in its *Transactions*, and later in separate publications.[74]

These brief lives represented a limited measure of success for Hailes' idea of a 'biographia Scotica', but they were essentially piecemeal contributions. There is little evidence that scholars shared his zeal to the extent of being willing to collaborate. Not every scholar had Hailes' private resources, for he envisaged a work 'on a large and liberal plan',[75] probably individual lives published as part of a series. One feature of his lives is worth noting. Engraved portraits enlivened two of his biographies,[76] and they were to be an integral part of the biographical series proposed by Lord Buchan.[77] This use of illustrations was not new, and ultimately derived from the Renaissance genre of collected portraits paired with brief biographies. Large compilations had appeared in England in the decades before 1770,[78] and engraved portraits were published with the individual biographical memoirs that featured in *The Edinburgh Magazine and Review* from 1773.[79] Scots were included in

James Granger's unillustrated catalogue of English portraits combined with biographical notes.[80]

The first collected portraiture of Scots was produced by the eccentric historian John Pinkerton, whose *Iconographia Scotica or Portraits of Illustrious Persons* (1797) comprised a set of engravings of likenesses of Scots from Robert the Bruce to Colin Maclaurin, the celebrated Scottish mathematician (d.1746). His very brief lives of each character were no more than captions for the illustrations. Next he published *The Scottish Gallery; or, Portraits of Eminent Persons of Scotland* (1799), a similar album of kings and nobles. Despite the inauthenticity of some of the original portraits and the poor engravings, the books confirmed the potential of the illustrated collective biography. It was only with advances in reproductive techniques in the nineteenth century that engraved portraits came to be included in biographical dictionaries for a wider market than the connoisseurs at whom Pinkerton aimed. In Scotland this development resulted in illustrated dictionaries, but also in works such as John Kay's *Portraits* of a cross-section of Edinburgh society, which combined his amusing engravings with brief lives by James Paterson.[81]

Apart from the quixotic Buchan, the only scholar who actively shared Hailes' vision was William Smellie, polymathic printer and writer, and first editor of the *Encyclopaedia Britannica.* It was said that the publishers' decision to include biography in the second edition caused him to refuse to act again. In 1791 he described the dictionary's 'department for biography' as 'a most dangerous and injurious affair, when the characters of illustrious men happen to fall into the hands of petulance and ignorance'.[82] From the 1760s Smellie had supported biographical writing as vital for 'moral and historical instruction.'[83] His desire to contribute to the genre as a well-connected man of letters and reason led him to conceive an alphabetically arranged series of 'Literary and Characteristical Accounts' of authors, 'as a commencement towards a Biographia Scotica'. His subjects formed a glittering list of Enlightenment figures whom he had known personally, and many of whom had commissioned him to print their works. Although he was actively gathering material in early 1795, unfortunately, like Hailes, all he achieved before his death that summer was a handful of brief lives. His biographies of David Hume and others appeared posthumously in 1800.[84]

Hailes died in 1792, having promoted his scheme as late as 1791.[85] Despite his pioneering work, by the turn of the nineteenth century his conception of a national biography remained unrealised, apparently a catalogue of false starts and dead ends. The difficulty of researching and writing a life might have deterred some potential authors, for biography was a scarcely developed art. In any case, historical enquiry in a nationalist sphere was not of interest to the leading Enlightenment thinkers, whose interests generally lay in philosophical and sociological problems. The construction of British identity after the Union had tended to stifle Scotland's national identity. Hailes, Buchan and Smellie represent a shift of the Enlightenment away from universal themes towards national preoccupations.

The work which can claim to be the first Scottish national biographical dictionary appeared in 1805. John Stark, like William Smellie a printer with literary tastes, fittingly entitled it *Biographia Scotica; or Scottish Biographical Dictionary; containing a short account of the lives and writings of the most eminent persons and remarkable characters, natives of Scotland, from the earliest ages to the present time.* It was a brave first attempt to compress 362 lives within about 420 duodecimo pages, enlivened with engraved portraits of five Scots.[86] Stark's subjects ranged from painters and poets to statesmen and men of science. Innovatively he included all Scottish monarchs from Malcolm I to James VI, though oddly omitting Queen Margaret and James V. He also included Constantine I, II and III, whom scholarship had confirmed were not mythical. This helped to dispel the persistence in popular culture of legendary history.[87] Although the lives were generally very short, Mary Queen of Scots and Enlightenment figures such as Thomas Reid, William Robertson and Tobias Smollett received longer treatment. The account of David Hume described his historical writing and philosophical achievements, and emphasised the philosophical and courageous manner in which he faced his illness and death. Stark's little work betrayed some of the pitfalls of the dictionary form: uneven coverage, and hasty judgements on recently dead subjects. Not all of his readers can have agreed with the assessment of Lord Braxfield, lord justice clerk during the critical 1790s: 'A well tempered integrity of conduct, and a steady and vigorous application of the law, will immortalise his memory in the annals of his country.' Other assessments dated quickly, but are interesting in their own right. He judged that when the philosophical works of the recently deceased Aberdonian divine James Beattie were superseded and almost forgotten, three of his poems 'will be read with tears of rapture, while a taste for poetry prevails'.[88] Critical opinion now recognises the influence of works such as *The Minstrel*, but gives more weight to his aesthetic essays.[89]

While Stark's judgements have inevitably been eroded by changing opinion, the *Biographia Scotica* testifies to his patriotic enterprise in writing the first national biographical dictionary. Its compact form, modest scale and lack of literary pretension mark it as a functional work of reference. It was essentially the forerunner of the popular compilations that have appeared occasionally ever since, many of which have continued the tradition of collecting lives with a moral or patriotic purpose by emphasising national achievements and virtues.[90] By contrast, after Stark the goal for the rising generation attempting a dictionary remained Hailes' model of a repository of lives recorded in lapidary essays. In 1819 the historian Patrick Fraser Tytler, who was then working as legal counsel in the exchequer, published his life of the Admirable Crichton. A further project suggested itself: to revive and execute Hailes' plan of a 'biographia

Scotica', 'including the lives of eminent Scotchmen during the sixteenth and seventeenth centuries'.[91] In choosing as his first subject Thomas Dempster, the first creator of a Scottish historical pantheon, Tytler perhaps sought to emulate Hailes' interest in Scots scholars abroad. In the event, the collaborative aspect of his project did not materialise, and Tytler devoted himself during the next decade to research for his seven-volume *History of Scotland* (1828–43). In 1823, the year he helped to found the Bannatyne Club, he published some lawyers' lives,[92] but the main by-product of his research in the period from Alexander III to James VI were three volumes of *Lives of Scottish Worthies* (1831–3). Devoting most space to Robert the Bruce, James I and William Wallace, he also wrote about several chroniclers, poets and authors, and a wizard.[93] Tytler can be credited with writing the first substantial accounts of some of these men, but he was necessarily very selective, and the long essay form was an unsustainable basis for a national biography across the span of Scottish history. He cannot have been encouraged by accusations of episcopalian bias and unpatriotic views,[94] but it was probably the demands of constructing his new narrative and analytical history that prevented him from adding to the biographies as a result of his studies after 1833.

It fell to another historian and miscellaneous writer, Robert Chambers, to produce the first substantial national biographical dictionary: *Lives of Illustrious and Distinguished Scotsmen from the Earliest Period to the Present Time . . . Forming a Complete Scottish Biographical Dictionary*. It marks the fruition of Hailes' conception of the 'biographia Scotica'. First appearing in instalments from 1832, it was published whole in 1835 in four octavo volumes, containing about 550 alphabetically arranged lives in its 2,300 pages. Chambers alluded to the failure of both Hailes and Smellie to do more than write a few articles of biography for their respective schemes, and drily admitted to proceeding 'rather under the influence of a peculiar enthusiasm, than any wiser or more considerate motive'.[95] It helped that he was an erudite and prolific writer with an eye for telling detail and shrewd judgement, which he had already displayed in *Traditions of Edinburgh* (1824) and a history of the '45 rebellion (1831). Another advantage was that his publishers, Blackie, placed at his disposal the material which they had already prepared for a similar unrealised scheme.[96] They declared that most of the writing and all the 'literary superintendence' would be the work of Chambers, and that some lives would be written by those best qualified to do so.[97] The several hands in the manuscript drafts[98] confirm that Chambers was helped in transforming the existing material into a completed work, and he acknowledged the 'zeal and talent' of his assistants.[99] Even allowing for this help, his success where others had failed was remarkable, and the dictionary became the standard work for many decades.

His *Illustrious and Distinguished Scotsmen* was a gallery of worthies: statesmen, clergymen, men of learning in all disciplines, judges, medical men, soldiers, sailors and a handful of women,[100] but it did not claim completeness. Chambers included only fourteen monarchs[101] and excluded all the Stuarts after Charles I, monarchs and claimants alike, presumably as being Scots only by descent. Unlike some English publications he excluded famous villains, unless they were also distinguished in some other way. His choice of subjects was to an extent determined by the source material available in earlier collective biographies, but he omitted most of Dempster's subjects and far exceeded the *Biographia Britannica*'s Scottish coverage. He benefited from recent biographical works,[102] as well as histories by Hailes and others. For recent subjects he used newspapers and drew on his own personal knowledge of the subjects and the recollections of family and friends, a method that had yielded riches for his *Traditions of Edinburgh*. Generally he exercised the concise style necessary for the dictionary genre, although occasionally he quoted sources at excessive length.

Not the least of his achievements was to combine lively insight with factual accuracy. His anticipation of criticism for withholding his own views on the controversies in which some of his subjects engaged points to contemporary expectations that historical writing could serve party political purposes.[103] Instead Chambers tried to show his subjects' 'prepossessions' or prejudices, and their failings. For example, he carefully evaluated the 'obvious dereliction of principle and consistency' displayed by Robert the Bruce, 'the most heroic as well as the most patriotic monarch which Scotland ever produced'.[104] Although he was praised for according even treatment to the protagonists in controversial episodes,[105] he did not always completely succeed, for example in a sympathetic account of Mary Queen of Scots which betrays his personal fascination.[106] Chambers was ready to make moral judgements, such as his distaste at the drinking 'by all ranks to dreadful excess' in Enlightenment Edinburgh, which contributed to Robert Burns' ruin.[107] Chambers' trenchant views of his subject's moral qualities gave his dictionary a distinctive voice.

He was addressing the expanding market for popular factual books, which he and his publisher brother William also stimulated with *Chambers' Edinburgh Journal* from 1832 onwards, echoing William Smellie's efforts in the democratisation of learning. During the early to mid-nineteenth century a growing appetite throughout Britain for historical and biographical writing helped the genre of the biographical dictionary to flourish. The *Dictionary* appeared amidst competing multi-volume works, some of which included collected lives.[108] It occupied a middle position between academic weight and popular history, permitting itself only occasional footnotes and confining its sources to brief endnotes. The deliberate omission of the scholarly apparatus of the encyclopaedic works of the previous century underlines the popular nature of the work compared with the monumental European dictionaries, such as the multi-volume Swedish dictionary (1835–57).[109]

Although it has yet to be established how popular Chambers' *Illustrious and Distinguished Scotsmen* was, it was perhaps significant that Blackie decided to publish a second edition in 1855, during the period of growing Scottish nationalist feeling. Retitled as *A Biographical Dictionary of Eminent Scotsmen*, the original four volumes were reprinted, followed by a fifth volume of additional subjects, most of whom had died since 1834, written by the Rev. Thomas Thomson, a professional author of military and naval biographical works.[110] All the articles were rearranged into a single sequence for the reprint in five volumes (1864). For the expanded third edition in three volumes (1870), Thomson penned almost all of the additional 147 articles that brought the dictionary up to date, containing a total of 810 subjects.[111] The fourth and final edition in 1874–5 incorporated 30 new subjects to make a total of 840 entries, a considerable addition to the 550 subjects in 1835. By comparison, a more concise contemporary Irish compilation included 1,242 lives.[112]

Thomson enhanced the moral tone and firm judgements of Chambers' original dictionary, and wrote many of the lives 'to form incentive examples to young and ardent minds'.[113] His conviction of the unique prevalence of the Scots 'lad o' pairts' ensured that his moral exemplars included the lives of men from humble origins who had made good.[114] Whether considering positive examples or those with deep flaws, he drew moral conclusions with relish. The final years of James, earl of Bothwell were 'the most solemn of warnings to princes and politicians'.[115] However, Thomson's circumspect treatment of recently dead subjects was criticised for rendering them 'too perfect'.[116] His Free Church sympathies led him to give prominence to the ministers who came out at the Disruption.[117] Their leader, Thomas Chalmers, was awarded twenty-four and a half pages, by far the longest entry in the whole dictionary.[118] The extensive treatment of Free Church men could largely be justified by the importance of the Disruption and the contribution to national life of its proponents, but the impression of disproportion remains.[119]

Thomson acknowledged that owing to his lack of perspective when assessing the historical importance of recent lives, some were perhaps 'overrated'.[120] Among his new subjects was a noticeably high proportion of poets, few of whom are now remembered. The participation of Scots in the ascendant British empire also left its mark. Colonial administrators and agents, explorers, soldiers and writers formed suitable examples of patriotic achievement, although events connected with their careers could assume disproportionate significance compared to those of earlier figures. Sir James McGrigor, an eminent military surgeon who died in 1858, was accorded twice as much space as Mary, Queen of Scots.[121] Soldiers in particular were worthy additions to the national pantheon because they embodied the historic martial identity and prowess of the Scots, displayed in the wider arena of empire.[122] Thomson wrote during a period of great interest in the Scottish, and especially Highland, martial past.[123]

Soldiers also embodied the dual Scoto-British identity, a vital aspect of Scottish national identity which collective biography reflected and perhaps, to an extent, helped to shape.

From 1855 Thomson's alterations to Chambers' selection reinforce the impression of a preference for the presbyterian and Whig sides of the struggles of the seventeenth and eighteenth centuries.[124] He also pruned minor figures whose merit had appeared greater to Chambers in the 1830s.[125] Of the nine women whom by 1875 he had added to Chambers' five, all were writers, except the mathematician Mary Somerville (1780–1872), 'perhaps the most remarkable woman of her age'.[126] The limited selection of female subjects reflected prevailing attitudes towards women's historical significance. Even in a more accommodating dictionary the view of their achievement remained narrow.[127]

The development of Chambers' work would repay investigation, taking into account his original choice and treatment of subjects, and how his biographical approach was altered by his Victorian editors. The assumptions Chambers brought to his work also deserve attention, for although he was lauded as 'a patriot among authors',[128] he shared the anti-feudalist view of Scotland's retarded pre-Union past. Although he could acknowledge the jobbery which facilitated the Union of 1707, he celebrated its benefits, including the role that it conferred on Scotland.[129] If his *Dictionary* was a notable example of patriotic publishing, it was as an expression of the North British historical identity into which Scottish identity had been transformed. As has been observed, 'Scots continued to trumpet the virtues associated with their national character, partly . . . because emphasis on national character remained the only plausible mode of chauvinistic boasting.'[130]

Collected lives continued to take many forms during the nineteenth century, including universal biography,[131] thematic compilations of essays and obituaries stretching unevenly beyond Britain,[132] and compendia of specialist British lives.[133] One work reflected the inflammatory tendency of some Scots, and many more English, to substitute 'English' for 'British' in writing or speaking.[134] Eight volumes of *Lives of Eminent and Illustrious Englishmen, from Alfred the Great to the Latest Times. On an Original Plan* appeared in Glasgow in 1837. Its novelty lay in the division of lives by period, each prefaced by a historical introduction. The work was reissued in the 1850s–60s under different titles, which attempted to express this difference from alphabetically arranged dictionaries.[135] From a Scottish perspective it is, however, peculiar. In an illustration of the submersion of Scotland's identity within the Union, the work included such eminent Englishmen as Robert Burns, David Hume and Joseph Black. In fact the Scots were well represented,[136] but the appropriation of their identity passed without editorial comment. Since no Scot before 1707 was included, the arrangement made clear that none could be considered an Englishman until after the union of the parliaments. It was the logical expression of the assimilationist argument.

Chambers' commemoration of Scotland's historic nationhood was followed in 1864 by William Anderson's *The Scottish Nation*, in three volumes. Building on his one-volume *The Popular Scottish Biography* (1842), Anderson combined biographies with entries on leading families and surnames, because, he argued, to an extent peculiar to Scotland, the country's history could be read from an account of surnames, families and honours. Group or family biography had been imperfectly realised in the *Biographia Britannica*, but it has been convincingly resurrected in the *Oxford DNB*. Another innovation was the inclusion of lists of a subject's works, which led Anderson to claim that as far as literary characters were concerned his work 'becomes as it were a *Bibliotheca Scotica* corrected and brought down to the present day'.[137] The 'bibliotheca' harked back to the seventeenth-century antiquaries' projects, and was to be continued in a British context by Leslie Stephen in the bibliographies attached to articles in the *DNB*. Of the portraits that illustrated many lives, Anderson boasted that they formed the first 'National Portrait Gallery worthy of the name'.[138] Although he wrote in a similar vein to Chambers, he was less discriminating as a historian.[139] His main achievement was to enlarge Scottish national biography to an unsurpassed degree. In addition to some 910 individual lives, the second edition (1882) contained about as many short lives within about 1,060 family entries, making an approximate total of 2,000 lives. Although this fell short of the 3,000 condensed lives in Irving's compact single volume, *The Book of Scotsmen* (1881),[140] Anderson's work was more substantial.

In retrospect, Anderson and Chambers can be seen as the high-water mark of Scottish patriotic commemoration. The British national biography reached its Victorian apogee in the *Dictionary of National Biography*, which between 1885 and 1900 gradually eclipsed the Scottish dictionaries, as well as English or British compilations, by virtue of the sheer scope and scholarship of its sixty-three volumes, and of its later decennial updates. The *DNB* claimed to include 'all men and women of British or Irish race who have achieved any reasonable measure of distinction in any walk of life'.[141] Thus it embraced the Scots, Welsh and Irish as well as the English. It eschewed illustrations but listed likenesses, source references and the subjects' bibliographies. For over a century it dominated the field as a work of reference and a literary and historical achievement. Inevitably its shortcomings became apparent as historical perspectives shifted and new or correct information was discovered.

Concerning the *DNB*'s treatment of Scots, Colin Matthew judged that although the later supplements contained fewer Scots, the landed, professional and governing classes were generally well represented, and more clergy were included than in the *Dictionary of Scottish Church History and Theology* (1993).[142] However, John Horden demonstrated the *DNB*'s selectivity: of about 36,000 lives in the volumes covering the period to 1970, the estimated 2,000 Scots formed a disproportionately low representation. Among the missing Scots were Kirkpatrick Macmillan, inventor of the bicycle, and Mary Slessor, pioneering missionary, both of whom were subsequently included in the *DNB*.[143] Horden argued that such omissions from a 'majestic piece of work' justified the need for a new, comprehensive dictionary of Scottish biography. He might have added that a Welsh national biography, which had addressed the similar concerns of a nation subsumed within the United Kingdom, was published in 1953.[144]

Not only would a Scottish dictionary include all the 'glittering figures' from historical studies and specialist biographical dictionaries, but also the many talented Scots (by birth, blood or association) who had never achieved proper recognition. Horden preferred the abbreviated format of the reference work to the interpretative essay of the *DNB*, because facts would outlast critical views, and brevity was necessary in order to write the lives of about 30,000 Scots without extensive funding.[145] Horden's proposed scope approximated to that of Boase's *Modern English Biography* of Britons dying between 1850 and 1900 who merited a newspaper obituary or inclusion in a specialist biographical work.[146] It has been observed that obituaries tend to summarise public aspects of a subject's life, recording rather than explaining, and not delving into personal matters or motivation, which are the proper concerns of biography.[147] Horden's proposals and the *DNB*'s coverage represent these alternative forms of collected biography.

His plea for the dictionary's computer data to be enshrined by the creation of 'national biographical archives' was far-sighted, and in proposing subject and place indexes not normally found in biographical dictionaries he anticipated the flexible interrogation of text that has become the norm for electronic reference works, notably the *Oxford DNB* online.[148] The proposals for a Scottish dictionary of 'prime authority', not merely an appendix to the *DNB*,[149] were bold but did not come to fruition. Although their author carefully avoided calling it a dictionary of Scottish *national* biography, the venture shared the fate of earlier attempts and secured neither funding nor a publisher. The popular market was catered for by *Chambers Scottish Biographical Dictionary* (1992),[150] a selection of over 2,500 condensed lives, whose inclusion of living subjects increased its popular appeal while postponing its value for historical reference. A new dictionary series commemorating deceased modern Scots faltered after one volume.[151] Meanwhile the landscape changed with the launch in 1992 of the project to revise the *DNB* completely and add a multitude of new subjects.

As a Scot, the founding editor, Colin Matthew, was conscious of the British dimension of the enterprise. He ensured that the *Oxford Dictionary of National Biography*, as the work was renamed for publication in 2004, included more Scots, as well as subjects from Wales and the north of England. Nevertheless, however the quality of the coverage of Scots subjects is judged, the *Oxford*

DNB is necessarily highly selective. Out of about 50,000 entries, the Scots by birth and association number about 5,700,[152] far fewer than the 30,000 lives of Horden's proposal. Figures of arguably lesser importance on the British scene, who have nonetheless been significant in a Scottish context, do not find a place, for example Sir George McCrae (1861–1928), local government servant and inspirational wartime battalion commander.[153] Similarly worthy Scots feature in the regional compilations popular in the nineteenth century,[154] and in the growing number of specialist biographical dictionaries by academic authors covering, for example, business, labour and the universities.[155] Both of these types only supply components of the wider national picture.

A group biography of a uniquely national character, the *Biographical Dictionary of Scottish Women* (2006), seeks to redress the gender bias of all preceding collected lives. With admirable concision it embraces over 1,000 women's lives in entries on about 820 women. Considered as a form of national biography, it demonstrates the requirement for the genre to achieve comprehensive coverage of greater and lesser subjects within its covers. About half of its subjects do not have a place in the *Oxford DNB*.[156] While the Oxford work strives to fulfil the requirement of comprehensiveness in the British context, it cannot do so in the Scottish. If a need remains for an up-to-date, scholarly and specifically national biography that respects Scotland's historical and cultural boundaries, instead of a monolithic dictionary, biographical databases could be created of subjects excluded from the *Oxford DNB*. Alternatively, group biographies that overlap with the *Oxford DNB* would add piecemeal to the national picture. For example, the 'Dictionary of Scottish Architects 1840–1940' (2006), which features systematic coverage of 6,700 subjects, demonstrates the potential for a group biography to achieve national coverage, and that a work which is available only online can be both scholarly and accessible,[157] by contrast with unmoderated biographies posted on the internet. Writing the biography of Scots by avoiding a single dictionary of Scottish national scope might gain in richness what it lacked in consistency, and in some ways fulfil Lord Hailes' vision.

Notwithstanding these possibilities, the *Oxford DNB*, with its greater and more sympathetic attention to Scotland and the character of its 'worthies' than the *DNB*, will probably enjoy a similar pre-eminence. It has diminished both the need and the opportunity for creating a unitary Scottish national biography. Problems of selection criteria, and even of the fundamental definition of Scottish identity in the twenty-first century, would have to be resolved in order to realise such a project. Above all, a new Scottish biography would demand a huge collaborative enterprise if it were to achieve suitably comprehensive coverage, and it would only be possible if unarguable historical and cultural needs were identified and agreed upon, and if financial resources could be found. However, given the repeated attempts to enshrine the collected lives of Scotland's worthies, it would be unwise to predict that a major 'biographia Scotica' will never again be attempted.

Acknowledgements

I gratefully acknowledge the assistance of the ever-helpful staff of the National Library of Scotland, William Ferguson, Bill Zachs, Elizabeth Ewan, John Horden and Henry Summerson, as well as members of the Scottish History seminar at Edinburgh University in 2003, who commented on an earlier version of this essay.

3
The Legacy of the Revolution in Scotland

ALEXANDER J. MURDOCH

The Revolution of 1689, as it can be identified in Scotland, has left a very different legacy from that in other parts of what became the United Kingdom. Any similarities of experience were perhaps closer to Ireland than to England and Wales, and that in turn has divided Scots across the centuries in interpreting this part of their history. Part of the project now known as the Scottish Enlightenment was about consigning Scotland's Gaelic-speaking history and culture to the past while denying it any historical significance in national terms.[1] By the end of the eighteenth century it seemed to represent the beginning of what became a national triumph through British union, which provided a model for what might be achieved in the United Kingdom established in 1801.[2] In subsequent centuries that legacy has prompted more critical perspectives of the impact of the Revolution on Scottish national identity and the sectarian divisions that have blighted so much of modern Scottish history. In the twenty-first century, the Revolution can be seen as a negative legacy of that sectarian conflict which has to be jettisoned in the search for a more 'usable' past.[3] Yet seen in the immediate context of the Revolution's legacy to eighteenth-century Scotland, a more positive history emerges. The revolution in Scotland is more directly linked with British union than it ever has been in England and Wales or in Ireland. That has produced both a strong historiographical tradition of portraying Scottish political incompetence and corruption in the period between winning political independence for the Scottish parliament in 1689 and that parliament voting itself out of existence in 1707. It reached its apogee with Henry Dundas' celebration of the positive effects of British union on the economic and social development of Scotland in his speech to the British Westminster parliament in 1799 prior to British union with Ireland.[4] It could be argued that this view became even stronger in the nineteenth century, and it is still defended robustly in the early twenty-first century.[5]

Just what was achieved by the Scots in 1689? This is still a contentious question. For some, the Revolution made British union, stymied since 1603, possible at last. From a Scottish perspective, the Revolution is often considered as a necessary prelude to union, and if events in Scotland are considered in a

British perspective, it is usually in that context.[6] Yet in Scotland the Revolution has continued to be perceived in sectarian terms into modern times, either in terms of the apotheosis of presbyterian Calvinism in Scotland with the return to the true faith of the Church of Scotland in 1690, or a descent into bitter sectarian conflict between Presbyterians, Episcopalians and Roman Catholics.[7] The emergence of the Jacobite movement came to demonstrate the strength of resistance in Scotland to what the Revolution, and the union with England, represented. It is less common to find the Revolution analysed in terms of establishing an independent Scottish political tradition that survived the union with England in 1707. James Halliday and William Ferguson both have made a case for celebrating the Revolution as representing the liberation of the Scottish parliament from the domination of an absentee monarch, much like those Irish historians who celebrated the political freedom of 'Grattan's Parliament' after the Declaratory Act of 1782, in contrast with the politics of post-Union Ireland after 1801.[8]

The analogy with Ireland almost a hundred years after the Revolution in Scotland does not quite hold up, as the institutions that survived parliamentary union in Scotland after 1707 differed markedly from those in Ireland after 1801. In Scotland it was the legal profession which dominated public life, whereas in Ireland after 1801 there continued to be a viceroy in Dublin Castle.[9] The purpose of this essay is to argue that although it was the ecclesiastical settlement in Scotland which made the Revolution there unique in Britain, it was the political repercussions of that development which made possible the semi-independent, devolved politics of eighteenth-century Scotland as part of Britain that created the most lasting legacy of the Revolution in Scotland.[10]

The most 'revolutionary' element of the Revolution in Scotland was the church settlement that was adopted in 1690, when the Church of Scotland was restored to Presbyterianism in a constitutional arrangement that is now more than 300 years old. As Tim Harris has pointed out, this really did represent revolutionary change in Scotland, even if the Revolution did not reach all parts of the country for a considerable period of time.[11] The first 'General Assembly' of the restored presbyterian Church of Scotland contained only eight clergy and six elders from north of the Tay.[12] An important issue in eighteenth-century Scotland would be just what the church of the Revolution would become and what it would represent. Despite the deep divisions between it and the predominantly episcopalian Jacobite movement that became so significant in Scotland during the first half of the eighteenth century, the Church of Scotland was very far from being a sectarian institution. This was a result of its political role in the development of a Scottish Whig constitutional tradition that Colin Kidd has described as Anglo-British, to distinguish it from the political traditions of the Scottish Reformation and the Covenanting movement of the seventeenth century.[13]

Historians from James 'Ossian' Macpherson to the late P.W.J. Riley subscribed to a black legend of mindless political infighting in Scotland from the moment William of Orange called the Convention of 1689 to the series of failed governments that ended only with the union of 1707. In his *Secret History of Great Britain*, James Macpherson advanced many of the modern Whig criticisms of the late seventeenth-century Scottish constitution, calling the Revolution of 1689 'a change of tyrants'. He defended the incorporating union of 1707 on the grounds that, as far as Scots were concerned, 'no expedient could be deemed unfortunate that put an end to their own government, as it then stood'.[14] Macpherson's withering contempt for Scottish politicians and Scottish institutions anticipates subsequent attempts to dismiss the legacy of the Revolution in Scotland in negative terms:

> There were radical defects in the constitution of the kingdom, which in the best times and in the ablest hands, could not fail to be productive of perpetual evils to the nation . . . The blow, which the royal prerogative received in Scotland, in the memorable year 1688, established licentiousness rather than freedom, in that kingdom.[15]

The Revolution and the Union

How far did the Scottish Revolution of 1689 affect the achievement of parliamentary union between Scotland and England in 1707? Dr P.W.J. Riley wrote two separate books, *King William and the Scottish Politicians* and *The Union of England and Scotland*; their separate publication implying a discontinuity that he did not himself accept.[16] Riley, like James Macpherson, believed that the union saved Scotland from the political 'licentiousness' unleashed by the Revolution, or at least made it possible to bring it to an end eventually; 'those who condemn what happened in 1707 as an act of violence against Scotland should reflect on the dire alternative, rapidly emerging after 1698'. This dire alternative was defined as 'anarchy, civil war and English conquest', without discussion of the fact that this was just the experience of Scotland during the Covenanting wars and Cromwellian occupation from 1638–60.[17] More recently, Mark Goldie has argued that Scotland and England became increasingly different, not similar, under the absentee monarchies of both the Restoration and post-Restoration regimes. This interpretation might be summarised as arguing that as England became exceptional Scotland did not. In other words, that as English power grew from the mid-seventeenth century, Scotland, like Wales and Ireland, was drawn inexorably into its orbit through military aggression, economic imperialism and the assumption that both validated inherent English cultural superiority.[18]

After 1689 the reign of William II was distinguished only by civil conflict, popular unrest and famine. Jacobite resistance ended in 1692, and efforts to generate colonial trade ended with the failure of Scottish expeditions to Darien in Panama. The whole reign was characterised by the Jacobites in Scotland as the 'Ill Years' of King William on account of the famine and bad harvests from 1695–1700, which resulted in a loss of population from Scotland through emigration to Ireland as well as increased mortality.[19] A dying king, who never visited Scotland, returned to the idea of union with England as an issue for the last meeting of his Scottish parliament. William's experience of the Netherlands as United Provinces would have made him familiar with the potential as well as the problems of political union. The Scots who travelled to England with William in 1688 and went on to return to Scotland never explicitly stated the influence of their experience of the United Provinces on them, but Andrew Fletcher of Saltoun's ideas of federal union, for example, clearly owed something to his knowledge of the Netherlands. Similarly William Paterson's ideas for the Bank of Scotland and Company of Scotland were influenced by his experience of Dutch finance, and the second duke of Argyll became interested in the ideas of John Law on public credit because of his family's contact with the Dutch and with William of Orange. William Carstares, William's chaplain, eventually returned to Scotland to begin the process of reinventing both the Church of Scotland and its colleges along the lines of equivalent Dutch institutions.[20]

The Netherlands provided a powerful model of a small country that had resisted conquest successfully through an elaborate system of international trade, finance and diplomacy, and there were significant numbers of Scots who saw the Dutch example and closer Dutch cooperation with England as an example that supported the idea of closer cooperation with England (but not necessarily a parliamentary union). As late as 1715–16, it would be Dutch troops, provided under the terms of a treaty for mutual defence, that would provide the military force necessary to comprehensively defeat and disperse Jacobite forces in Scotland in the aftermath of a domestic standoff.[21] The Scots Dutch brigades in the army of the United Provinces continued to recruit in Scotland until the 1750s, providing a military link to complement the educational links with the universities of Leiden, Utrecht and Groningen favoured by Scots who wished to pursue careers in the law and the church.

Did the legacy of the Revolution in Scotland weaken significantly after William's death in 1702? Certainly the opprobrium with which William's reign was viewed in Scotland contributed to the very different nature of the Scottish parliament elected under Queen Anne. It was defined by union negotiations. Previous negotiations had come to nothing in 1702. Their failure led to the election of a new Scottish parliament and the negotiations of 1705–6 through which Union with England was achieved, flawed and incomplete as it was. Patrick Riley has argued that:

> In 1702–3 the Scots were far less demanding than in 1706 and the explanation would seem to lie in the circumstances in which they were negotiating. The authorisation of 1702 had been pushed through a rump parliament in direct pursuit of an English scheme. The Scottish court, lacking experience of opposition on the scale they had yet to endure, had drifted just so far out of touch with reality . . . The fact was that they did not know the extent of the clamour they were expected to satisfy until they had met the Scottish parliament of 1703 and lived through three of its sessions.[22]

The Scottish opposition of 1703–5 could be seen to be working within a Revolution tradition in Scotland because it was grounded in the idea that it was possible for the Scottish parliament to choose a successor to Queen Anne as monarch of Scotland different from the Hanoverian succession adopted by the English parliament in 1701. Indeed it was this which prompted court attempts to review union negotiations in 1702. The obvious successor was Queen Anne's half-brother James. That was the real Scottish alternative, although the duke of Hamilton had a claim to the Scottish throne and certainly was enthusiastic in encouraging opposition to the court and the Hanoverian succession. Fletcher of Saltoun 'moved that if the queen died without heir, Scotland's throne should be separated from England's. But Fletcher left no doubt that this was a measure of last resort, by no means desirable', as it would almost inevitably involve war.[23] Indeed, 'At one point he suggested that Scotland should look to the Prince of Prussia as a successor to Anne, on the ground that this was a Calvinist line where the Hanoverians were Lutheran.'[24] What Fletcher revived in 1703 was the tradition of limited monarchy that had been pursued by 'the Club' and Sir James Montgomery in 1689, in turn a revival of the work of the Covenanting Scottish parliament of 1641.[25] Despite all efforts to portray Scottish opposition to the court in parliament from 1703–1705 as the greedy work of an awkward squad intent on personal advancement, that opposition was about limiting the power of the monarchy in Scotland, and that issue was central to the legacy of the Revolution in Scotland. Its most focused expression was the passage by the Scottish parliament of the Act of Security in 1703, declaring its right to choose the future monarch of Scotland.

In the end, the impasse over what was to give was broken by the representative of the Scottish political interest most associated with that of limiting the power of the monarchy and presbyterianism in both 1641 and 1689, the second duke of Argyll. The rival Hamilton family may have had a claim on the throne of Scotland, but they also were forever associated with the court, and it was the young second duke of Argyll who would bring the duke of Hamilton over to the court and the cause of the Union in 1705. His great-grandfather had been a dominant force in opposing Hamilton's ancestor as king's commissioner in 1641, and his father, the tenth earl and first duke, became one of William's most trusted supporters in Scotland. At the age of twenty-five the second duke became the key figure in persuading the Scottish parliament to vote to enter into negotiations for a treaty of union again and to put the nomination of commissioners to negotiate on Scotland's behalf in the hands of the queen. He did this through agreement with his rival Hamilton, promising that as a reward Hamilton would become one of the commissioners to negotiate the treaty. When this did not happen, Argyll also refused to serve.[26] So two Revolution families, Argyll and Hamilton, made renewed negotiations for union possible, even if they took no part in the subsequent negotiations themselves. Why did they do it? Self-interest? Undoubtedly, but also because they saw union as the only way to save the gains of the Revolution in Scotland from the threat posed by Jacobitism. Restoration of a Jacobite monarch in Scotland who could claim continuity at the beginning of his reign, following his sister's death, could only mean war. It would also mean the restoration of the absolutist monarchical tradition in Scotland represented by the Jacobites, overturning all that had been established in 1689–90, although many Jacobites in Scotland did not see it that way and sought assurances from the Stuarts that the authority of the Scots parliament would be enhanced if the Stuart dynasty was restored.

The Presbyterian Tradition

How did this relate to the Scottish kirk by law established by 1690? It partly reflected the secular Enlightenment values entrenched in the elite culture of those who formed the political nation in 1689 and who constructed the union settlement and the semi-independent national Scottish politics that sustained it over the course of the eighteenth century.[27] Dr Tristram Clarke has established the extent to which there was Scottish episcopalian support for William of Orange and the seriousness with which William and certain of his servants in Scotland, particularly James Johnston in his time as one of the secretaries of state, pursued the idea of religious 'comprehension' in Scotland, in which the Church of Scotland would unite moderate presbyterians and episcopalians.[28] The turbulent world of Scottish ecclesiastical politics during the Restoration period had produced many presbyterians who had been willing to accept indulgences from the Stewart regime and thus accept a degree of Erastianism. It also included episcopalians such as Gilbert Burnet or James Canaries, who might have accepted that bishops were not always necessarily at the centre of dispute in the Scottish religious tradition that was more about the attitude of the church towards the acceptance of civil authority than about episcopalian hierarchy.

The toleration for episcopalians that could not be secured by the Williamite regime before the union was imposed by the in-built English majority at Westminster in 1712, and like the law of civil patronage restored to the Church of Scotland in 1712, it was never revoked through any of the changes in civil government in Scotland over the course of the eighteenth century. The establishment of a 'Moderate' party in the Church of Scotland after 1712 represented continuity rather than change in Scottish church affairs from the Revolution into the eighteenth century. Even when episcopalianism became associated with Jacobitism explicitly after the Scottish rebellions of 1715 and 1745, the law of patronage and toleration of episcopalianism never came into doubt. Despite this, the act of 1746 relating to Episcopalian meeting houses apparently all but ended the independent (and Jacobite) Scottish Episcopalian tradition in that only 5 of about 130 ministers complied with its requirement for explicit loyalty to the Hanoverian dynasty.[29] Only clergy ordained by English or Irish bishops were authorised to hold public worship in future under the terms of a law not repealed until 1792, but at the same time the Church of Scotland became more attractive to those who had remained Episcopalian after 1690.

After the defeat of the Jacobite rebellion in 1746, the triumph of the Moderate party in the Church of Scotland meant a return to a system of 'comprehension' that reflected a distinctive reading of the Revolution legacy in Scotland by its leader William Robertson. His fellow Moderate Joseph McCormick was responsible for a careful edition of William Carstares' state papers, which presented Carstares as founder of a civil Church of Scotland that embraced a truly national role after 1755.[30] Yet while former episcopalians might find the church more attractive, it lost those members with liberal evangelical and conservative Covenanting sympathies over the course of the rest of the eighteenth century. When William Robertson was attacked so severely over the issue of Roman Catholic relief in Scotland in 1779, some of the anonymous death threats he received compared him to Archbishop James Sharp, a former presbyterian minister who became primate of the Restoration Church of Scotland as archbishop of St Andrews. Sharp was assassinated by presbyterian extremists in Fife exactly 100 years before William Robertson was forced by death threats to remove his family to Edinburgh Castle. In 1725, Sharp's tomb at St Andrews was vandalised and his remains removed, never to be seen again.[31] Clearly 'comprehension' remained a live issue in the Church of Scotland from the Restoration through the Revolution to the triumphs (and disappointments) of the Scottish Enlightenment.

This was evident in William Robertson's celebration of the legacy of the Revolution in a sermon given to mark the centenary of the Revolution in Scotland on 5 November 1788, a day on which the General Assembly of the Church of Scotland called upon its ministers to remind their congregations of what they termed 'this special interposition of Divine Providence in their favour'.[32] Robertson's sermon was only one of those given to celebrate the legacy of the Revolution in 1788 in Scotland, linking liberty with the creation of a British state and the Church of Scotland post-1690; William Peebles, *The Great Things which the Lord Hath Done for this Nation, Illustrated and Improved* (Kilmarnock, 1788); John Robertson, *Britain the Chosen Nation* (Kilmarnock, 1788) and Alexander Ranken, *A Discourse on the Advantages of the Revolution of 1688* (Glasgow, 1788) amongst them.[33] Unlike the others, Robertson's reflections remained unpublished until Professor Richard Sher identified the text and published an essay based on it in 1990.

Robertson's sermon was suppressed after his death out of fear that what could be seen as understandable analogies between the British Revolution of 1688 and events in France in 1788 might appear disloyal to the very British constitution and state Robertson celebrated. The careful scholarship of Sher draws a contrast between the suggestion by Robertson's fellow minister at Old Greyfriars, John Erskine, that Robertson was not in sympathy with a Scottish national day of thanksgiving to mark the centenary of the Revolution, and a memoir by Henry Brougham (Whig lord chancellor of Britain after 1832), that recorded the impression that Robertson's 'exultation was boundless in contemplating the deliverance of "so many millions of so great a nation [France] from the fetters of arbitrary government"'.[34] Robertson in 1788 could not foresee just how different continental revolution after 1788 would be from the legacy of 1688, but it is clear that Robertson did not perceive 1688 in sectarian terms. His entire career can be seen as a 'Moderate' return to the Erastian tradition of comprehension that could not be established initially in Scotland after 1689, but formed the basis of its legacy to Scottish politics and culture in the eighteenth century.

Robertson's centenary celebration of the Revolution can be seen as emphasising the value of 'comprehension' that initially was resisted by those in the Church of Scotland who looked back to the seventeenth-century covenants as a precious legacy. It can also be argued, however, that comprehension had succeeded by 1788, despite the efforts of Robertson's enemies, and the Jacobite tradition in Scotland had come to an end with the death of Charles Edward Stuart.[35] Coincident with the establishment of a true 'Moderate' party in the church which saw its role as national rather than sectarian, Jacobite families in Scotland found their way back to favour, and the eventual restoration of forfeited estates in 1776 and 1784, by demonstrating their loyalty to the Hanoverian dynasty they defended against French attack in the Seven Years War of 1756–63 and the war with France from 1778–83 that saw British colonies in North America rejecting British authority.[36]

Although there was significant support for American rebels in Scotland after 1776, it came from those subscribing to the same presbyterian Covenanting tradition that questioned Robertson's commitment. At elite level, the landowning class and the urban merchants, and professionals like Robertson who saw their culture as one with them, closed ranks behind the British state and the young king whom a Scottish peer had taught to 'glory in the name of Briton' at his coronation in 1760.[37] The third earl of Bute was a grandson of the Campbell champion of 1689 in Scotland, the earl of Argyll, who was created a duke in the last year of William of Orange's reign as king of Scotland, but Bute's surname was Stuart, which sustained the accusations of Scottish crypto-Jacobitism that marked the launch of the political career of John Wilkes. George III was seen as a monarch who was foreign both through his German ancestry and his education by a Scottish nobleman, and thus unable to comprehend English liberties. Yet his supporters could point to the role of a foreign prince who was a Stuart in the person of William of Orange as the personification of what had been achieved in the three British kingdoms after 1688. The Highland regiments who defended the British empire in North America after 1757, and who after 1775 fought to retain it in many cases, included officers and men who had fought in the Jacobite army at Culloden in 1746.[38]

The peasantry north of the Tay in Scotland became associated with loyalty to Britain rather than opposition to it within a generation of 1746. The city and university of Aberdeen became centres of commerce and enlightenment rather than Jacobitism, as the Campbell political interest offered its protection from the invasive state intervention encouraged by the duke of Cumberland after his victory.[39] The north-west Highlands became a source of strength to the British army rather than opposition to it, and all sections of Scottish life from moderate presbyterians to former Jacobites benefited from what by 1788 had become their full admission into British public life. The only exceptions were lowland presbyterians such as John Erskine (or John Witherspoon), who saw these developments not as the final victory of the Revolution but as the corruption of the presbyterian legacy of liberty from the Revolution by agents of those who had opposed it, now altered and made Erastian by conforming to a new establishment which was crypto-episcopalian in fact if not in name.[40] Yet even in the presbyterian heartland of the west of Scotland, the legacy of the Revolution became increasingly secular in the years after the Union, as the Campbell/Argyll political interest, rather than the church, came to be identified with what was still called the 'revolution interest'.

Tobias Smollett, writing from London to friends in the west of Scotland after completion of the relevant volume in his history of Britain, confessed that he now viewed the legacy of the Revolution differently from the principles in which he had been bred as a youth as a west of Scotland Whig.[41] These were principles represented by his grandfather, Sir James Smollett, member of both the 1689 convention and a commissioner for negotiating the union of the Scottish and English parliaments. Although Sir James was a presbyterian and a Whig, he recorded in later reminiscences that he was reluctant to represent his home burgh of Dumbarton in the Convention of Estates in 1689 because he could not see how the future James VIII could be barred from the Scottish throne on account of his father's actions.

> I was convinced he [James VII and II] had done many things against law, yet the pure child his son, if he really was such, was innocent, and it was hard to do anything [that] could reach the sone for the father's fault . . . when this question about forfaulting came to be touched, I could not go in it, so that thereby I was exposed to the wrath of several people. But afterwards when the crown was settled, I was well satisfied and went into all measures wherein my conscience allowed me for establishing the government both in church and state.[42]

Thus Smollett's presbyterian/Whig politics were not explicitly within the Scottish Covenanting tradition, and his later identification with legal and burgh politics in Edinburgh in the service of the Dalrymple family and still later, the Campbell/Argyll political interest, makes him a good example of the kind of politics represented by those who associated themselves with the Revolution and its legacy in Scotland. It was the key event in the evolution of the Whig tradition in Scotland from sectarian to secular foundations that formed the basis for the transformation of the Scottish kirk and the national education system it maintained over the course of the eighteenth century.[43] This was a process that involved loss as well as gain in terms of the clarity of Scottish national identity, but at its best it represented the creation of a confident and cosmopolitan public culture that overcame the deep scars of sectarian conflict that had blighted the country's history under the later Stuarts.[44]

The Jacobite Legacy of the Revolution

Of course the Revolution in Scotland was not glorious because it was not bloodless, although it was far less bloody than what unfolded so tragically in Ireland. The Highland War that threatened the Williamite regime in Scotland was a sorry affair despite the dashing heroism of Bonnie Dundee, checked by the stolid determination of General Hugh Mackay of the Dutch army. After Dundee's death the Jacobite army was led by the bland General Cannon, who arrived from Ireland, not to strengthen the Highland rebellion to the point where it could overthrow the government, but to lead it to stalemate in the great glen. The horror of the murders at Glencoe in February 1692 stained the Revolution legacy in Scotland with the blood of innocents and founded a Jacobite tradition which, almost by default, became the custodian of Scottish national identity in the eighteenth century.[45] Nor did it end with defeat at

Culloden in 1746, as its transfiguration into sentimental tradition became a foundation stone of European Romanticism into the early nineteenth century through the phenomenal success of the novels of Sir Walter Scott.[46]

Jacobitism became associated with the Highlands and both became associated with the antithesis of the Revolution tradition in Scotland, yet the Campbells established and led a 'Highland Interest' that ended up preserving the country's political identity in the eighteenth century and preventing its reduction to the status of conquered province, which briefly threatened after the denouement in 1746.[47] As the Campbells (represented by the dukes of Argyll) were presbyterian and Whig, the Macdonalds and the Camerons remained Episcopalian or Catholic and Jacobite, as did the Gordon family in north-east Scotland to some extent. The Campbells weren't alone, however. In Highland terms the 'Revolution Whigs' were led by the Mackays, Munros, Grants and the Sutherland family in the north as well as the Campbells of the south-west, although the interest was always 'Argathelian'. The Forbes family of Culloden outside Inverness equally represented Whig presbyterianism in the north, and it was no mistake that the final pitched battle that ended Jacobitism as a meaningful force in Scottish and British politics was fought near the family's house at Culloden, where Duncan Forbes, lord president of the Scottish court of session, had held out in the government interest from the very beginning of the rebellion.[48] In the central Highlands, the Murrays of Athol were deeply divided in 1689, as they would be in later rebellions. The great Jacobite general Lord George Murray was a son of the duke of Atholl, but then so was the colonel of the Black Watch, Lord John Murray, and with the support of the Campbells those who were dukes of Atholl remained true to the government interest, although in public life they always followed the lead of the dukes of Argyll.[49]

From the very beginning in 1689 the government interest in the Highlands was associated with money and patronage. Was there anything more to it than this? Were the 'government clans' and the Campbells in particular nothing more than a mindlessly selfish kin interest group intent on maximum exploitation of their hotline to the government? It is impossible to portray the leaders of these interests as idealistic, yet the argument of this essay is that it is wrong to think of all the Revolution Whigs who over the years became associated with the court interest in Scotland as corrupt.[50] All politics are corrupt. All politicians in office become tainted by the imperfections of their decisions and actions. The longer politicians hold power the more they are defined by its possession. As the years elapsed from 1688 to the death of the last credible Jacobite claimant to the British throne in 1788 (the year of Charles Edward Stuart's death), the Revolution Whigs in Scotland as elsewhere in Britain became associated with office and power, and their Jacobite opponents with opposition, intrigue and, of course, treason.

The Campbells felt the power of the Stuarts through the execution of the earl and marquess of Argyll in 1661 and the ninth earl in 1685. They were acutely aware of the fact that if the wheel turned once more after 1689, they would suffer in the most immediate manner. As late as 1752, at the time of the 'Appin murder' trial of James Stewart for the murder of a Campbell government factor on a Jacobite annexed estate, the third duke of Argyll's address to the condemned man sought to justify the ferocity of the verdict by reference to the ruthless nature of the Stuart dynasty in the seventeenth century. He gave the 'true original source' of Stewart's crime as the 'barbarous cruelties and lawless oppressions practiced in the Highlands' and 'that obstinate and almost incurable disaffection and aversion to the Government in several Highland clans, and, in particular, your own, ever since the happy Revolution and the establishment of the crown in the Protestant line'. In discussing the rebellion of 1745, Argyll drew a picture of the horrors of absolutist monarchy that sought to justify any effort to defeat it.

> If you had been successful in that rebellion you had been now triumphant with your confederates trampling upon the laws of your country, the liberties of your fellow-subjects, and on the Protestant religion. You might have been giving the law where you now have received the judgement of it; and we, who are this day your judges, might have been tried before one of your mock courts of judicature, and then you might have been satiated with the blood of any name or clan to which you had an aversion.
>
> I have thought it my duty to put you in mind of these facts, only to mark out those wicked paths which have led you to destruction . . . this murder has been visibly the effect and consequence of the late rebellion.[51]

The Jacobites countered, of course, that theirs was a patriot cause and their king represented a dynasty that literally defined Scotland, going back to the ancient line of kings defined in the Declaration of Arbroath.[52] Yet the failure of the dynasty to reside in Scotland, despite the forays of James II there before he became king, and the reconstruction of Holyrood Palace as a symbol of Stuart authority, made it increasingly difficult to portray the Stuarts as Scottish. The initial burst of enthusiasm from Charles Edward Stuart in 1745 included an emotional appeal to the traditionally Jacobite Highland clans that included the adoption of Highland dress by the prince, yet Charles Edward eventually abandoned the Highlands as completely as his father abandoned north-east Scotland in 1716.[53]

Although the Jacobite court continued to attract support, the long years between the rebellions of 1715 and 1719 and the dramatic and initially successful rebellion of 1745 naturally made Jacobitism less of a force in Scottish and British politics, as Sir Robert Walpole consolidated the Whig interest in Britain in a manner that alienated enemies of corrupt politics but could be claimed by Walpole's defenders to represent a final victory for Revolution principles.[54] During that time it was a Scottish Jacobite scholar, Father Thomas Innes, who published the work that demolished traditional Scottish ideas of national identity based on possession of the most ancient monarchical dynasty in the world. In its place, Innes produced a theory intended to prove the primacy of absolutist monarchs ruling by divine right as God's representatives on earth.[55] Even if the Jacobite court had to leave France as a result of British and French diplomatic rapprochement, Jacobitism increasingly represented the pale British reflection of the robust pretensions of a Bourbon dynasty still basking in the radiance of the sparkling career of Louis XIV.[56] Yet there were a great many Scottish Jacobites like George Lockhart of Carnwath, who had adopted to the changing ideological context of post-Revolution Britain. The monarchy was at the centre of the constitution, but in Britain the national parliaments, churches and laws all shared sovereignty with the monarchy, and in Lockhart's view, if the Stuart monarchy was restored in Scotland, a restored Scots parliament would play a central role in formulating the new restoration settlement. The Revolution involved 'only an alteration of one, though indeed a material, part of the constitution'.[57] Though it can be argued that the Stuarts never quite caught on to this, with their 'good looks and not very remarkable intelligence', as Ronald Hutton put it,[58] there was a Revolution legacy for the Jacobites who supported them, even in Scotland. It was apparent to everyone in Scotland as early as 1689 that after the Revolution, nothing would ever be quite the same again.

The Revolution Whigs in Scotland and the Semi-Independence of Scotland in Great Britain, 1689–1801

The Revolution began the process whereby the Stuart dynasty was deposited in the waste bin of history, having served God's purpose in calling them from Scotland to a wider stage by demonstrating just how reprehensible absolutist monarchy could be, or at least that is how David Hume came to present it in his history of Britain.[59] Yet the very Revolution that marked the beginning of the end of what claimed to be the world's oldest dynasty ensured the preservation of Scotland as a nation. Caught in the halfway house of sharing a monarch with the United Provinces as well as the rest of Britain, Scotland's parliament eventually agreed a movement towards political integration with England and Wales. At the same time, other stars in the Williamite universe moved in opposite directions. The Netherlands began to become distant and detached after 1702, while Ireland became ever more a colony of Britain.[60]

In Scotland, the Revolution Whigs made the Union and their own fortunes. To emphasise either aspect of this development to the exclusion of the other is misleading. The Union was not an act of statesmanship, but most of those who pursued its achievement in Scotland saw more than their own enrichment in the process. By the time that generation passed away, even the most fervent Jacobite, having experienced defeat in 1746 as final as that their predecessors, the Scottish Covenanters, had experienced at the hands of Cromwell in 1652 at Worcester, accepted the work of the Revolution as complete. Even if the parliament that made the Revolution in Scotland in 1689 voted itself out of existence eighteen years later in 1707, in that time the independent existence of the Scottish legal system had been secured and its existence written into the very treaty of union, which guaranteed Scottish rights and privileges within a political union.[61] The legacy of the Revolution fragmented as differences arose between Revolution Whigs, who saw the future for Scotland in a British union in further integration and 'completion' of the union through the adoption of superior English institutions, and those who perceived Scotland's status and laws within the Union as separate but equal. In 1746–8 there was a need to present their politics rather differently in the face of heavy-handed intervention by the Pelham ministry and the military led by the duke of Cumberland.[62] It was a polarity that has run through the centre of modern Scottish history to the present day.[63]

This division within the Whigs in Scotland went back to the emergence of the 'Squadrone' or 'New' party in the Scottish parliament after 1689, briefly given real intellectual power by the accession of Andrew Fletcher of Saltoun in 1703, but soon sullied by the difficulties of preserving political integrity while holding office in 1704 and after. The Squadrone persuaded the Westminster parliament in its first British session to abolish the Scottish Privy Council in 1708 as a means of completing the Union, and thereby removed the logical centre from Scottish public life until the Scottish Office was created in the late nineteenth century.[64] In contrast the followers of the court interest who supported the Revolution were increasingly identified with the duke of Argyll, and by 1725 this arrangement was formalised by Sir Robert Walpole. The second duke of Argyll had the manners and demeanour of a courtier and, by all accounts, the arrogance of the mighty at court as well. He and his brother Archibald presented themselves as working within the Revolution interest while also upholding both the ancient Scottish martial tradition and the distinctive traditions of Scottish laws.[65] There were times when disagreements between the two groups became pronounced, but also times, particularly when Jacobite rebellion threatened or had occurred, when their essential unity of purpose became more apparent. This was particularly clear after the last Jacobite rebellion in Scotland.

In many ways the abolition of heritable jurisdictions in Scotland, guaranteed by the treaty of union, became perceived as the means of completing the Revolution and securing the rule of law in Scotland. The act became something of a hobby horse for the English lord chancellor, the earl of Hardwicke.[66]

Hardwicke became convinced that the Jacobite Rebellion of 1745 had been possible in Scotland because of the power landowners there wielded through their control of the law at local level, and although he could not question the Whig credentials of his colleague the third duke of Argyll, he remained deeply suspicious of him, and in a sense he was right. The Jacobite rebellions of the eighteenth century were all Scottish in origin. In contrast, Ireland, cockpit of Jacobitism in 1688, experienced civil peace for a century afterwards. The Jacobite rebellions in England were centred so far to the north that they seemed part and parcel of unrest in Scotland, as was demonstrated by the Jacobite surrenders at Preston in 1715 and at Carlisle in 1745.[67] The Campbells had represented a quick fix when Walpole delegated Scottish affairs to them in 1725, but twenty years later their time should have been up and their former colleagues from the Walpole ministry saw the consolidation of their authority in Scotland as an extension of what they had already achieved in the cabinet.[68]

Nevertheless, the third duke of Argyll made a point of presenting the passage of the Heritable Jurisdictions Act as something other than the extension of English legal authority over Scotland. His gloss was that it represented the completion of the integration of two separate but equal legal traditions that formed part of the creation of Britain. The ambitious young Scottish Whig MP Andrew Mitchell, impatient with the legacy of Walpole, left the most influential account of Argyll's speech to the House of Lords in favour of the bill. His description of it as 'the most exotic speech I every heard' has been frequently quoted, yet reading Mitchell's account closely tells us more about Argyll's understanding of just what the Scottish Revolution tradition represented.[69]

According to Mitchell, Argyll 'began by telling the house that the people of Scotland were against the bill' and 'then gave a detail to show that the laws of Scotland were very imperfect, that before the union there were perpetual feuds and civil wars among the Nobility' and 'that there was no treason law till after the union everything being deemed treason that the administration and privy council were pleased to construe to be so'. Far from representing feudal absolutism red in tooth and claw, Argyll argued that the jurisdictions and powers of the nobility had been useful in preserving 'the Constitution ag't the attempts of the Crown', and 'he expatiated much on the iniquity of the Privy Council, and the great abuses introduced by the manner of managing the Parliament of Scotland' [under the Stuart Restoration regime].[70] The Revolution tradition in Scotland, in other words, was formed in the crucible of exposure to the raw edge of Stuart absolutism, from which Scots were delivered by the Revolution. That Revolution was Scottish, despite the feuding of the nobility, as it was formed in resistance led by nobles (such as Argyll's ancestors, of course) against the Stuart kings and their creatures. That Revolution had been safeguarded by the Union, which Argyll represented in its Scottish context. Mitchell reported the duke of Argyll as arguing that abolishing heritable jurisdictions did not break the treaty of union; indeed 'he exhorted the Ministry to do more, and to make laws not from the Scots Statute book, but desired to be governed by Acts of the British parliament, he added that by this Scotland would become rich and its inhabitants industrious'. Although Mitchell presented Argyll as defending the pre-Union establishment, he found himself disapproving of Argyll's praise of the Heritable Jurisdictions Act as encouraging British integration; 'the dreadful description he made of Scottish policy and government, set in contrast to the wise policy and just laws of England, must give a high idea of the candour and capacity of the Speaker to an English audience, who generally think every other nation their inferiors'.[71] For all Whigs in Scotland, the Revolutionary legacy was a unionist one, but the debate remained for over a century just what that union should come to mean.[72]

This provides some background information relevant to the account left by the third earl of Marchmont of a chance meeting with Argyll at a bookseller's earlier in the year that the heritable jurisdictions bill was taken through parliament by the government. Argyll asked Marchmont if he had been told that Argyll had prevented his nomination as one of the sixteen representative peers for Scotland in the House of Lords for the 1747 parliamentary elections, which Argyll denied, 'because his view had always been to have the country represented by the peers in the best manner possible'. Argyll justified his support in terms of the Revolution interest in Scottish politics (Marchmont's grandfather had been Lord Chancellor after the Revolution). 'He said both our families were forfeited families' (meaning that both had their estates confiscated by James VII and II), and Marchmont agreed that both families had 'ventured their lives in the same cause', which was that of the Revolution.[73] This could be dismissed as the hollow gossip of wily politicians seeking to reassure each other of their loyalty even as they sought advantage over each other, but this is to misunderstand the impact of the 1745 Jacobite Rebellion on Whig ideology and thus the Revolution interest in Scotland. It was united not just by the reinvigoration of the old Jacobite threat, but by the introduction of British state imperialism in the form of the duke of Cumberland's army in the aftermath of Culloden and the determination of influential members of the British government to sort out the 'Scottish problem' once and for all.

By the 1750s Scots had responded by proactive participation in the British state, which survived the obloquy heaped on the first Scottish prime minister, Argyll's nephew, the third earl of Bute, from 1761 until well after he gave up office in 1763. Statesmen and legal figures such as William Murray, Lord Mansfield or Alexander Wedderburn, Lord Loughborough (later earl of Rosslyn), or Henry Dundas, Viscount Melville were only the most prominent of a legion of Scottish politicians, diplomats and, especially, officers, who became an integral part of the burgeoning British state in the era in which it lost one empire only to gain another by the early nineteenth century.[74]

Yet the phenomenon of Scots at the centre of British government changed after the end of the Napoleonic wars, as a growing number of Scots, many of them veterans who demanded British political rights, saw the Revolution legacy and the fruits of union with England as the preserve of a narrow oligarchy which selfishly guarded its own interests to the detriment of the majority of the population. Nevertheless, the idea of a separate legacy of the Revolutions of 1688–9 in Scotland safeguarded by the union persisted. In 1760, opponents of aristocratic political influence by the Queensberry family in the burgh of Dumfries defined their rights in terms of the Claim of Right of 1689 passed by the Scottish Convention Parliament,[75] and in 1793 the medical student Alexander Aitchison at the 'British' convention of the Associations of the Friends of the People in Edinburgh described 'our rights as Britons' in terms of 'Magna Carta and the Claim of Right',[76] thus marrying English and Scottish traditional liberties by representing English liberties as rooted in medieval history, whereas liberty in Scotland was very much a Revolution legacy. Gordon Pentland's article on the Scottish Reform movement in 1830–2 emphasises an important strand of support that presented the political reforms of 1832 as completing the Revolution of 1689.[77] In 1842, when the Church of Scotland established in the aftermath of the Revolution in Scotland found itself under threat from the determination of the Scottish court of session to assert its authority over it, it too passed a Claim of Right in its General Assembly summoning the legacy of 1689 in a fruitless attempt to defend its place at the centre of public culture in Scotland.[78] While the Disruption of the Church of Scotland did not mark the end of the Revolution legacy in Scotland, it represented the end of the public culture it created far more than the parliamentary political reforms of 1832 had done. The Revolution had been more of a revolution against absolutism in Scotland in alliance with a radical Covenanting tradition in 1689 and 1690 than the restoration of traditional liberties that it had been in England. With the Disruption of the Church of Scotland in 1843, the legacy of the Whig Revolution in Scotland was also disrupted and fragmented, as the attempt to square the circle of deep sectarian conflict in a society that required public institutions trusted by all its inhabitants ended in renewed conflict between Scottish ecclesiastical and legal establishments scarcely understood by those governing the British state that had been created in part to prevent that very tragedy.

Acknowledgements

I am very grateful to Professors Tim Harris, Allan Macinnes and Daniel Szechi for their comments on earlier drafts of this essay, and to the Research Seminar in Scottish History at the University of Edinburgh for an opportunity to present an earlier version of this text to a critical audience.

4

The Life and Death of the Notorious Captain John Porteous

KENNETH J. LOGUE

INTRODUCTION

The study of 'the crowd', 'the mob', popular direct action – or of popular disturbances, the more po-faced description I have used myself[1] – remains, as it was twenty-five years ago, not well developed, especially for Scotland in the pre-industrial era. Following the pioneering and inspiring work of George Rudé,[2] Richard Cobb[3] and especially Edward Thompson,[4] there have been some developments, often critical of the above, outwith Scotland in work by Stevenson and Quinault and others.[5] In Scotland, to the early work of S.G.E. Lythe,[6] valuable and developing work has been added by Christopher Whatley,[7] who has contributed to our understanding of popular protest in Lowland Scotland in the eighteenth century in general[8] and in the context of such as the king's birthday celebrations,[9] by W.H. Fraser[10] and by R.A. Houston,[11] who also began to explore the murky politics of the trade incorporations and town council in Edinburgh.[12]

As the inspiration and motivation for my work in this area came originally from Edward Thompson's work,[13] the most interesting contribution to the overall debate on eighteenth-century popular protest and 'popular politics' in the past twenty years has been Thompson's own essay revisiting his own concept of the 'moral economy' of the crowd.[14] There he defines anew his concept of 'moral economy' and what it was that he was describing and analysing.

> My object of analysis was the *mentalité*, or, as I would prefer, the political culture, the expectations, traditions, and, indeed, superstitions of the working population most frequently involved in actions in the market; and the relations – sometimes negotiations – between crowd and rulers which go under the unsatisfactory term of 'riot.'[15]

He then defends his 'moral economy' against a variety of attacks on this concept.[16] His most successful riposte is against those who bring Adam Smith to their argument in a supreme piece of historicism. Smith may have described the concept and operation of the market in goods;[17] the pre-industrial crowd *experienced* it. The trouble for his opponents is 'the vulgarity of crowds. They were not philosophers. They did . . . have substantive and knowledgeable arguments about the working of markets, but about actual markets rather than theorised market relations.'[18] And the Edinburgh crowd that lynched Captain Porteous of the city guard on 8 September 1736 were not philosophers either. It seems clear – at least on the basis of our knowledge to date – that there was in Edinburgh that night a version of Thompson's 'moral economy' at work. Not in the usual context of food riots or 'meal mobs' but in, as Thompson put it, 'the relations . . . between crowd and rulers which go under the unsatisfactory term of "riot"'. Walter Scott, a high Tory coming at it from a slightly different angle, put it in much the same terms in his depiction of the riot in *Heart of Midlothian*. What we do know is that when John Porteous, late captain of the Edinburgh city guard, ended his life hanging at the end of a rope slung over a dyer's pole, victim of a bloodthirsty but otherwise disciplined Edinburgh crowd, he set off a train of political events that eventually ended the political career of one of Britain's most powerful men and sent shockwaves through the body politic of the new and potentially fragile kingdom of Great Britain – formed by the relatively recent parliamentary union of England and Scotland in 1707. He also set in train a mystery as to the identity of his murderers; this mystery has not yet been adequately explained.[19]

Captain Porteous

John Porteous was probably born in the 1690s; his actual birth date has not been established, but he was appointed as a drill master to the city guard of Edinburgh in 1715, and subsequently an ensign in 1718. Prior to that his career already seems to have involved service in the army of Queen Anne in Flanders – something he took up after suspicions that he had, at worst, physically mistreated both his parents and, at best, lived the life of a ruffian on the streets of Edinburgh. Having said that, our sources for his early career are *post hoc* and somewhat biased: William Roughhead described the principal of these as 'so violently partial as to defeat his own design'.[20]

However he got himself to Flanders, Porteous is reported to have been involved there in the death of his captain and to have fled back to London, where he made a living variously as 'a tailor, a bully in a bawdy house, a street walker, a gentleman and a beggar'.[21] It was on his eventual return to Edinburgh in 1715 that his career as drill master and then ensign in the city guard began, due largely – according to gossip – to his relationship with the provost's housekeeper, whom he later married. From this point his chequered and ultimately doomed career began: 1726, appointed captain; 1732, violently put down a crowd protesting at the appointment of a minister to the West Kirk; 1735, he and another captain, John Fergusson, were dismissed for fighting each other but were later reinstated.[22] All of this was a prelude to John Porteous' short and brief walk on the stage of history.

In 1736 he was again captain of the city guard. Even allowing for the biased 'histories' published after his death, Porteous does seem to have been an unpopular figure, almost certainly hated by 'the mob', that disparate and inchoate group of citizens who occupied the lower levels of Edinburgh's highly stratified mid-eighteenth-century society and who from time to time exercised the only power they had – their collective weight and anger – for good or ill against the powers that be. As Thompson suggests, they had their own 'political culture, expectations, traditions, and superstitions', and ways of asserting these when the need arose.

Porteous' job was to maintain law and order, and he and the Edinburgh crowd frequently clashed. He was described by one commentator as

> middle-sized, broad shouldered, face a little pock marked, and round; mild and gentle featured, nothing of the fierce or brutal; brown complexion; insolent to inferiors; easy and equal with his equals; humble and submissive to his superiors; cunning; a master at insinuating and gaming [sic] on the young and unwary; quick to detect weakness in another and take advantage of it; cold over an insupportable pride; contempt for religion; readiness to fly into a rage.[23]

Allowing for the bias already mentioned, a vivid picture is presented of a small-minded man with more power than was good for him.

Execution of Andrew Wilson

Ever since the still largely unpopular union of the English and Scottish parliaments of 1707, smuggling to avoid excise taxes had been a widespread activity, the perpetrators of which enjoyed popular support. The Scots showed considerable hostility towards the English system of customs and excise, which they resented as foreign and contrary to the Union agreement. Serious rioting had occurred fairly recently in Glasgow in 1725 against the Malt Tax.[24] The unpopularity of 'English' customs and excise duties made illicit trade both widespread and 'legitimate', and smuggling was endemic along the quieter shores of Scotland. Andrew Wilson was one such smuggler – or entrepreneur – who had suffered for his trade at the hands of the revenue officers. He had retaliated with an attack and robbery on the customs house in Pittenweem, Fife. He was caught and, along with a colleague, George Robertson, convicted and condemned to be hanged in the Grassmarket. Many believed that his actions were more like justified theft than aggravated armed robbery and hardly merited public execution. Sympathy for their fate may have been further increased by the fact that they were convicted largely on the 'king's evidence' of one of his fellow smugglers.

When sentence was due to be carried out on 14 April 1736, John Porteous was in command of the city guard, with instructions to maintain order.[25] Sympathy for Wilson was particularly high, on top of his positive reputation as a smuggler. On Friday 9 April, Robertson and he, along with two other prisoners, had tried to escape from the Tolbooth. One of the men did make his escape, but Wilson, next to make the attempt, got stuck in the cell window, preventing his other colleagues' escape. The following Sunday, 11 April, while Wilson and Robertson were in the church of St Giles to hear the traditional pre-gallows sermon, Wilson violently engaged the attentions of his four armed guards, reputedly yelled 'Geordie, run for thy life', and made enough commotion and confusion to allow Robertson to escape, aided by the passive response of the rest of the congregation and the more active intervention of other bystanders.[26]

Wilson, however, was not to escape – in spite of rumours that his friends intended a rescue. As captain of the city guard, Porteous was aware of the rumours about a possible rescue and, mindful of that, he was less willing than usual to allow a prisoner in his charge to cheat the gallows. The Magistrates, also aware of the rescue rumours, had ordered Porteous to request military support on that day. This is likely to have been seen by Porteous, who already had the full complement of seventy city guards at his disposal, as an insult to his capacity to keep the peace and is unlikely to have improved his humour. Roughly treating Wilson, on 14 April he duly marched the prisoner from the Tolbooth up the Lawnmarket and down the West Bow to the Grassmarket: a route that Porteous himself was to witness as a prisoner five short months later. Every execution was a spectacle, almost an entertainment for the people of Edinburgh: Wilson's notoriety and his popularity meant the place of the execution in the amphitheatre of Edinburgh's Grassmarket, overlooked by tall tenements rising against the castle's backdrop, was filled to capacity. The area around the gallows was a sea of faces; every window and other vantage point around were occupied; people of every class were gathered to see Wilson hanged. John Porteous was determined to ensure that he was.

There was as yet no sophisticated, mechanised 'drop' to ensure a quick end (that would have to await the ingenuity of another Edinburgh celebrity, Deacon Brodie): just a ladder from which the condemned were pushed so that they slowly strangled. At the appointed time the hangman John Dalgleish helped Wilson up the grim ladder, the Magistrates in their window high above the Grassmarket gave the word and Wilson was launched into eternity. There were no roars of popular approval: the crowd was silent. After about fifteen minutes Porteous seems to have grown anxious, and he asked permission of the magistrates to cut the body down before the usual half hour had elapsed. This was denied, but a few minutes later the hangman decided to cut Wilson down anyway. There were often attempts by friends and relatives of those hanged in this crude fashion to cut the body down as quickly as possible and whisk it away for a sympathetic doctor to attempt resuscitation. This may have been the intention on this occasion. At any rate, no sooner had he set foot on the ladder than the hangman was struck by stones thrown by the crowd – in the usual fashion, but possibly as a diversion – and he retreated to the protection of the city guard. At this, some of the crowd pushed forward themselves and Wilson's body was cut down, perhaps with a view to attempted resuscitation, or at least to secure his body for his relations and friends. Others in the crowd turned their attention to Porteous and his city guard and began to stone them. While this was going on the guards' attention was distracted and Wilson's body was rushed off.

What happened next is disputed. John Porteous later claimed that he tried to restrain the guard as he retreated up the West Bow under attack from a hostile, stone-throwing crowd. During this retreat, and under such provocation, unknown members of the guard discharged their muskets into the crowd, several of whom were killed or wounded. When the smoke and dust had cleared, six people were dead. According to their captain, the guard had acted only in self-defence. While a few witnesses, rather half-heartedly, supported much of Porteous' version of events, many more told a different story. This version generally had John Porteous waving his musket angrily and threateningly at the crowd by the gallows as it pushed towards him and his men. When a stone hit him, he retaliated by firing on the crowd at point-blank range, killing the first of the victims. He then ordered his men to fire, threatening some of them with his own firearm. This they did, but over the crowd's heads, resulting in injuries to spectators at the high tenement windows. Then he ordered them to fire properly, into the crowd. When they did so, two more victims fell dead. When the crowd retreated in some panic at this time, Porteous ordered the guards' withdrawal up the West Bow, but turned his men back to face the crowd and again threatened them. A third order to fire was given, and three more members of the crowd were killed where they stood. The guard then completed its march up the West Bow, passing through the ranks of the regular troops stationed in the Lawnmarket, and back to the guard house in the High Street.

The Arrest and Trial of Porteous

As in many such cases, what actually happened cannot now be determined with any certainty. Many witnesses attested to Porteous having fired on the crowd.

Porteous denied it, and produced his unfired firearm to prove it. Others said they had seen him grab one of his men's muskets which, if true, explains his own being unfired. Several people later attested to the 'bad humour' of Porteous, his feeling of insult at the calling in of regular troops, his general hatred of the crowd's boldness and his opposition to their sympathy for the condemned smuggler. But then they would say that, after the event – would they not? The only truth we can agree to at this remove is that shots were fired and six people did die, with many more injured.

The Provost and Magistrates had few doubts, however, and also many political reasons for not having any such doubts. Porteous was arrested that afternoon and charged with murder.

The Magistrates would have liked a swift trial, but the Lords of Judiciary were out of Edinburgh, on circuit. Provost Wilson could have tried the case in his capacity as sheriff, but he chose not to do so – either because he might have been called upon to give evidence, or because this course of action would have given him the responsibility for condemning or acquitting Porteous, neither of which prospects he relished. Furthermore, the senior political and legal officers in Scotland – Lord Advocate Duncan Forbes and Solicitor-General Charles Erskine – advised that the magistrates should await the return of the Lords of Judiciary.

The delay did nothing to cool tempers, particularly among the populace of Edinburgh and the surrounding districts, and when the trial began on 5 July 1736,[27] with Lord Justice-Clerk Andrew Fletcher, the senior judge in Scotland, presiding, feelings were already running high. The trial took place with a large, vocal and somewhat biased crowd in attendance outside the court. This was not likely to 'encourage' the witnesses and the fifteen jurors to lean towards Porteous' account of the riot. Nineteen prosecution witnesses swore that Porteous fired into the crowd on 14 April. Sixteen defence witnesses were less certain, but all stated that they had not seen him fire. Eight of these said that the first shot had been fired by other guards, and four of the guards swore that Porteous had not given the order to fire. The defence in essence proved that Porteous had not given any order to fire during the second phase on the West Bow, but did not press the point that the city guard had been expecting trouble and had been severely provoked by the crowd. Because of the climate of opinion, it is unlikely that this would have carried much weight in any case, and the jury duly and unanimously found Porteous guilty of murder. He was sentenced to be executed in the Grassmarket on 8 September 1736 and secured in the Tolbooth – the Heart of Midlothian – the city's gaol close to the church of St Giles, and the place from which Porteous had escorted the smuggler Andrew Wilson to his own execution only five months earlier. The Edinburgh populace – and more polite opinion, too – was satisfied. Political and legal opinion in London was much less so. The feeling there was that the verdict must be unsafe in the circumstances, and – less overtly – that this was an unfortunate example of the forces of law and order not being protected when rebellious Scots took the law into their own hands.

A Political Miscalculation

Whatever was happening in Edinburgh and for whatever cause, the normally sure-footed Earl of Islay, Walpole's political manager in Scotland, made a grave political miscalculation. He sought to placate London opinion without reference to the depth of feeling in Scotland, and in Edinburgh in particular. Islay seems to have encouraged the trial judge Fletcher to have a petition for clemency drawn up and signed by a cross-section of Scottish political opinion and society. This was forwarded to London. Porteous himself was advised to appeal to Queen Caroline who was, in the extended absence of George II in Hanover, acting as regent. Porteous' confidence in his political betters was rewarded when a deferment of his execution for six weeks was granted by the Queen, who appears to have become an enthusiast for the condemned captain as a victim of, at best, unfortunate circumstances, if not of an outright conspiracy. Her position, however, did not do any good for Porteous' reputation as a social-climbing toady.

The Lynching of Captain Porteous

The deferment arrived in Edinburgh on 2 September, six days before the date set for his execution. Among the ordinary people of Edinburgh and the surrounding area, this was – to say the least – not well received. For a substantial group including, it seems, some from Andrew Wilson's home area in Fife, it looked as if their revenge for the death of the smuggler Wilson was about to be denied them. Rumours of a plot to murder Porteous began to spread almost immediately. By 4 September, the new captain of the city guard, Robert Lind, reported his concerns to Provost Wilson. He was asked to investigate further, and he reported back on 7 September, the eve of the original date of execution. Lind claimed his report confirmed these rumours. Provost Wilson denied this, and subsequently sacked Lind for contradicting him. The only precautions actually taken were that extra guards were called out for the next day, 8 September.

There were thus only fifteen guards on duty – ironically unarmed since the tragedy of 14 April – on the evening of Tuesday 7 September. At around 9 p.m., a crowd began to gather in the Portsburgh, west of the Grassmarket, beating drums and gathering force, until eventually it reportedly reached 4,000 in number. Apparently well-organised and disciplined, and certainly purposeful, the crowd entered the city proper through the West Port, which they immediately secured behind them, preventing or certainly delaying any military intervention from that quarter. They crossed through the Grassmarket eastwards to the Cowgate, where they secured their flanks by closing both the Cowgate Port and the Netherbow Port. The latter cut the city off from the Canongate and Holyrood, where regular troops were stationed.[28]

The crowd then made its way up the High Street to the city guard house, overpowered the guards, seized their arms and proceeded up the street to the Tolbooth where the hapless Porteous was still expecting a further reprieve from his friends in high places: he was reported earlier that evening to have been relaxed and confident.

As the crowd progressed towards its goal and began to attack the Tolbooth, the civic authorities were virtually paralysed, both by the prospect of what the crowd was clearly bent on doing and by the prospect of the danger to themselves of trying to do something about it. Some cowered in the old City Chamber in the corner of Parliament Square, behind the Tolbooth itself, others in a nearby tavern. They all felt, probably correctly, that they were in great danger of being attacked if they showed themselves. Troops were stationed in the castle, but the crowd at the Tolbooth stood between them and the Magistrates. And they, the troops, would not act without warrant from the civil authorities. The military were all too aware of the precedent set at Shawfield, Glasgow, ten years earlier, when soldiers had been prosecuted for firing on the crowd without being ordered to do so by the civil authority. This was a common refrain throughout eighteenth-century Britain. In Edinburgh on 7 September a form of 'catch-22' operated: troops would not intervene without civil authority; the magistrates would not ask for troops because (unlike the troops) they would have to live with the potentially fatal consequences. It does seem likely that the Magistrates would have quite liked military intervention *without* authority (and thus with *deniability*).

The Magistrates eventually stopped dithering (or did they wait for a decent interval to elapse?) and decided to send Robert Lindsay, MP for Edinburgh and a former lord provost, to ask General Moyle, officer commanding, based at Holyrood, for military assistance. Critically – or deliberately? – he did not take with him the necessary warrant signed by the Magistrates, and Moyle, whom he reached by about 10.45 p.m., would not act without one. By the time a messenger had been sent to and returned from Andrew Fletcher, the Lord Justice-clerk, who lived some miles off, the warrant he brought was worthless. John Porteous was already dead.

The Tolbooth withstood the crowd's assault until about 11.30 p.m., time enough for military assistance to have intervened if a warrant had been obtained. Oblivious to this, but fully determined, the crowd persisted with its attack on the Tolbooth's defences and finally broke through to the inner iron gate, which would almost certainly have thwarted their efforts for a further hour or so. But they also came upon the gate-keeper and, with him, his keys. The Tolbooth was theirs. They released all the prisoners, including seven of the city guard arrested with Porteous: their objective was Porteous and Porteous alone.

Porteous showed courage and presence of mind in the circumstances. He was roughly dragged out of the Tolbooth at the head of the crowd, up the Lawnmarket towards the castle and then down the steep West Bow towards the Grassmarket. Someone – according to tradition – broke into a cordiner's shop on the way and left a guinea on the shop counter for a rope to hang their victim. This was the end of any gallantry on the crowd's part. A long dyer's pole had been set up near the usual place of execution in the Grassmarket as a makeshift gallows. Without further ceremony the unfortunate Porteous was strung up. After a few minutes he was brought down so that – probably to add further humiliation – his night-shirt could be wound around his neck. When they strung him up the second time they forgot to tie his hands, and as he struggled to prevent his own strangulation someone broke his arm and shoulder with one of the city guard's own Lochaber axes. This was now a cruel and heartless attack bordering on torture: Porteous' last few minutes were not at all pleasant. While the lynching went on, some of the crowd taunted Porteous: 'Where is your reprieve? Shew it us and we'll save you'; 'Now the Queen can wipe her back-side with her reprieve.' Not yet dead, Porteous was brought down from the pole for a third time, attacked around the head and body and had one foot burned with a torch before being finally hauled up again. Shortly after that the torment was over as his neck was broken. John Porteous died shortly before midnight on the very eve of the date set for his judicial execution. By all accounts the crowd then melted away, leaving the body twisting slowly at the end of its pole.

Who Killed Captain Porteous?

The cruel death of John Porteous had serious political ramifications. Political opinion in London was alarmed for two reasons. Why were the rioters so disciplined, dangerous and effective, and why did the authorities fail to crush the riot or bring the culprits to book? These questions were not answered at the time, and it is difficult to do so now. There are, of course, other questions too – and we can only hazard a guess at some of the answers. Linked to the contemporary concerns about the nature of the riot, we are interested in a number of slightly different questions. Was this a 'simple' example of eighteenth-century urban popular direct action? Or were other forces at work? Was this somehow an extension of incorporation/burgh politics? Were the Jacobites really the cause of it all? How did so many do so much with hardly a soul to bear witness to it?

Lots of theories have been advanced about the motives of those behind the lynching of Porteous. They were involved in a Jacobite plot or an extreme

Presbyterian conspiracy; they were smugglers seeking revenge; they were a wild drunken rabble; or they were simply the determined friends of those killed on 14 April. It is possible that elements of all these were present in the crowd of 4,000 or so that broke Porteous out of the Tolbooth and accompanied him to his painful and cruel death. It is, however, also likely that the core of the planning and organisation was the work of a small group of Edinburgh tradesmen and journeymen. They may or may not have had some connection to the internecine and Byzantine politics of the Edinburgh town council. Some tantalising material is emerging on this[29] about the politics and infighting – and the prestige sought – within the craft incorporations and between the incorporations and the town council. For instance, quoting Houston, 'while a craft incorporation was politically weaker than a lord provost, it still had something to offer the city's leader'.[30] Membership of an incorporation was valuable to a city politician and businessman because of the connections it brought. Another contemporary commentator claimed that the traders and craftsmen of Edinburgh largely controlled the town council and were in a position to overawe the magistrates.

> These Incorporations of Craftsmen are the very root from whence all the abuses and tumults spring. That they are an invincible obstacle in the administration of justice and punishment of offenders I can vouch from my own experience; for no magistrate who inclines to continue so dare punish any craftsmen for any fraud or crime peculiar to that craft; and I have known instances where it was dangerous to punish them for open outrages.[31]

Perhaps there is something of this in the background to the death of Captain Porteous?

Back to the small group of possible ringleaders. They probably included John Maxwell, a journeymen carpenter, who gave detailed and damning evidence against Porteous at his trial and who worked for Colin Allison, a master carpenter. Allison must have been well known to Provost Wilson: not only had he been employed on several council projects in both 1736 and 1737, but he had in fact been paid over £300 on 10 September 1736 while the council was still conducting its inquiry into the riot.[32] Maxwell and three other of Allison's journeymen, and several journeymen and apprentices of Samuel Neilson, a master mason, were indicted along with nineteen others for the murder of Captain Porteous. But they all absconded – along with about seventy other tradesmen, journeymen and apprentices – and they were subsequently reported to have left the country. These were all, as far as we can see, respectable working men, certainly not the stereotypical 'rabble' of day-labourers, unemployed and other rootless proletarians. This was the traditional 'Blue Blanket', flown at the head of a just crowd, out to right a grievous wrong. This is surely a version of Edward Thompson's 'moral economy': justice should be done, and if the powers that be will not carry it out, then the local populace will. This is not incompatible with the suggestion by Chris Whatley that 'most riots in Edinburgh in the later-seventeenth and early-eighteenth centuries tended to reinforce rather than weaken the social order by uniting participants from all ranks in popular opposition to "outsiders"'.[33] Wilson's re-election as Lord Provost on 5 October 1736[34] indicates that whoever else he alienated it was not the craftsmen of his home city. It would appear, therefore, that the Porteous riot supports this thesis – with only a few exceptions in the upper and politically active echelons of society. So: a mixture of 'moral economy' and social solidarity. We probably need to know a lot more about Edinburgh society, the life of the incorporations, the politics of the town council, and how all of these were inter-related before we can successfully unpick the full story of the riot.

On the judicial front, in the end only one trial of any consequence resulted: that of William Maclauchlane, footman to the Countess of Wemyss. In spite of evidence of his presence at and around the lynching – standing out from the crowd in his mistress' livery – countered only by evidence that he was seriously drunk, the jury acquitted him. No sign of respectable disgust at the awful events here.

More Political Miscalculation

Something we do know a bit about, however, is the wide and serious political consequences of the riot. The events in Edinburgh were sufficiently serious that they threatened to undermine the political influence of the great earl of Islay at Westminster and, indeed, the whole position of the Walpole administration, which was already reeling because of the gin and turnpike riots in England. In the spring of 1737, Islay warned Lord Justice-Clerk Fletcher of the trouble he was facing in England as a result of the fallout from Porteous' untimely death.

> The House, & indeed vast numbers of people here are so exasperated at the Edenburg [sic] mob that whatever is proposed, however violent & unjust, is popular, & its impossible to judge what effect this violence may have . . . This is the substance of yesterday's work which was the most furious & most unjust attack that I ever saw in my life. We shall do all for the best, but we must play the cards as they lie, & the main strength must be gathered & reserved for the getting the better of the enemy in their further attempts of more real mischief, if it should happen.[35]

Islay's letter was a reference to the campaign that the opposition had launched in Parliament. The apparent breakdown of law and order gave the opposition in the House of Lords, led by Lords Carteret and Bathurst, the opportunity to push for a Parliamentary inquiry into the whole Porteous affair. The Lords ordered Provost Wilson, the other four Edinburgh magistrates, Patrick Lindsay MP, Captain Lind of the city guard, General Moyle and others, to appear before the house in order to answer questions. The Lords also demanded that the leading Scottish judges should be ordered to appear before the bar of the house, and there was even some discussion about amending the criminal law of Scotland to bring it into line with that of England. Islay saw these actions as a direct challenge to his political influence over Scotland, to his ability to protect his agents and dependents, and to the independence of the Scottish legal system, which had been guaranteed by the Union. His elder brother, the proud and fiery duke of Argyll, was even more enraged, especially when Lord Chancellor Hardwicke and the Duke of Newcastle began to support the opposition's efforts to punish those responsible for letting the Porteous riot get out of hand.

In April 1737 Hardwicke and the opposition peers supported the introduction of a bill to imprison Provost Wilson for a year, to debar him from holding civic office in future, to disband the city guard and to pull down the Netherbow Port, which could prevent troops in the Canongate entering the city.[36] Islay managed at least to save the other four Edinburgh Magistrates – who were all his supporters, unlike Provost Wilson – but neither he nor Argyll was satisfied. In Parliament, within the administration and at court, the two brothers tried to point out the dangerous implications of this bill, which would infringe the liberties of the Scottish capital, punish the innocent more than the guilty, attack the Scottish legal system and alienate a considerable body of Scottish opinion. These warnings went largely unheeded, despite the fact that Islay's argument had the backing of Lord Hervey and Queen Caroline. The leading ministers showed a propensity to placate the opposition and public opinion in England rather than their normally docile Scottish allies – perhaps indeed because they were normally so docile, and thus, they miscalculated, could be taken for granted. When the Bill was pushed through the Lords, by a vote of 54 to 22, only seven Scottish peers were prepared to vote with the majority. Islay abstained, but his brother broke with the Walpole administration and went into opposition. In a passionate speech, which reveals incidental insights into eighteenth-century beliefs about the central political importance of property, Argyll declared:

> I have opposed the present Bill, my Lords, because I look upon it to be an invasion upon property in that part of the kingdom. And on that account my Lords, were it upon no other, I have more reason to oppose it than any man in this House, nay perhaps, than

> any man in the United Kingdom: because there is none whose property is there so extensive as my own. I likewise look upon it, my Lords, as an encroachment upon liberty, and on this account, no man has better reason to oppose it.[37]

In the House of Commons the Scottish members refused to follow the Government's lead, as most of them usually did. Opinion throughout Scotland appeared so outraged at the bill that even the Government's staunchest supporters and most reliable political agents in Scotland, Duncan Forbes and Charles Erskine, were prepared to lead the campaign against the bill. The regular opponents of Walpole now fully realised the scale of the rebellion against the ministry and changed tack. Whereas the opposition in the Lords had promoted the Bill in order to condemn the government for its failure to maintain law and order, the opposition in the Commons argued on 'patriotic' grounds that the Bill was a fundamental attack on the liberties of a parliamentary constituency and a threat to the balanced constitution. William Shippen, the spokesman for the small 'Jacobite' group, protested:

> Sir, the plain and natural tendency of the Bill is, to turn the metropolis of a once independent kingdom into a military garrison. And, Sir, it has always been my opinion, that the execution of the laws, by a military force, is the surest symptom of a distressed administration and a consumptive constitution.[38]

The opposition to the Bill was so great that it was only saved in the committee stage by the casting vote of the chairman, a government placeman. Only one Scottish MP, Brigadier Anstruther, was brave enough to support the bill. When asked 'if he would dare go to Scotland again, he said he would go to Edinburgh and piss on the magistrates'. Years later he was to suffer for his audacity. In 1751, when acting as governor of Minorca, Anstruther was accused of misgovernment. In the subsequent parliamentary inquiry, all of the Scottish MPs voted against him.[39]

Walpole was at last conscious of the strength of Scottish opinion against the Bill, and feared that the peaceful management of Scotland would collapse if Islay was seen to lack real influence with his ministerial colleagues. Without withdrawing all support for the Bill, he advised the Commons:

> If, after it is committed, gentlemen would think fit to make such amendments upon it as may leave the privileges of the incorporation of Edinburgh untouched, and remit the most penal part of the punishment of the Lord Provost; and if these amendments should be founded upon reason and equity, I shall by no means be against them.[40]

The Commons took the hint and the Bill was emasculated. Of the punitive clauses, only that which debarred Provost Wilson from public office was retained, although Edinburgh was now fined £2,000, which was to be paid in compensation to the widow of Captain Porteous. Even then the Bill only survived on the casting vote of the chairman of the Committee of the Whole House. Hardwicke and Newcastle were piqued at these suggested amendments but agreed to accept them, though Argyll refused to be mollified by the government's concessions. Nevertheless, the Lords accepted the changes. When Provost Wilson returned to Edinburgh he was greeted by ringing bells and celebration bonfires.

Argyll's hostility and the alienation of much Scottish opinion were to help bring down Walpole's administration in 1741–2. Islay remained loyal to the ministry, but he lost credit in Scotland and could not prevent an increase in opposition MPs in the general election of 1741 after it had been seen that he could not exert enough influence on his ministerial colleagues. In an effort to assert its authority and to placate opinion in England, the Government, this time supported by Islay, decided to renew the attempts to bring some of the rioters to justice. An act was passed that offered a reward of £200 to anyone who would come forward with sufficient evidence to convict any of those who had helped to lynch Porteous. This act was probably doomed to failure, but it might have caused little offence in Scotland if the ministry had not insisted on a clause that commanded it should be read in every church in Scotland on the first Sunday of every month for a year. This clause provoked considerable resistance and incited a major pamphlet debate. One pamphlet, *A Memorial for the People of Scotland*, protested that the act would make 'the Ambassador of the King of Kings do the drudgery work of scoundrel messengers and heralds, rendering their persons and ministries odious, base and contemptible before all the people'.

A large and increasing number of ministers refused to read the Act, regarding acquiescence as Erastian heresy. Some who did read it found themselves addressing empty churches. Walpole retreated, and no-one was arrested for failure to comply. Neither was any further information about Porteous' killers ever uncovered.

Some Conclusions

The Edinburgh rioters of 7 September 1736 can be said to have won an almost complete victory over the forces of law and order in Britain. They had shown the power of an urban populace when united in a common aim and determined to implement its notion of justice. The riots exemplified both the notion of 'moral economy' in action – the political culture, the expectations, traditions and superstitions of ordinary people asserted against the powers that be – as well as emphasising the social cohesion of the greater part of a city like Edinburgh. They had also revealed some serious weaknesses in the instruments of law and order at the disposal of an eighteenth-century British government anxious neither to make too many enemies nor to provoke a backlash it could not be certain of controlling. The successful maintenance of law and order owed much more to the willingness of those outside the ruling political classes to be ruled and the delicate ties of the local community than to naked force or Acts of Parliament that could be deployed by central government. When that willingness was taken for granted, or the political class misjudged the values and traditions of those they ruled, the crowd could take matters into its own hands. This John Porteous discovered to his cost.

ACKNOWLEDGEMENTS

I am indebted to Alex Murdoch for encouraging the writing of this piece. Much of it is based on material developed some years ago in conjunction with Professor H.T. Dickinson but since worked on outside the purely academic environment. I am grateful to Professor Dickinson, Professor Whatley and Dr Murdoch for comments on drafts of this piece. The errors are, of course, all mine.

5

The King's Men or Glengarry's?: Discipline in a Newly Raised Highland Regiment during the Napoleonic Wars

Ronald M. Sunter

The long war waged by Great Britain against revolutionary and Napoleonic France necessitated the rapid expansion of an army which had greatly contracted since the conclusion of the War of American Independence. Men were sought in every corner of the kingdom, and nowhere more energetically than in Scotland, particularly the Highland portions of that country. Colonel's commissions were awarded to individuals who would undertake to form a new regiment, and existing formations were rapidly expanded with the formation of additional battalions and companies. Some of this expansion was for the regular army, but more was for the fencible regiments, who were essentially war emergency troops who would be disbanded at the latest when peace was concluded and whose service was restricted in some manner. Scotland, in contrast to England, began the war without a militia to provide a defensive force. Scottish fencible regiments were intended to fill that gap. There was, however, very little difference between the two types of soldier, who received the same pay and allowances, wore similar uniforms, were armed with comparable weapons and were subject to the same regulations. Many of the Scottish fencible troops, however, were initially recruited under conditions of service which made it very difficult to march them out of Scotland, save in the case of an actual invasion of another portion of Great Britain, and although these conditions could be amended with the consent of the fencible soldiers (with a number of units agreeing to go to Ireland or other European portions of the empire), most did not, and the entire episode suggests the inadequacy of the cabinet responsible for their authorisation.

Colonels charged with the raising of a new formation, whether regular or fencible, were given a very limited time to muster the nucleus of their battalions. In the case of a unit intended to be completed to 1,000 men, for example, the critical number was the first five or six hundred, who could then be relied upon to attract their own friends and neighbours into the service. The field and company officers belonging to a new formation were given their commissions in return for their best efforts to recruit a portion of the necessary manpower, and indeed such demands in more modest numbers were even made upon the most junior officers as a condition for receiving their commissions. Many of the new regiments were nominally Highland in composition. The Highlands were seen at the end of the eighteenth century, before the Clearances changed that picture, as the great reservoir of untapped military manpower, but how was this potential to be realised?

Those gentlemen with a Highland estate and the ability to influence tenants were attractive candidates for the award of new commissions; and a chief of a name, supposedly able to encourage his clansmen to look upon the army with favour, was an even better catch, but there could be some real disadvantages with such men as officers, which only tended to be appreciated considerably later. One of the new formations which illustrates this was the 1st or Strathspey Regiment of Fencible Highlanders, formed by Colonel Sir James Grant of Grant, a Highland chief who was very conscious of the advantages of securing the services of his fellow Highland proprietors when raising his regiment.

Several chieftains were approached unsuccessfully[1] before Alexander McDonnell of Glengarry consented to become one of the Strathspey regiment's captains.[2] Alone of all the officers of the Strathspey regiment, Glengarry obtained all of the men of his company by his own efforts, and was the first captain to report the completion of his sub-unit.[3] Sir James Grant presumably congratulated himself upon his own astuteness in securing this influential gentleman of name who had proved to be such an able recruiter for his regiment. Captain McDonnell of Glengarry, however, turned out to be the most troublesome officer in the regiment and was extremely unpopular with many of his fellow officers, notably the lieutenant-colonel, Alexander Penrose Cumming of Altyre, who commanded the battalion in the absence of Sir James Grant, whose political duties conflicted with his military ones. The friction between Glengarry and the lieutenant-colonel became so serious that the former finally left the Strathspey Fencibles to command a fencible battalion of his own which saw service in Ireland, during and after the Rising of 1798 and the accompanying French invasion of that troubled island. The growing friction between Captain McDonnell of Glengarry and the Strathspey regiment may be traced in the Seafield Papers, and although admittedly this gives but one side of the dispute there is little reason to question the essentials of the quarrel.

The picture that emerges from the surviving manuscripts is of a very disruptive company whose soldiers demonstrated real allegiance only to their own chieftain and not to the military machine of which they now formed a part. According to the battalion's field officers, Glengarry's soldiers undermined the discipline of the entire formation. A major part of the problem was due to the reluctance of Glengarry himself to attend to his frequently boring regimental duties, and his extended absences on official or unofficial leave. Even when the chief was with the regiment his conduct did little to encourage discipline. As early as July 1793, the commanding officer of the Strathspey Fencibles,

Lieutenant-Colonel Cumming, was complaining that 'there is one company the bane of our comfort & some other bad spirits in others'. The blame for this rested with the absent company commander. 'I have wrote Macdonell a positive order to join forthwith on accot. of the turbulent state of his men & hope he'll not think of disobeying.'[4] The letter seemed to do some good, for Glengarry made a brief appearance at headquarters before moving to take command of the detachment stationed in the port of Peterhead.

During his stay at Peterhead, Captain McDonnell continued to pester the commanding officer to authorise furloughs for his men and for himself, which Colonel Cumming refused on the ground that Glengarry 'had the advanced post of honor & danger, that if any insult was offered by a Privateer, he wou'd cut a very bad figure indeed by being absent from his post'.[5] Cumming made it plain to Sir James Grant that even with Glengarry present in Peterhead his company was 'in very bad order indeed'. Captain McDonnell's reason for requesting leave was 'on the footing of indispensible business at Glengarry & his sister's situation there, overrun with company'. That there was something very far wrong with Glengarry's company appears to be confirmed by a second field officer of the Strathspey regiment, Major John Grant, who expressed the same opinion in a letter to Sir James Grant, reporting the assembly of the regiment at Aberdeen preparatory to marching to Glasgow, that 'the MacDonald company are to be here on the 20th . . . I am told there is very little discipline established among them'.[6]

Major Grant may have only been reporting the opinion of Lieutenant-Colonel Cumming at this stage, but it was amply confirmed by events and appears to have been a view that was fairly general among the officers. Writing from his home at Forres, Colonel Cumming informed Sir James Grant that

> I had the satisfaction of seeing a deserter of ours go past under an escort a few days ago. It is Captn.Macdonell's little piper who left them at Nairn & 1 hear he is a very wicked little dog. However disagreeable it must be . . . I wou'd suggest your not passing him, as well for the crime as for the example of the people of these countries from whence he comes. We never can have a better opportunity of showing them what must happen from breaches of discipline . . . in the present temper of these people it is fortunate you have such a fair opportunity.[7]

It is unclear, however, whether Sir James Grant chose to make an example of the piper, for he was still desperately short of manpower from the intense competition for recruits in Scotland at this time, and was in fact engaged in raising a second regiment of Highlanders, the 97th Inverness-shire regiment,[8] a regular army formation, while continuing as colonel of the Strathspey

Fencibles, and severe punishment of a soldier would necessarily have discouraged recruitment.

Sir James Grant, and indeed Lieutenant-Colonel Cumming, treated Captain McDonnell with great consideration, granting him seven weeks leave in June and July 1793, and again giving him leave to attend to his affairs in October, since these were so pressing,[9] much to the annoyance of other officers due for leave who were obliged to remain with the battalion. The departure of the captain gave command of his company to his senior subaltern, Lieutenant James Macdonell, an officer who perhaps had had enough of his chief, for he was actively seeking a commission in a line battalion. Captain McDonnell departed for his home upon condition that should Lieutenant Macdonell secure the regular commission that he was seeking, or the commander-in-chief order a full muster of officers to be present, he would return to duty, failing which he would tender his resignation. On 29 October Lieutenant Macdonell was duly gazetted ensign in one of the independent companies,[10] and immediately appointed to a lieutenancy in Seaforth's Highland regiment. The lieutenant continued to command Glengarry's company for a few days longer in the absence of his chief before Colonel Cumming sent him off to Seaforth accompanied by a number of soldiers whom the Strathspey regiment did not want, drawing the following reprimand from the commander-in-chief, Lord Adam Gordon, who wrote to Sir James that 'tho' I agree that useless men are always to be got rid of, you will please to acquaint your Lt-Colonel that, for the future, that must be done with permission and approbation'.[11]

One of Colonel Cumming's motives was to rid the Strathspey regiment of a volunteer, or aspiring officer, who was completely unacceptable to him in this capacity. Cumming had already written to Colonel Sir James Grant on the subject of this volunteer.

> I wish you wou'd make us free of the other Macdonell, calling himself the Volunteer. I have been obliged to discharge him from appearing at the parade, as he was nasty, ill-dressed & dirty beyond suffrance. He is nothing but a beggerly eat-meat on the Regt.[12]

When faced with a choice of discharging a simple-minded soldier named Macdonell and the volunteer Macdonell, Colonel Cumming chose to keep the former, insisting that 'the vagabond Volunteer' was the best candidate for discharge, and that he would 'keep the fool, who is the best man of the two. The other has lost his bayonet, knapsack & many other articles & is a most worthless subject.'[13]

Notwithstanding the lieutenant-colonel's opinion, Captain McDonnell of Glengarry wrote to Sir James, urging that Volunteer Macdonell be advanced to the vacant ensigncy[14] occasioned by the departure of his lieutenant for the Seaforth Highlanders and the promotion of the existing ensign, and indeed Glengarry had received a promise from Sir James that he could name his own subalterns.[15] Sir James, however, would not agree without first consulting the battalion commander, who left him in no doubt about the unsuitability of this candidate, declaring that he was 'astonish'd how Glengarry cou'd make such a proposition with regard to him, as no officer in the Regt. cou'd keep company with him. His behaviour here has been more blackguard than ever and there is at this moment a town's prosecution agst him.'[16] Lest this be thought mere prejudice against a poor Highland gentleman, it is worth pointing out that there were a considerable number of officers promoted after service in non-commissioned ranks in this and other fencible regiments. Colonel Cumming, however, was happy to report that the volunteer had been otherwise provided for, he having agreed to enlist in the Seaforth Highlanders with Lieutenant James Macdonell.

> He was a most useless member to us and I think on your representing the situation to L(or)d Adam (Gordon), his being a Gentleman's son, & our being unwilling to punish him, he'll see the propriety of our getting free of him. He's not lost to the service and we can easily replace him.[17]

Archibald Macdonell, the volunteer, and the other recruits whom Lieutenant Macdonell took to the Seaforth Highlanders were clearly doubtful military assets symptomatic of the very real difficulties in recruitment in Scotland at this period where excessive demands were made upon a small population.[18]

Captain McDonell of Glengarry, despite his undertaking to return to the regiment upon his lieutenant's departure, did not appear in any hurry to do so, thus necessitating the appointment of another experienced officer to assume command in Glengarry's absence. The officer named for this task, Lieutenant John Grant of Auchterblair,[19] despite being a near relation of Glengarry through his wife, was informed by the outgoing Lieutenant Macdonell that Glengarry would certainly not permit another officer to involve himself with the pay of his company.

> Capt. M. had no regard or esteem for him & that he was certain he never intended giving him the pay etc. of his company. On these considerations Grant very properly declined meddling with their money or accots. It is now more than ever necessary that you (Sir James Grant) order Capt. Macdonell to join immediately, as no officer here will meddle with the money of his company & sorry I am to say, that it appears, that no accot

> whatever of debit & credit has been kept with them & no regular discharge by any man except what I ordered in the bread money rolls. This is contrary to the rules of the service . . . The Captn. of the company by this neglect may get himself into a very awkward situation as the men might call on him for very large sums, & in the event of his death or insolvency, you or I are obliged to be in his place. For these reasons I wou'd advise you to order him up immediately & let his company be put in such a state . . . as will not discredit us[20]

Writing from Glasgow in December 1793, Lieutenant-Colonel Cumming informed the colonel that although Captain McDonnell was still not present for duty, he had nonetheless managed to disrupt the discipline of the regiment by putting ideas into the heads of his men to the effect that they should be able to draw the allowance called bread money when they were on furlough. 'Had it not been instantly checqued [this] might have had disagreeable consequences.'[21] Sir James Grant at last wrote to the absent captain, ordering him to rejoin the battalion and resume command of his company. This appeared to have the desired effect, for Glengarry hastened to Glasgow, claiming to have been detained in a remote part of the Highlands and not to have received the previous correspondence sent to him. He might thereafter be physically in Glasgow, but he still declined the duties of his command, for he now claimed to be sick. Glengarry informed the commanding officer on 23 December that he was 'prevented by indisposition from doing duty' but that he would nonetheless 'be under the necessity of taking charge of my company from Lieut. Grant Achterblair'.[22] Glengarry had reached the station of his regiment at Glasgow on 15 December 1793, but had not reported for duty. Two days later, he was seen by Lieutenant-Colonel Cumming on horseback and out of uniform, and according to Cumming's complaint:

> He never came near the Mess but has taken up his abode in the Saltmarket . . . Finding he kept away from us, I directed the Orderly Serjeant . . . to go to him with my comp[liment]s & to desire he wou'd read all the orders since he left the Regt. He was at the same time put in orders for picket this day. He did not come to the Parade . . . I answered him by hoping he wou'd confine himself to the house till he got well . . . I am convinced as are all the Regt. we never shall have pleasure or satisfaction in him & for God's sake take the first opportunity of letting him resign.[23]

Glengarry's excuse for absenting himself from duty was that he was indisposed with a cold, which must indeed have been of a very severe nature, since according to his own statement he had caught it about 10 June, and it was now late December![24]

Early in January 1794 Captain McDonell at last consented if not to appear on parade, at least to use the quarters provided for him, and Colonel Cumming reported to Sir James that

> the Laird is coming round . . . To show him that I wished to put no hardship on him, I desired the Adjutant to tell him that . . . he had liberty to ride out in the middle of the day, which I thought would be agreeable to a person used to much exercise . . . I hear he has discharged his dirty lodging & now occupies his Billet at Hemming's Hotel.[25]

Colonel Cumming surmised, however, that the gallant captain would not make his appearance on the parade ground until after Cumming's departure on leave, when another field officer would assume command in Glasgow, but within days Colonel Cumming again had reason for complaint about his unsatisfactory subordinate, for the soldiers of Glengarry's company were again misbehaving, encouraged by

> their captain's presence in the city. 'They were beginning their old tricks but we soon knocked it on the head. Favor & kindness is thrown away on many of them. The Captn. has not yet appeared, but has promised to do so tomorrow.'[26]

Apparently Glengarry did consent to return to his duty, for there is an absence of further complaints from the senior officers of the battalion for several months. They had more pressing difficulties than an officer reluctant to carry out his duties at this time, for discipline in all of the Scottish fencible regiments was being undermined by the determination of the government to breach the terms of the enlistment contract in order to send these regiments out of Scotland. Many battalions, including the Strathspey Highlanders, declined to extend the terms of their enlistment, with the Macdonell company at the very centre of resistance. 'We are convinced were it not for Macdonell's company the whole wou'd come right round, but they will not,' the commanding officer lamented.[27]

In this crisis of its own making, the government looked with favour upon the application of any officer prepared to form a new fencible regiment with extended service that would take it to Ireland. One of the officers so named was the troublesome Captain McDonell of Glengarry. 'I heard today,' Lady Grant reported to her husband, Sir James, 'that Glengarry had made an offer to raise a Regiment of Catholics: if it be so I wish him success.'[28]

The offer to raise his own corps from among his Catholic clansmen would lead to advancement in rank, of course, but this may not have been the only reason for Glengarry's eagerness to bid the Strathspey regiment farewell. Glengarry had quarrelled seriously with his subaltern, Lieutenant John Grant of Auchterblair, and the medical officer of the battalion, yet another Grant, who filled the vacant ensigncy in Glengarry's company. In the course of this dispute Glengarry 'had submitted to receive words from the little D[octo]r that no gentleman wou'd put up with & which words the D[octo]r was highly justified in using,' Colonel Cumming reported gleefully.[29] The exchange of correspondence between Lieutenant Grant of Auchterblair and Glengarry survives in the Seafield Papers, and apparently commences with Glengarry's written enquiry of this man, who had been de facto commander of his company for some time, if he 'would have objections silently to resign the charge of the Glengarrie Companie, and return to the Grenadiers or whatever other Companie might suit him best'.[30] This missive produced the following response from the short-fused Lieutenant Grant:

> I have this afternoon received your ill-bred card. The meaning of which I can scarcely comprehend. The Commanding Officer was pleased to appoint me to Capt. McDonell's Company under the impression that I might be usefull to it. As to resigning it silently, or otherways, it does not depend on me. Should I be ordered to another I shall obey with pleasure, as I cannot say that the commencement of any military condition with you promises me much satisfaction.[31]

Captain McDonnell of Glengarry once more lay low, again pleading illness as his excuse for absenting himself from the company. Colonel Cumming insisted that Lieutenant Grant should remain with this company, as he was 'the only man in the Regt. fit to command them, and I'm sure too he is well liked by the men'.[32] Eventually the quarrel was patched over when Glengarry backed down after a face-to-face confrontation with Lieutenant Grant, the details of which Colonel Cumming happily passed on to Sir James. It appeared that Lieutenant Grant had

> insisted on knowing what he hinted or alluded to, in his expression to you. He answered, by saying, that there was no man he had a greater regard for than Mr. Grant & that the only objection he had, or knew to him, was that the men of the company did not like him. This to Mr.Grant was & is the highest praise, as it is easy to conceive (if the assertion is a fact, which I doubt) that the officer who keeps them tightest to their business, wil[l] not be

> a favourite. At the same time I am convinced Achterblair is the best officer in the Regt. for them & that the real good men of the company prize him.[33]

Lieutenant Grant of Auchterblair was due for leave, and Colonel Cumming told Sir James Grant that 'I shall post the D[octo]r in his room, who is next to him in spunk & propriety, but on his return I must insist that he is again placed in that company, as the young cub is by no means fit to manage them.'[34]

Much more seriously for the discipline of the Strathspey regiment, Glengarry was once more fraternising with the soldiers of his company, and as Lieutenant-Colonel Cumming related:

> [He] is again returned to his playing & joking with the men in the ranks, and yesterday there was hardly one of them that he did not entertain with whiskie. This behaviour you may easily conceive, frets & disgusts all the officers, who are certain neither the company or Regt. will ever do good while he is with us.[35]

There was, however, a very good reason for this fraternisation far exceeding the normal relations of a clan chieftain with his people, and for the singularly inappropriate conduct for an infantry captain.

The complaints about Glengarry continued, and on 14 January the captain appeared on parade 'wrapped in a great coat which he seems to have very little occasion for . . . he has a cursed trick of laughing & speaking to the men, which does much harm,'[36] according to Colonel Cumming. Captain McDonnell continued his bizarre conduct after Colonel Cumming's departure for his home at Forres, the lieutenant-colonel transmitting the information to the colonel of the regiment, Sir James Grant.

> I had a letter from the Paymaster yesterday, telling me Macdonell is going on in his accustomed folly, such as coming on parade in brown breeches, plain hat, sash & gorget, and when reprehended for it, saying he did not like the duty & wou'd resign, if he cou'd only be allowed to name his successor. I rely if he offers to resign to you, that you'll not refuse him, for the Regt. will never be quite the thing while he is in it.[37]

There was, however, reason in Captain McDonell's strange conduct, for he had used his most recent leave to press his claim for his own fencible regiment, and was ultimately successful in securing one of the new regiments for service in Ireland. Glengarry resigned his commission in the Strathspey regiment in May 1794 upon being gazetted colonel of his new regiment. His former colleagues must have breathed sighs of relief, but they had not seen the last of Glengarry.

Command of Glengarry's former company passed to Captain John Grant of Rippachie,[38] formerly captain-lieutenant of the colonel's company and thus first in line for promotion. Dr. Peter Grant continued to act as subaltern of Glengarry's old company in addition to his medical duties with the regiment until July 1794, when the dispersed nature of a fencible battalion, whose units were then found at Kirkcudbright, Stranraer, Girvan and Wigtown, besides two companies and the regimental headquarters at Paisley, made it inconvenient to have the medical officer doing a subaltern's duty at an out-station. It was contemplated that Dr. Grant should be replaced by a Lieutenant Macdonald, who had been recruiting in the Highlands; Colonel Cumming believed that his name would make him more acceptable to a company consisting mainly of Macdonells and Macdonalds.[39] The Strathspey regiment, like every other formation in Scotland, was in the summer of 1794 striving to augment its numbers in line with an expansion ordered by the War Office, and certainly there was no thought in the regiment of discharging any substantial number of the men.

All that changed in October 1794 when Colonel Alexander McDonnell of Glengarry wrote to the political manager of Scotland, Henry Dundas, to report on his success in raising the Glengarry Fencibles.[40] In this letter Glengarry made it plain that if he had his way, the Strathspey Fencibles would lose more than a captain. Having now enlisted more than 300 men for the new battalion in spite of intense competition from other regiments, Glengarry wished to add to their number the company he had formerly brought to the Strathspey Fencibles. Glengarry assured Dundas that if only he could 'procure the same advantages to him as those other new Colonels get, at least leave to get his own men drafted out of the Grant Fencibles . . . [it] would enable him to have his Regit. in the course of a few weeks ready for inspection & be the means of rendering them in a very short time fit for service'.

Elaborating his arguments to the minister one week later, Glengarry argued that he had

> brought about a hundred men into the Grant Fencibles, all my own Tennants sons who follow'd me from mere attachment, you cannot therefore be surprised if I should have every inclination to have as many of them or any others out of the Regt. as would chuse to follow me . . . Which would be the means not only of compleating but also of discipling, my Regt in a very short time.[41]

This of course raises the question of whether the addition of a company whose discipline had never been of a high order and which had already strenuously resisted extending its service to Ireland would make an efficient regiment when joined to Glengarry's new recruits. Clearly, however, it establishes the reason for the joking and whisky-treating of the rank and file during Glengarry's last few weeks with the Strathspey regiment. Glengarry's argument was that the other colonels of new fencible regiments committed to service in Ireland had been given permission to try to recruit up to 200 men each from existing fencible regiments whose service was restricted to Scotland. Glengarry, therefore, should have a right to take an entire company from the Strathspey fencibles if they could be persuaded to volunteer, together with any other men who might be willing to follow him, an argument that had no appeal for the senior officers of that regiment.

Glengarry did not await permission from Henry Dundas before making an assault upon the Strathspey regiment. Captain John Grant, a senior captain stationed at Paisley, reported to Sir James that the primary target was the men whom Glengarry had brought to the regiment when it was formed, who were now a major portion of the garrison of Stranraer. Aided by the future Roman Catholic bishop of Ontario, an official of Glengarry's estate had visited the men to persuade them where their duty lay.

> Glengarrie's ground Off[ice]r . . . Achindroun was there, and supposed tampering with the men. Priest McDonell lately told Major Grant that he was going to see some friends in the neighbourhood of Stranraer, no doubt for the same purpose. Glengarrie is here [Paisley] just now . . . he plainly owns he is trying & laying every oar in the water to get the Company detach'd, and says he thinks he has a good claim on them. This however can never happen without your consent. I thought it my duty to inform you of what was going on which will not make these lads more submissive to discipline than formerly.[42]

Captain-Lieutenant Allan Grant, the commanding officer of the detachment at Girvan, reported the passage of Glengarry and the Catholic priest, the Reverend Alexander Macdonell, who had a major part in the raising of the Glengarry Fencibles, through his town, en route to Stranraer. Glengarry had been preceded by a messenger 'to announce his being on his way to visit his late ragamuffins. When he arrived at Stranraer [he] made them all conveen'd & paraded & he and Lieut. McDonald drunk several bumpers of spirits with the men on the street.'[43] It was unfortunate for Sir James Grant that the senior officer of the three companies at Stranraer was absent from the town at this critical moment. Sir James hastily ordered the absentee, Captain Simon Fraser of Foyers, to return to Stranraer, but the latter found upon his arrival that he was too late to undo the damage that Glengarry had inflicted, although as

Foyers pointed out, only sixteen of the soldiers had signed a paper undertaking to go with their chief 'on being promised land, cow's grass etc. etc.'. There were, however, other promises that did not require written agreement, and one suspects that the implied threat to the families of the Macdonell soldiers would have had some effect. In any event, discipline, which was never the strong point in Glengarry's former company, broke down completely. Several of Glengarry's former soldiers, led by Corporal Andrew Macdonell, appearing to believe that their departure from the Strathspey regiment was certain, went to the quarters of two of the senior non-commissioned officers of the lieutenant-colonel's company who shared the Stranraer duty with them and 'dragged one of them out of bed and cut him in a dreadful manner . . . Next morning I [Captain Simon Fraser of Foyers] . . . ordered a Court Martial and had Corpl. And[rew] McDond. reduced to the ranks . . . In short that Company are quite set agog by the Colonel's visit.'[44]

Captain Fraser describes the incident more fully in his letter of 13 November, emphasising the fact that the men's mutinous behaviour had been provoked by Glengarry's visit, and now reporting that all of the 'Sergeants, Corpls. and about thirty of the Privates of that Company have enrolled themselves to go along with him, on his making them promises of farms on their return to the country'.[45] These were the same men who had come close to mutiny at Linlithgow earlier in the year, when they were being pressed to extend their service beyond Scotland.

According to the report of Captain Fraser,

> Glengarry left some money to be given to the companies here in drink, which was accordingly given them early in the day to prevent them going about the streets in the night . . . [N]otwithstanding of this precaution severals of them . . . went down to the different quarters of the Serjts. of the name of Grant, dragged them out of bed, cut and abused a Serj. Don[al]d Grant of the Lt. Coll's company, and swore they would pour whisky down the throats of all those that did not drink to Glengarry's health. Capt. Grant & Lt. MacDon[al]d, hearing of their behaviour, went to send them to their quarters and threatened to confine a man that spoke insolent to them. Upon which a Corpl. that was of the party stept forward and said the man would not be confined, that they were in sufficient number to prevent them . . . Capt. Grant finding them in this humour thought it most prudent to go home. I arrived here the morning thereafter. There being a sufficient number of officers to sit a Court Martial I ordered one and had the Corpl. reduced to the ranks. I did not think proper to try any of the privates by a Court Martial as we must have ordered them to receive

> corporal punishment, and dreading we would not be allowed to put that in execution. I am told Glengarry corresponds with some of the men since his departure from this, that he desires them not to alter their minds, that he is using his interest to bring about an exchange.[46]

Needless to say, Colonel Sir James Grant resented Glengarry's tampering with the uncertain loyalties of his soldiers, and his letter caught up with Glengarry at Dalwhinnie on his way north. The latter excused his conduct at Stranraer by insisting that

> had I understood that the drafts were only intended to be permitted (if agreeable to the Colonels) for compleating and disciplining the new Fencible Corps, I would not have troubled you on the occasion. You were inform'd of the truth by those who told you I had gone to your Fencible Regt. The nature of my present duty call'd me the length of Girvan & as I was then within a few miles of Stranraer (where I had a relation whom I wished to see) I went there, & to be introduced to him, was the reason I beg'd of Mr. McDonell to accompany me (who at all events was but in the way of his duty) as there is a whole Company of Catholics there. But Sir Jas. I beg leave to say, he who told you my Ground Officer at Laggan Achendrone had gone to Stranraer was grossly mistaken.[47]

Glengarry, however, had gained the ear of Henry Dundas, who wrote from London in November 1794 urging Sir James Grant to give up the men whom Glengarry had brought to the Strathspey Fencibles. 'I do not think it right to prevent them from doing so, and you need not be uneasy about the augmentation for it will not be expected or wished that you should augment them above 600 rank and file.'[48] It was the king's command, signified to all the fencible colonels in Scotland by the deputy adjutant-general in Edinburgh, that although men might be permitted to transfer from the old fencible corps to the newer regiments with extended service, which were to be established at a strength of 1,000 men each, the older regiments giving up men were not to be allowed to fall below 500 rank and file.[49] Men were now very scarce in Scotland, and if Glengarry had his way Sir James Grant's Strathspey regiment was in considerable danger of falling below that strength. Sir James, nonetheless, was extremely reluctant to risk offending the powerful minister, Henry Dundas, and on 20 November instructions were sent to the senior officer with the regiment, Major Grant of Glenmoriston, to permit Glengarry to recruit among the soldiers of the Strathspey regiment, but the authority so given was strictly limited, as Sir James' letter makes clear.

> I have . . . received a letter from Mr. Dundas desiring that I may allow any men from among those who were raised for my Fencible Regiment by Glengarry to go into his new Regiment upon their expressing a willingness and earnest desire to do so. It is my duty to obey what I consider as a communication of his Majesty's commands, more especially as Mr. Dundas's letter is in answer to one I wrote wishing my Fencible Regiment to remain untouched. I therefore authorise you upon application from Glengarry to discharge any of the men raised by him . . . who are willing and desirous to serve in his Regt. specifying that as the condition on which they are discharged. You will . . . limit this permission as to Glengarry to those alone who were raised by himself.[50]

The Strathspey Fencibles were thus deprived of an entire company of soldiers, but arguably the departure of Glengarry's men was essential if discipline was to be preserved in Sir James Grant's regiment. In support of this contention it can be pointed out that there was a final incident prior to the departure of those soldiers who had agreed to go with their chief. Stranraer was of course then, as now, one of the ports of embarkation for Ireland. Through this town passed many units being sent to reinforce the Irish garrison troops, among them Colonel Campbell of Munie's regiment. According to Major John Grant of Glenmoriston:

> A most unpleasant affair happened here . . . betwixt the MacDonalds and a Division of . . . Munie's Regt. On their marching into town one of the officers of that Corps pushed one of the MacD's out of his way. He said nothing till the Division halted then he went up to the officer and struck him, more of them gathered and a battle ensued betwixt some of them and the officers, two of whom were very much hurt. I delivered over the man who began the business to Glengarry as a Prisoner and gave in a crime with him which I think ought to shoot him but I this day went to Portpatrick to see Col. Buchanan who commands Munie's Regt. to know what he wished to do in the affair or if he wrote to the Commander in Chief on the subject; he said he did not and wished rather to hush up the business. As those men are now going away from us, and I am sure every man in this Regt. wishes they may never return to it again, I have said nothing to the Commander in Chief on the subject.[51]

The decision to cave in to ministerial pressure and permit an entire company to be discharged had a damaging effect upon the war readiness of the Strathspey Fencibles, now faced with a substantial loss of manpower and with other recruiters exerting their powers of persuasion with the rank and file. Cumming, Sir James Grant's lieutenant-colonel, was convinced that this concession would prevent 'our ever being compleat'.[52] Glengarry wasted no time once he had secured official backing, and by 3 December Major MacAlister, one of his field officers, was at Paisley to collect those men who volunteered to go with their chief, which Major Grant, the acting battalion commander declined to permit until Glengarry himself was present. By 5 December, Glengarry had arrived and Major Grant could delay no longer. The major had been informed by the Reverend Alexander Macdonell,

> who is the principle manager that the whole of his recruits signed a letter some time ago wishing to go with him if they got leave . . . if it is a thing that must be I think the sooner we are quit of them the better. Perhaps they may not all go, but by the Priest's account I think it likely.[53]

Grant of Glenmoriston, the senior major of the Strathspey Fencibles, accompanied Glengarry's recruiting party when it left Paisley for Stranraer, where Glengarry's old company was garrisoned, and where no less than sixty-seven of the men agreed to go with their chief. Major Grant commented that 'there are only three of his own Recruits that did not go along, [and] one of these after all the rest were settled with came to me and insisted he should be allowed to go with him as he had changed his mind. I refused him till I had your further orders . . . He wanted three more but I have put a positive negative on them.'[54] Glengarry, for his part, in his letter of acknowledgement to Sir James Grant, indicated that he had received seventy-five soldiers from the Strathspey Fencibles, while emphasising that he was having great difficulty securing his numbers and alleging that he was entitled to a further five of the Strathspey men.[55]

Glengarry informed Henry Dundas in March 1795 that although his new regiment had been inspected at a strength of only 500 rank and file, the latest recruiting returns indicated that the corps now totalled over 600, which was still well short of its intended establishment of 1,000.[56] According to the War Office records, the strength of the McDonell Fencible Regiment, then at Kilmarnock, was only 580 rank and file a month later.[57] Even by 1 June the strength of the regiment had only reached 628,[58] and the War Office, acknowledging that there were no more fit and willing men available, had reduced the establishment to 630. Such an involuntary reduction must have been a great disappointment to Glengarry, for with the larger establishment went places for additional field officers, and there was at least the possibility of forming a second battalion by splitting the first. This was not to be, and the Glengarry Fencibles sailed for Ireland with a single small battalion.[59] The Irish establishment, moreover, was markedly more generous with commissions than was the home establishment. An infantry regiment that could muster little more than 700 men on the Irish establishment, consisting of ten companies, had several supernumerary officers, including a second lieutenant-colonel and a second major. The benefits of such patronage, however, appear to have eluded Glengarry. The regiment from whence came most of the trained soldiers of the Glengarry Fencibles, the 1st or Strathspey Fencible Regiment, never really recovered from the loss of manpower. It found itself with its establishment reduced and, with an entire company to make good, competing increasingly desperately for such manpower – or, rather, boy-power – that its recruiters were able to find until its disbandment in March 1799 upon its refusal 'to serve in Ireland, or Europe, unconditionally'.[60]

The trouble with the Glengarry men demonstrated to the administration and the military alike that there were serious problems in permitting a company officer enjoying the status of a chieftain of a clan to form his company from his own clansmen or tenants, extending even to the naming of the original commissioned officers. Such men were totally dependent on the chieftain in civil life, and not surprisingly looked upon their military service as an extension of their civil condition. However familiar this would have been to those who remembered the Jacobite armies earlier in the century, it was clearly not in the interest of a regiment of the crown to have sub-units within it who regarded themselves first and foremost as the followers of their company commander, particularly when that captain showed little or no capacity for command. The new regiment that Glengarry raised, the Glengarry Fencible Regiment, owed its formation much more to the efforts of the reverend Alexander Macdonell, the Roman Catholic chaplain of that corps, than it ever did to Glengarry himself, the nominal colonel, and the chaplain and many of the soldiers who served in this corps were obliged to emigrate to Canada when the Glengarry Fencible Regiment was disbanded and they found that their military service did not in fact translate into secure possession of a farm holding. It must be acknowledged, however, that the Glengarry men were much more effective soldiers when in a regiment of their own than they ever were in the Grant regiment, whose officers left their colonel in no doubt that the loss of manpower was for the best. 'It is a pity the Macdonells went the way they did, tho' we are well free of them,' the lieutenant-colonel contended,[61] while the second major of the Strathspey Regiment, John Grant of Achindoun, in a letter to Lady Grant of Grant, commented that he wished 'we had never seen' the Macdonells 'as a part of us'.[62] The lack of discipline that coloured these opinions was a direct consequence of the manner of their recruitment by their own chief, to whom they still looked for patronage to the detriment of their military duty as members of the army of the crown. In other circumstances this might not have become the problem that it did for the Strathspey Regiment, where the chieftain who recruited his own following for the service showed real ability as a commissioned officer, but unfortunately this could not be said of Alexander MacDonnell of Glengarry.

6

Scotland and the Ministry of All the Talents, 1806–1807

DAVID J. BROWN

The death of William Pitt in January 1806 finally brought to an end the already weakening government that had held office since May 1804. After some attempts to avoid the inevitable, the king asked Lord Grenville to form a government, and this took office in February, with Grenville at the Treasury, Lord Spencer as home secretary and Fox as foreign secretary. This 'Ministry of All the Talents' also included Lord Sidmouth's supporters, but the friends of the late Pitt, once Grenville's allies in office, were not invited to participate. This exclusion was considered a great insult to Pitt's memory, not least by Melville, and it introduced an immediate bitterness into the Pittites' attitude to the new ministry.[1] Yet, paradoxically, the Pittites for some time genuinely but mistakenly believed that Grenville would eventually have to turn to them for protection against the radical plans of Fox's followers. Their wait for his call did much to condition their actions.[2] The exclusion of Pitt's adherents, combined with the first appearance of Fox's followers in office since 1783, meant that the regime that Henry Dundas, Viscount Melville had built up over the intervening years was about to come under hostile scrutiny.

From the outset, almost all the Scottish political nation assumed that there would be a change in the government of Scotland. Nobody seriously expected that the Dundases would continue their direction of elections and patronage under the new administration. Instead it was widely anticipated that the management of Scotland would be passed to the Scottish Foxites.

The major decisions of the new government regarding Scotland were made in February, and Melville, convalescing at Bath after a short illness, was almost a bystander. Before knowing that Pitt's friends were excluded, Melville had wanted the king to form a strong government, including Fox and Grenville. He felt that it should be supported by everybody. Only if this government then attacked his friends would he support systematic opposition, and in this event, with his Scottish allies, he had no doubt of success.[3] At the formation of the new administration, the earl of Moira, commander-in-chief in Scotland, married to the countess of Loudoun and a friend to the prince of Wales, was made master-general of the ordnance. He also claimed to have the management of

Scotland. Even as Pitt's ministry had seemed to be failing in January, Moira, expecting high office, had tried to recruit Melville's aid.[4] Now he renewed his attempts. If Melville and his friends supported government, Moira as manager would only allow a few sackings of Scots office holders to reward 'the most hungry' of the Scots Whigs. Otherwise Melville's friends would not be disturbed.[5] Moira lost little time in announcing this to the Scots MPs, informing them that he would be '*a father*' to them, as Melville had been.[6] Melville's reaction was cautious. With his impeachment before the House of Lords for malversation of naval funds pending, he was unwilling to dabble in politics. Further, he was aware that Moira could have little influence in Scotland without his support.[7] He wrote a letter ostensibly showing that he would acquiesce in any temperate government of Scotland by Moira.[8] Privately, Melville prepared for a period of retreat, even contemplating the surrender of the Edinburgh seat to Henry Erskine, the leader of the Scots Foxites,[9] and he began to calculate how his friends might stand if they could not reach accommodation with the new government.[10]

Other factors were also coming into play. By now the English Pittites had resolved to act together in a body. Unless their interests were attacked or issues were agitated hostile to Pitt's principles, they would generally support government. In this they wanted Melville's Scots friends to join them.[11] With occasional lapses, throughout his long career Melville had been opposed both to the idea of factious opposition and to the concept of party, and the Pittites' strategy appealed to him. He believed that eventually the group of Pitt's followers would split up,[12] but meantime he avowed a wish to associate with any of Pitt's friends who might feel obliged to keep together to protect Pitt's name and the principles for which he had stood.[13] Still reprobating party politics,[14] he was nevertheless taking his share in one of the major developments of the period, the gradual evolution of a British Tory party, gathered around the memory of Pitt. A few days later he wrote: 'Our Scotch friends must be the last to abandon that standard.'[15] It is clear that Melville regarded his Scottish allies – the duke of Buccleuch, the earls of Dalkeith and Hopetoun, and the rest – as a strong group. He had little fear that a hostile government could injure them, and he saw them all as gathered together upon principles rather than for the pursuit of political advantage.[16]

Melville and his son Robert were agreed on this general line, and on 10 February Robert informed Lord Moira that the Scots Pittites would be acting with their English brethren and that if government should split, they would support Grenville.[17] Moira misunderstood this, believing that it constituted a refusal to support government. Unwilling to become involved in expulsions of Melville's friends – inevitable if they opposed government – he decided to 'resign' as Scottish manager. Privately, he offered to help protect some of Melville's allies from the Foxites.[18] Moira's withdrawal was no real upset to either Melville or his son, neither of whom had been convinced that he really would have had the management of Scotland.[19] Their coolness ended Moira's plans. It seems that he had averted a purge of Melville's friends from their offices in the first days of the government,[20] and the actions of Melville and his son were disapproved of by their Scots allies, who now feared that Scotland would be managed by Lauderdale.[21] This did not happen, although the truth emerged in a confusing fashion, with a swirl of rumours and false stories.[22] Already on 12 February, Melville's nephew William Dundas was preparing to meet Grenville, and the next day Robert Dundas wrote that Grenville was not going to commit Scotland to Lauderdale.[23] A few days later, William Dundas wrote to the premier, explaining that he was opposed to having Moira as Scots manager and that Buccleuch only favoured him because he feared that any regime run by Lauderdale would be characterised by sackings of his opponents. Instead Dundas pointed to his own preference for Scottish patronage to flow directly from the Treasury and the Home Office.[24] Grenville followed up this letter by calling Dundas to a meeting on 24 February, at which the Scot detailed the attitudes of Melville's friends towards government. Grenville in turn indicated both that he had no plans for a general sweep of Scottish placeholders and that Lauderdale would not be his sole adviser in Scots affairs.[25] Grenville and Spencer had decided to keep the management of Scotland in their own hands.[25] Here, as far as Melville's friends were concerned, matters rested. They knew that the activities of Pitt's heirs in England might draw them into open opposition, and Melville feared that Fox's politics might have a similar effect.[27] Fox himself, engrossed in foreign affairs, took little direct concern in Scottish matters before his untimely death in September. For a while there was peace.[28]

The decision by Grenville and Spencer to retain Scottish patronage in London was not to the satisfaction of Melville's Scottish opponents. Lauderdale, the marquis of Douglas, Moira and the marquis of Stafford (husband to the countess of Sutherland) had met to suggest the measures that they considered necessary in Scotland. The two Foxites on this committee, Lauderdale and Douglas, pressed for the replacement of Melvillite office holders, and Lauderdale provided a list of them on 12 March.[29] Moira acquiesced in this idea 'rather from an indifference to all projects short of his entire management of Scotland'. Only Stafford was firmly opposed to sackings. Although outnumbered, he already had the ear of the premier's brother, Thomas Grenville, who was similarly unenthusiastic about the resentments that removals would create. Lord Grenville shared his brother's views and for the moment chose not to act.[30] During and after these discussions it is quite clear that a wave of fear swept the ranks of the Melvillite office holders in Scotland.[31] Initially, however, the only changes were in the law. While Spencer had private reservations,[32] the elevation of Henry Erskine to be lord advocate in place of James Montgomery was inevitable. The solicitor-general's appointment was more problematic, and the replacement of the long-serving Robert Blair with the intemperate John Clerk was made over the strongest protests from Lord Justice-Clerk Charles Hope.[33] In the court of session Lord Methven, who had died in January, was replaced by the Foxite Charles Hay, now Lord Newton.[34]

Grenville was under some pressure from his Scottish allies to make at least some changes, and attention quickly focused on two of Melville's relatives: Alexander MacLean, the receiver general of the land tax; and George Buchan, the solicitor for the stamp office in Scotland. Melville was relatively unconcerned at the prospect of their dismissals, but Justice-Clerk Hope, then in London, protested 'that there was something so unhandsome & revolting in the time of doing this, when Lord M's back was at the wall'.[35] This intervention seems to have gained the pair a short respite, for they were not removed until later. Hope also learned that Grenville and Spencer were disposed to interfere as little as possible in Scottish elections. In practice this became an agreement that government would actually assist Melvillites in some seats, or at least be neutral.[36] Unsurprisingly, the Scots Whigs wanted more than this. Some rewards were more easily bestowed, and the earls of Breadalbane, Cassillis, Eglinton and Lauderdale all received British peerages. Grenville had, however, to reject one request of the Scots Whigs: that the earl of Sempill be restored to the army and his cashiering of 1793 reversed.[37]

Quite apart from the benefits to be anticipated from the new government, the position of the Scottish Whig party was stronger than it had been for some time. The noble families of Hamilton, Douglas and (from May 1806) Argyll were all led by Whigs. The marquis of Bute and the earl of Breadalbane, once Portland Whigs, lent their support to the new administration, and there were other supporters among the nobility, including the earls of Elgin, Selkirk, Sempill and Stair. The public leaders of the Scottish government party were almost all Foxites. There *were* men who saw their allegiance as being primarily to Grenville and Spencer, notably the families of Stafford (Sutherland) and Cassillis, but they were not in the forefront of business. Likewise, many of those who had drifted, or were to drift, from the old government party to the new order found it easier to pay their court to the former Pitt supporters Grenville and Spencer, rather than to the long-reviled Fox and his adherents.[38] It is likely that government's wish to retain the support of these men explains why they continued to delay the purge demanded by the Foxites.

Fox and Grenville could also count on the general support that the Scots politicians could be relied on to give to the government of the day. The earl of Galloway, long disenchanted with Melville, supported government on the basis that it was the king's administration, although he was also happy to pursue family advantage.[39] The duke of Queensberry acted on the same principles. Several MPs were like Colonel William Dickson, sitting for the Linlithgow Burghs, who '*supports* the present administration (as he did the last)'.[40] Given that Melville's friends were not in outright opposition to government, a strange truce could prevail in Scottish politics. In this way Melville's relative, Sir Charles Ross of Balnagown, MP for Ross-shire, could profess support for administration even while he opposed friends of government in his local politics.[41] There were some embarrassing defections from the ranks of Melville's friends, however. William McDowall of Garthland, MP for Renfrewshire, indebted to successive governments for loans secured on his West Indian estates, would have been obliged to give Grenville some support. Instead his adherence was enthusiastic and he even tried to persuade Grenville to give him the keepership of the privy seal, held by Melville.[42] Later he advanced a private parliamentary bill to alleviate his debts at the expense of his sureties, who included a furious Lord Chief Baron Robert Dundas.[43] Altogether more humiliating was the conduct of William Dundas. Even as Pitt's administration was winding up, he had obtained the promise of a reversion of an office held by his own brother, the chief baron. This was bad enough in Melville's view, but he had no sooner received it than he signalled to Pitt's friends that he felt bound to adhere to the politics of the Staffords, whose Sutherland seat he sat for. Despite his protestations, he was in effect separating himself from the Pitt party. Melville was livid. It was a disgrace on William, and he was removed from the family's confidential councils.[44]

Grenville's policy of tolerance, of not besieging the Scots Pittites provided that they did not oppose government, was frustrating to the Scots Whigs and their allies. They could see that people like Sir Charles Ross and James Brodie of Brodie, MP for Morayshire and another apparent convert, were likely to be only fairweather friends. They could only look askance when, for instance, Grenville indicated to Lauderdale in April that he would not countenance plans to unseat Melville's son-in-law George Abercromby in Edinburgh, nor would he help the Foxite William Maule in his attack on the sitting MP for the Montrose Burghs, who was both a Melvillite and a government supporter.[45] The first solace to the Scots Whigs came in early May as Melville's trial was under way, when government finally acted to remove the two initial candidates for dismissal, Alexander MacLean and George Buchan. The process of replacing MacLean by Sir William Cunynghame began on 6 May, and Buchan was similarly ousted in favour of James Gibson.[46] The events following Melville's impeachment confirmed to the Scots Whigs that this was too little, too late.

Melville had resigned as first lord of the admiralty in April 1805, following the revelation of apparent misappropriation of naval funds in the years when he was treasurer of the navy. The select committee investigating his case had taken much evidence since July 1805, including some showing that not only he had received loans from his friend Alexander Trotter, the paymaster of the navy, but that he must also have been aware of Trotter's misuse of public money.[47] In the end, the managers of the impeachment reduced this evidence to ten charges against Melville. Melville was angry at the extent to which the investigators had examined the most innocuous of his private affairs. Worse, as early as February he was conscious that despite a public perception that he was 'wallowing in wealth', the projected legal expenses of his defence were already beyond his means.[48] He had never been truly rich, and most of his costs would be met by a massive loan from his brother-in-law, the earl of Hopetoun.[49] He never saw his impeachment in any light other than as a political 'persecution', and nowhere in his intimate correspondence with his son Robert is there even a suggestion that he saw himself as guilty of any impropriety. His friends had always regarded him as incompetent in his personal finances and attributed his problems to this.[50] There is little doubt, however, that he was afraid of revelations about his use of secret political funds and that this lay at the heart of his refusal to discuss some of his expenditures. Yet it is unclear whether this refusal stemmed from fears that discussion would hurt him personally or that it could damage public policy.[51] The power of Fox and Lord Sidmouth in the new government had quickly convinced Melville that his prosecution would be extended and expensive, and that the Lords might not give him a fair hearing.[52] Robert Dundas discussed all this with Grenville on 10 March, and Grenville agreed to ensure that the trial was not delayed. Grenville himself had avoided taking part in the proceedings against Melville, but he did not feel at liberty to dictate his wishes to colleagues. 'It is evident therefore,' reported Melville's son, 'that there is no chance of its being made a government question in your favor, & the utmost we can expect or attempt is to neutralise them.'[53]

The trial was held in Westminster Hall from 29 April to 17 May, and the judgement of his fellow peers was pronounced on 12 June.[54] In one of those intriguing demonstrations of cross-party currents that have so often marked post-Union Scottish politics, Melville was defended by, among others, his long-term electoral opponent, the Whig lawyer William Adam. The defence offered was skilful, demonstrating repeatedly that Melville personally had broken no law. Nonetheless, his friends were concerned. Lord Kellie wrote, 'my mind cannot be easy – seeing so many doubtfull folks among us!',[55] and he despaired at some of Melville's supposed supporters, who did not stay for the end of the trial.[56] In fact the final votes by the assembled peers saw Melville acquitted on all the charges, but the majorities were at their lowest on the two that alleged his connivance at Trotter's misuse of funds.[57] This effectively meant that the suspicion of his guilt would linger, and indeed the stain was never effaced. This was not immediately apparent, however. Melville was jubilant, and a large part of the Scottish political nation joined in celebrations. Melville's nephew, the lord chief baron, reported: 'I really believe no event almost ever occurred which has excited such warm & general feelings of joy in Scotland. The Scotch papers will show you part, & but a part of the expressions of rejoicing in public.'[58]

The rejoicings included a well-attended public dinner in Edinburgh. and there was also a general illumination of the city.[59] The most immediate loser from Melville's acquittal was Lord Moira. Having early described the impeachment as unjust, he had voted against Melville in the Lords.[60] His association with Melville's friends dropped stone dead. He would continue to wield electoral influence in Ayrshire and in politics around the prince of Wales at the apex of the Whig party, but the wide influence that he had enjoyed within the Scottish political nation since 1803 was at an end.

The celebrations of Melville's acquittal were a further shock to the Scots Whigs, and they again pressed for a purge of Melville's friends from their offices.[61] Nonetheless, on 28 June the Whig candidate for the Edinburgh seat, James Mansfield, lamented:

> The Melvellits [sic] are more high than you almost can imagine and unless ministers means [sic] to have a Melvillite Parliament returned they must take stronger measures than they yet seem disposed to do, it is really most distressing to think of the scrapes they have brought all their friends into by their ill timed moderation . . . However we have accounts today that the rejoicings in Scotland for the acquitted felon has [sic] roused them. I shall believe it when I see them act.[62]

The vote of congratulations to Melville by the Society of the Writers to the Signet was the prompt for Lord Douglas to write to Lord Grenville about 'the sensation a late acquittal has excited in the metropolis of Scotland' and to press for the long-proposed dismissals. In particular he pointed at the improper conduct of Melville's son, Robert Dundas, as keeper of the signet, involving that society in politics.[63] Grenville's response was to restate his position: that Scotland should not be governed as a separate part of the empire, but that it should be ruled directly by ministers in London. He was determined to rule in a spirit of moderation, although showing countenance only to those who were friendly to government.[64] This was not the reply that Douglas wanted. Privately, Lord Spencer began to think that government might indeed have to give more aid to the Scots Whigs.[65] One near-immediate outcome was the dismissal in late July of the duke of Gordon as keeper of the great seal and his replacement by Lauderdale. Gordon's tenure of the post had been the subject of speculation since the government had commenced, and while his sacking was conducted with much politeness, the message was plain.[66]

Lauderdale met Spencer on 16 July and renewed the request of his Scottish allies for a purge. Some Melville supporters were to have their arms twisted, and several revenue officials were to be sacked and replaced by Scots Foxites. Others were to be rewarded in different ways. Grenville agreed to this wider purge of Melville's friends,[67] but apart from Gordon's loss of the great seal, nothing had taken place by 6 August, when Henry Erskine again pressed for action. He specifically asked for four removals from law offices and advised that 'their being *speedily* made is absolutely necessary for changing the political current in this part of the kingdom'.[68] On 12 August Spencer confirmed that Grenville had agreed in principle to more sackings but wanted details on the proposed appointees, because he was wary of being seen to fill all the posts by people in the same line of politics.[69]

Simultaneously Grenville and Spencer seem privately to have considered the idea that they did indeed need a Scots manager of some sort. Perhaps at their bidding, Lady Stafford asked Colin Mackenzie, the Sutherland family's Scots agent, to be the government's confidential adviser. Mackenzie, an Edinburgh-based lawyer with an estate by Peebles, initially declined the task, although later he did relent enough to provide some intelligence about the Scots elections.[70] Even later still he would provide government with fascinating private insights into the Scots legal community and its attitudes to law reform. In the meantime, however, he surveyed alternative candidates for the post of adviser, discussing and dismissing the separate pretensions of two court of session judges, Lord Armadale and Lord Glenlee, before advancing the original proposition that the post should go to the newly appointed deputy clerk register, Thomas Thomson. Thomson was, Mackenzie explained, a Foxite, but moderate in his politics. Grenville was enthusiastic and thought the suggestion worth pursuing.[71] Nothing seems to have come of it, however, and Thomson was left to the successful pursuit of an altogether more honourable career as an archivist.

Independently of these public and private discussions about the management of Scotland, William Honyman, Lord Armadale, was planning his own grasp for power. The son-in-law of the late Lord Justice-Clerk Braxfield, Armadale had been assisted to a seat in the court of session by Melville in 1797 but the two had fallen out in 1803.[72] Now in June 1806, Chief Baron Robert Dundas sent Melville a warning: Armadale was preparing to use his position as a director and stockholder in the Bank of Scotland to oust Melville from his position as governor. Allegedly the plan was to install Lord Douglas in Melville's stead, and Armadale would then manage Scotland as Douglas' sub-minister.[73] How precisely this might have worked is still unclear. Historians have only begun to investigate the influence that the banks could exert in Scottish politics through their control of credit, and it is not fully understood.[74] It is quite clear, however, that Melville's counter-attack, an endeavour to purge Armadale and his associates from the bank direction, was anathema to the Scots Whigs. If he succeeded, wrote Lauderdale, 'we will lose all chance of the Town of Edinburgh, and indeed much of our influence all over the country'.[75] Government seems to have woken up only too late to the threat posed by Melville's attack, and in March 1807 its friends were expelled from among the bank's directors.[76]

The wreck of Armadale's ambitions lay in the future, however. On 18 August Erskine again returned to the charge, pushing Spencer to make changes as 'the best means of checking the prevailing influence of Lord Melville and his party'. He reported that the earlier removals of Buchan and MacLean had been explained away by Melville's friends, who variously claimed either that Melville would soon form a political alliance with Grenville, or that government was not strong enough to consider removing more of his friends. Spencer was given a brief history of the political division in Scotland between Dundas and his opponents in the years after 1784. Some of Melville's friends now supported government, 'Others affected a moderation to avoid the consequences of direct opposition; but the greatest part have hoisted along with Lord Melville the standart [sic] of defiance and the *real* friends of administration are confined to the original opposers of Lord Melville.'

In this way, Erskine proceeded to explain that the Scottish Foxites were loyal to government 'as a united cabinet'. It was essential that those appointed after the removals should be unconnected with Melville. Even apparent converts should not be trusted. Erskine detailed his candidates, whose appointment would 'give a check to a formidable opposition which cannot be defeated but by measures of the most marked as well as decided hostility'.[77] In early September, Spencer and Grenville were agreed that it was time for removals and at the end of the month announced that these were imminent,[78] but a week later Erskine was still complaining of the strength of the Melville interest and the manner in which they misrepresented their relationship with government in order to maintain their influence in Scotland.[79] For whatever reason, Grenville and Spencer had done nothing further regarding Scotland before parliament was dissolved, and even after the elections their Scottish friends were still advising them to signal that Melville's power was at an end.[80]

The dissolution was a shock to Melville, who saw it as an indication of the extent to which the king was now subdued by 'a sturdy faction, acting under the auspices of the apparent heir of the Crown'.[81] Ironically, it was equally unwelcome to Henry Erskine: 'This early dissolution will play the deuce with us in Scotland. I hope the loss will be made up in England.'[82]

There were contests in twelve Scottish seats[83] and extensive activity in over a dozen others. Much of it involved struggles between Melville's friends and the Scots Whigs, and from the Whig viewpoint the result fully justified their opinion of Grenville's early temporising policy towards the Dundas interest.

The Aberdeenshire contest between Ferguson of Pitfour and Hay of Rannes was rooted in an old county feud, with the duke of Gordon backing Pitfour and Lord Fife supporting Hay. Hay enjoyed government support, and in the end the poll was close, with Ferguson winning by only two votes.[84] In Banffshire, Sir William Grant easily overcame Sir James Duff, who was supported by Lord Fife and government.[85] Further south, the Whig Robert Ferguson of Raith had canvassed Fife since February, and Melville advised Robert Dundas to support William Wemyss' candidate.[86] In fact Wemyss stood himself, hoping to profit from his relationship to the Grenvillite Lord Stafford. Grenville in fact was persuaded of his unreliability, and government support ultimately secured the county for Raith in a victory that gave the Whigs much satisfaction.[87] The Lanarkshire contest between Sir Charles Douglas, backed by Melville and Buccleuch, and Lord Archibald Hamilton, was an easy victory for the latter, a staunch Whig. Similarly, the Hamilton family overcame a challenge for the Linlithgow Burghs led by Sir Charles Ross against their candidate, William Maxwell. In both seats, however, the Hamiltons felt that Grenville had not been as forceful in their support as he might, particularly after their warnings about Ross's likely duplicity.[88] In West Lothian, Henry Erskine renewed an old family claim to the county, and he had government support.[89] It did him no good against the Dundas–Hopetoun interest, and he latterly turned his attentions to the Dumfries Burghs seat. Here Buccleuch backed Colonel Alexander Dirom, well-disposed to Melville but also inclined to support government.[90] Queensberry, belatedly hearing that Dirom did not consider himself connected to government, threw his weight behind Erskine.[91] This, with the support of the opportunist Provost David Staig of Dumfries, carried the burghs after a tight contest.[92] In Dumfriesshire itself, Queensberry's support guaranteed the success of Melville's relative, Captain William Johnstone Hope.[93] This support was given despite government's wish for the success of Hope's opponent, Sir John Lowther Johnstone.[94]

The Aberdeen Burghs were contested by James Farquhar and John Ramsay, a Foxite, who won despite government's declared neutrality. In the Stirling Burghs Sir John Henderson evicted the Melvillite Alexander Cochrane, while in the Glasgow Burghs a complicated contest saw Archibald Campbell defeating the ministerial candidate, Boyd Alexander. The Tain Burghs contest was essentially a local feud between Sir John Sinclair and Lord Seaforth, whose candidate won.[95]

Elsewhere, several struggles did not come to a poll. Threats of opposition in Clackmannanshire led George Abercromby to leave his Edinburgh seat to secure his home county.[96] The attack did not materialise. The Whigs had early hopes for the Edinburgh seat, but these were ruined by government's failure to ostracise the Melville party. The Whig candidate could only bewail the fact that 'this procrastination has been fatal to my views, and has allowed the Melvellits [sic] to rivet themselves so fast in this city that I might as easily attempt to give the Hill of North a shove, as to attempt to move this city at present'.[97]

The Scots Foxites contemplated opposing Robert Dundas in Midlothian, but eventually decided against.[98] In Kincardineshire, a confused contest saw Melville's allies backing two successive candidates (one had to drop out) against the Whigs, who successively fielded three (one died, a second dropped out). In the end, William Adam carried it for government.[99] In Perthshire, Colonel Alexander Campbell canvassed against Colonel Thomas Graham of Balgowan.

Government declined to take sides in the struggle and Campbell, although well-disposed to Melville, did not have his support.[100] In the end he withdrew.

As Whig electoral manager, William Adam made a report on the Scots elections. A recent analysis of this has suggested that of the MPs returned, twenty-eight were government supporters, fourteen were opposition and three were doubtful. It was a relatively poor showing for government in comparison to its performance elsewhere in Britain and, given the known 'fairweather' status of some 'supporters', may even have exaggerated government support.[101] The Scots Whigs, hindered by government's equivocal stance, had failed to break the entrenched Melville interest in the Commons.

Lord Advocate Henry Erskine had initially been apprehensive about the extent of Melville's continuing influence with the Scottish peerage,[102] but the results of the peerage election of 4 December were more to government's satisfaction. Ministers circulated a list of sixteen candidates. This was a return to the unpopular practice of the 1770s and a break with Dundas' more subtle method of channelling knowledge of the government's wishes indirectly through Buccleuch and others.[103] There was some confusion in that one government candidate, Lord Kinnaird, initially declined to stand and was replaced in the list by Lord Saltoun.[104] Later Kinnaird changed his mind, and for a time seventeen candidates appeared to have government support.[105] Of these government candidates, eight had been in the previous parliament.[106]

Melville wrote to several peers with his own list of thirteen candidates, avowedly supporting them because they were friendly to the politics and principles of the late Pitt.[107] The confusion in the election that followed arose both from the fact that several candidates were on both Melville's and the government lists, and from the government's insistence that its candidates should as far as possible exchange votes with their fellows rather than with other candidates.[108] There is little doubt that the operation of this hurt Melville's friends. Some who were not on the government list found that others who were would not exchange votes.[109] Others of Melville's 'friends' tried to steer a neutral course.[110] Lord Napier, loyal to Melville, was unhappy at what he perceived would be the effect of Melville's letter. Melville responded that it would only influence the friends of Pitt, but he was afraid 'that even in the exalted order of the peerage there are still more who look to the present powers, rather than to past services'. Melville's letter would at least identify his and Napier's friends. A major problem arose from those friends of Melville who, although well disposed to Pittite candidates, would, from personal ties, also vote for certain other candidates. In effect, those on the government list not only had the full advantage of acting as a party but could also benefit from a trickle of votes from Melville's allies. Melville could only advise that his friends should carefully supervise the exchange and transfers of votes between them.[111] The unusually high number of twenty-four candidates also contributed to making the contest unpredictable.[112]

In the end, government was pleasantly surprised when fifteen of its candidates were elected. The sixteenth, Sempill, was hopelessly unpopular with his fellows,[113] and Saltoun, who had trailed along after Kinnaird's re-emergence as a candidate, was latterly dropped entirely by government.[114] Of Melville's list, only seven were elected, and all but Lord Aberdeen were already on the government list. The remainder, including staunch Pittite noblemen such as Strathmore, Kellie, Haddington and Napier, were brushed aside.

The overall result of the 1806 election – the survival of a large if damaged Melville interest – worried the Scottish Whigs, but they had little immediate justification for their apprehensions. The fear, in the aftermath of Fox's death in September, that Pitt's English followers were talking to the king, had been the spur to Grenville to press George III to grant a dissolution as a decisive show of government's influence over him.[115] The Talents had gained ground in England, and this, combined with the belief that the king was now reconciled to his ministers, served to demoralise the Pittites in the south. This had already been seen in Scotland, where Melville was reproached by the countess of Abercorn: 'I hear you return 30 out of 45 Scotch members but with all that power, I fear you are a *languid party*.'[116]

Melville was repeatedly urged to come to London to join opposition, but he declined. He had no love for government after their attacks on him, but nor would he indulge in factious opposition. He had originally believed that George III had disliked his new ministers, but the king's granting them a dissolution of parliament had removed any such belief as a rational basis on which to conduct opposition. Melville was nevertheless angry with Grenville for his participation in the prince of Wales' virtual usurpation of the crown, and he certainly had a disposition to speak out against the prince. He was well aware, however, that other politicians, mindful of the rising sun, might not be enthusiastic about following him in this.[117]

In late January 1807, Robert Dundas approved of his father's aversion to 'contentious opposition' but felt that Melville should give some lead to his followers. He disliked the indiscriminate opposition of the Pittites, but he did not think that the country would gain from their not attending parliament. He wanted Melville to concert with the leading Pittites, and he shared his father's doubts about making an issue of the prince's activities. Unlike his father, he did not believe that enmities between the Pittites and the various parties in the government would necessarily be permanent, and for his proof he pointed to the bewildering variety of alliances and unions that had taken place since 1782.[118]

Melville had in fact already changed his plans. Spencer Perceval, now a prominent Pittite, had apprised him of the weakness and apathy among the opposition. Perceval wanted Melville to come forward and persuade his associates to attend parliament. As a postscript, Perceval wrote of the king's being surprised by Grenville's demand for a dissolution. Because the Pittites had not communicated to the king any willingness to form an alternative government, no assumptions could be made about the royal attitude to Grenville based on his having allowed the dissolution. Quite simply, the king had had no choice.[119] This letter, the first detailed account that he had had for some months from an insider at the centre of the political scene, was a revelation to Melville. He now felt obliged to come south to give some direction to his friends, and it is clear that his motivation was the news of the circumstances in which the king had granted the dissolution. If the king's real opinion of his ministers was uncertain, this might give a wholly different complexion to the prospects for such Pittites as opposed government.[120] It would also allow Melville to oppose the king's government while simultaneously remaining true to his long-held principles of supporting the king's wishes in politics.

Initially, Melville had thought that his son might lead his friends in criticising government for their mishandling of the organisation of the volunteers for national defence, a subject that had certainly caused disquiet in Scotland.[121] In fact the Scots Pittites were almost immediately presented with a focus for opposition much dearer to their hearts in February 1807, when ministers at last began to proceed with their plans to reform the court of session.

So far we have said little of the Talents' actual administration of Scotland. In truth there seems little to tell. Without an extended purge of office holders, they had little opportunity to change personnel, and this in turn prevented any serious changes in the workings of the system. It is clear that government was receiving warnings of corruption in the Scottish excise service, but it does not seem to have followed up these allegations.[122] In the last days of the government the resignation of the customs commissioner, David Reid, allowed Grenville to appoint an Englishman, Edward Earl, a deputy searcher from the London customs office. Earl's was not a political appointment, and he was talent-spotted by Richard Frewin, the chairman of the English Customs Board, who then recommended him to Grenville.[123] Needless to say, by the time he arrived in Edinburgh he was a Grenville supporter, and as an outsider he was not welcomed. His subsequent career suggests competence and diligence. In time, the next government would receive complaints from his subordinates and others about his meddling ways, but he seems to have been too isolated to cause serious trouble to the Dundas interest.[124]

Perhaps unsurprisingly, given the preponderance of lawyers among their leadership, the Scots Whigs had concentrated their plans for reform almost exclusively on the Scottish legal system. In late 1806 they had carried through a minor reorganisation of the sheriffdoms,[125] but their main focus was on the court of session. The problems here were certainly pressing. The court had not functioned efficiently for some years, and there was an enormous backlog of cases pending. Perhaps as embarrassing, there was a rising number of judgements being appealed to the House of Lords, with a consequent inconvenience to that court. These problems had not appeared suddenly, and there had been abortive proposals for reform before, most seriously in 1785 and 1805. The solution now mooted by the Scottish government party was to remodel the court of session along English lines, splitting it into three chambers with concurrent jurisdictions, bringing jury trial into civil causes, and introducing an intermediate chamber of review.[126] It was Grenville who announced the plan in mid-1806, and he had already discussed it with Lord Armadale.[127] The later bill was drafted by John Clerk, the solicitor-general, and Adam Gillies, a Whig advocate, with some advice from Lauderdale.[128] Grenville's outline proposals were actually in the hands of the Edinburgh lawyers before he informed the judges, and this caused much offence.[129] It typified the Whigs' determination to prevent potentially obstructive judges becoming involved in the work, and in the coming months the lord justice-clerk and others would complain of being kept at a distance by crown officials.[130] In June 1806, a committee of the House of Lords resolved on the reform of Scottish civil justice, and the Scots judges were duly informed.[131] Then the wrangling began. The bill was drafted over the summer, with no apparent consultation with the judges or with the former lord chancellor, Eldon, an acknowledged expert in the field. The drafters had a reverence for English law forms and no small part of the outrage in Scotland derived from the belief that they were attempting to abolish Scottish law.

When it finally appeared in February 1807, the bill was badly drafted and the objections to it were substantial.[132] The lord chief baron, Robert Dundas, complained at length about not being consulted. He objected to the chamber of review, and to the idea of three chambers, asserting that Scotland could not find legal talent enough to fill them. Of the bill generally:

> It seems to me to do, what your Lop. denies & disclaims – Abolish the law of Scotland, & introduce the law of England so far as regards jury trial, in all cases whatever; with an implied, obscure & very doubtful exception of such actions only as are strictly feudal, & affect the real rights & estates of the landed interest of Scotland.[133]

The lord justice-clerk, Charles Hope, was similarly blunt.[134] Before seeing the bill, he warned that jury trial in civil causes would be unpopular in Scotland. In commercial disputes it would be hard to find jurors who were not in one way or another connected with the parties involved.[135] He preferred a two-chamber system for the court, warning that the three-chamber plan was generally regarded as 'a job . . . merely to create another President'.[136] Nor did he support the chamber of review, designed to reduce appeals to the Lords. It would merely be another opportunity for delaying cases and would not function equitably. Further, it would violate the treaty of union. Grenville politely brushed Hope aside,[137] and when Hope finally saw the bill he had little time to comment. His verdict was pointed: 'As the bill stands at present, I have no hesitation to say, that I am decidedly of opinion, that the objections to it are insurmountable, and I am positive that I could easily convince your Lordship.'[138]

Grenville was determined to press matters and left only three weeks between the first and second readings of the bill.[139] Meetings of the writers to the signet and of the faculty of advocates were held to consider it, and government worked hard to 'pack' them with its supporters.[140] In fact the faculty was deeply divided, and while it did vote approval of the reforms proposed, the advocates only narrowly voted for the principle of a chamber of review, with the minority including a number of the younger Whig lawyers. An apparent majority in favour of splitting the court into three chambers actually disguised fairly equally divided opinion.[141] The fifteen court of session judges were also divided. Eleven of them agreed to send a memorial to the House of Lords detailing objections to the bill, but the four Whig judges disagreed.[142] The senior Scots judges were summoned to London to state their case, but they were followed hotfoot by three of the dissenters.[143]

By now it was beginning to dawn on Grenville that all was not well with his plans. Following a series of particularly persuasive parliamentary speeches by Eldon, he announced on 18 March that the clauses introducing trial by jury in civil cases would be removed from the bill. In fact it was already too late, for Grenville was given notice of his dismissal that same day. Reform did not go away, but in the long run perhaps the most important effect of Grenville's endeavours was to foster a divergence between the older Scots Whigs under Erskine and Lauderdale, and the younger under Francis Jeffrey. This division would become much clearer over the next decade.[144] The Scots Tories could take no credit for the demise of Grenville's bill. Melville had spoken against it,[145] but more time would have seen it being passed comfortably into law by the government majority. It would have been a perfect example of a Scottish group using English support to foist a measure of doubtful popularity on their fellow countrymen.[146]

Grenville's fall – 'the mucking of Geordie's Byre', the marquis of Huntly called it[147] – was quite sudden and had little to do with the opposition. The government had proposed a plan for limited Roman Catholic emancipation and this, together with Grenville's attempts to entice the Pittite George Canning into government, had led Lord Sidmouth to tender his resignation. In a repeat of his actions in 1801, George III managed to use his influence against the proposal. Several cabinet members prepared to resign even as he further demanded a written assurance that the Catholic question would not be raised again. Grenville and Spencer would not give this undertaking, and the king dismissed them on 18 March. Ministers remained in office for another week while their successors were chosen.

It had been a year of very mixed fortunes for Melville and his friends. Pitt's death had been a terrible blow to them, but paradoxically it had served to strengthen links with their English allies. Grenville and Spencer had never fully faced up to the problem of what to do with Scotland and against all the evidence they had persisted for too long in a policy of neutrality to Melville, reining in their natural allies, the Scots Whigs. In the end it was unimportant in British terms, since government's English majority was large enough to allow the luxury of indulging a significant body of opposition in Scotland. This initial neutrality by government is part of the explanation for the survival of so strong a party around Melville, but attention has also to be paid to Melville's own explanation; twenty years of support for William Pitt's government and principles had done much to weld together a formidable body of the most powerful men in Scotland. Even for a determinedly hostile government, it would have been a tough nut to crack. The Scots Pittites never forgave Grenville for the few attempts that he did make to disturb them. In the short time available to them, the Talents Ministry had achieved only qualified Scottish successes. As a clear success, they had undoubtedly augmented their electoral strength in the constituencies and among the peerage. Their minor tinkering with the Scottish revenue administration had no immediate impact. In the field of the law we have noted their reorganisation of several sheriffdoms. Much more significantly Grenville had also released the genie of court of session reform. This would never be rebottled, and the new government was forced to keep the issue open, although it proposed a different remedy for the problems. The first serious reforms of the court would pass into law in 1808.

For Melville personally, it had been a miserable interlude. In 1804 he had returned to government at Pitt's insistence and had abandoned a pleasant retirement very much against his inclination. Now, three years later, not only was his old friend dead but his own reputation as a statesman, painfully built up over a quarter of a century, had been brought low by the impeachment. With feeling, he would describe the outgoing administration as 'that abominable vermin'[148] and he looked to its successor for vindication.

7

Moderates and Wild Men: Politics, Religion and Party Division in the Church of Scotland, 1800–1843

IAIN F. MACIVER

What's in a name? Or rather, names, for one of the two rival ecclesiastical parties within the earlier-nineteenth-century Established Church of Scotland, prior to its climactic Disruption in 1843, which are the subject of this study rejoiced in a multiplicity of titles, of which the Evangelical party, by which it has come to be known, was actually a comparatively late arrival. In 1800, this party was most frequently referred to by itself or others as the Popular or Orthodox party. Opponents also disparaged it as the Wild party or Wild Men of our title, or as the Highflyers, but sympathisers, like the judge and diarist Lord Cockburn, could also refer with some affection to 'the Wild'. By contrast, the rival Moderate party remained under a single banner, though towards the end of the period of this study they sometimes referred to themselves as the 'Constitutional' party to emphasise their loyalty to a legal and political establishment which they saw under attack by their rivals, the opponents of the 'intrusion' represented by lay patronage, thus 'Non-Intrusionists'. It is to the fortunes of the Moderate party in particular that this study is directed, though with a good deal of reference to the organisation and actions of their opponents.

Both groups, in imitation of secular politics, regarded themselves as parties, though with their loose structure, and the fact that through most of this period they operated and were visible mostly in the short, annual General Assemblies of the kirk and seem to have organised primarily for this forum, meant that they bore little resemblance to the highly organised and spin-doctored secular political organisations of today. According to John Gibson Lockhart (who was himself a son of the manse), in General Assembly the rival parties stuck in quasi-parliamentary fashion, 'with the most senatorial pertinacity, each to his own side of the Senate-house – the right side of the throne being occupied exclusively by the *Moderates*, while, on the left side, sit, equally pure and uncontaminated, the representatives of the *Wildmen*'.[1] For the two decades from 1800, this right–left division did reasonably reflect at least the general political alignment of the parties, though the Evangelicals, regarded as broadly Whig, and remaining firmly labelled so up to 1832, increasingly came to display more internal political division. This was to become a factor in the eventual disruption of their broad coalition, those who came to form what was called a 'Middle Party' in the early 1840s being mainly supporters of Peelite conservatism.

Another area of considerable contemporary consensus was the belief at the opening of the century that the Moderate party did not only dominate the higher courts of the Church, but that it was a particularly tightly organised group. Its controlling nexus was largely based on the clerical university professoriate, and its dependent parishes. St Andrews University, in particular, had the direct patronage of nine kirks. Up until the 1830s, possession of certain strategic city churches, particularly in Edinburgh, was seen also as important for the party, but the hard core of its strength lay in rural Scotland. In 1800, both parties were heavily clerical in leadership and ethos, but the Moderates were to remain especially so. They also remained crucially dependent for leadership on their fortresses in the universities, which were to fall increasingly under siege. Hence Lockhart's description in 1819 of the Edinburgh minister, Dr John Inglis, as 'chief of the Moderate or Tory party', quickly corrected by the rider, 'or rather, perhaps, the chief of a small college of cardinals by whom that party is managed'.[2] The Moderates remained collegiate in leadership, but it was to become an increasingly narrow and embattled collegiality.

Even if this ever constituted an effective clerical cabal, the Moderate leadership's federal structure, based on regional fiefdoms in Edinburgh, St Andrews, Glasgow and Aberdeen, could create problems in coordinating action in the Assembly and elsewhere. Their geographical dispersal rather contrasts with the Popular/Evangelical party, whose Assembly leaders prior to 1832, Sir Henry Moncreiff and Andrew Thomson, were Edinburgh ministers, and whose wider post-1832 leadership, of whom the internationally celebrated Thomas Chalmers was the undoubted primus inter pares, came to be concentrated in or around the capital.

In the early period of our study, the most spectacular example of poor judgement and bad coordination by the Moderate leadership was the notorious Leslie case in 1805. Professor John Leslie, a scientist of European reputation, was elected by the town council of Edinburgh to the chair of mathematics at the university against the rather less impressive Thomas M'Knight, nominee of the Edinburgh Moderate leaders, Drs. Finlayson, Grieve and Inglis. In an attempt to stop Leslie, the latter tried to use the Presbytery's right of *avizandum* (a claim to judge professorial candidates' doctrinal orthodoxy) and charged him with following the heretical and sceptical views of David Hume on causation. Leslie, supported by clerical and academic friends (notably the philosophers Dugald Stewart and Thomas Brown), indignantly rejected the charge of atheism. He asserted that his own religious principles were sound, claimed that Hume misapplied the theory, and bitingly reminding his critics that they had based a heresy-hunt on a note in his *Essay on Heat* that 'refers entirely to the relation between cause and effect considered as an object of physical examination'.[3]

The dispute dragged on into the Assembly of that year, when the case against Leslie was poorly handled by the St Andrews Moderate leader, Principal George Hill, who normally led the party in the supreme court of the Church. In his defence, Hill had inherited an unholy mess created by his Edinburgh colleagues, but effectively the argument was already lost. After some initial hesitation the Evangelicals had weighed in strongly on Leslie's side. The result was a humiliating defeat for the Moderate leadership in a vote in which many doubters in their own party refused to follow their lead.

Despite the determination of Moderate sympathisers like Lockhart to dismiss the Leslie episode as 'of too limited and personal a nature to be considered as anything more than a passing tempest',[4] it was a very crucial episode. If anything can be said in its favour as far as the party were concerned, it served to confirm that the Moderates were, despite attacks by their opponents to the contrary, now firmly rooted in confessional orthodoxy, making it difficult for the latter to hark back to John Witherspoon's jibe 'that it was the characteristic of a Moderate man never to speak of the Confession of Faith but with a sneer'.[5] However, this did not prevent Witherspoon's satire being reprinted for propaganda purposes in the inflamed atmosphere preceding the Disruption.[6]

Whatever the feelings of more latitudinarian Moderates, the historian William Robertson, regarded by his successors as the founding father of the party, had always firmly resisted any attempts to tinker with the church's touchstone of scholastic Calvinism, the Westminster Confession of Faith, thus depriving his 'Orthodox' party critics of this avenue of theological attack. George Hill, the inheritor of Robertson's mantle in the ecclesiastical context at least, was the author of the standard textbook of Scottish theological halls, and not only firm but active in his orthodoxy. He saw confessions as absolutely vital to established religion, as they were expositions of truth prepared by teachers of religion to guide their own ministrations and protect their flocks against error; and subscription was a pledge to the civil magistrate that they would not, without his knowledge 'make any change upon that system of doctrine which has not received his sanction'.[7]

Most fair-minded Evangelicals recognised this change (if change it was): asked about his view of the Moderate party in 1834, David Welsh, the last moderator of the Assembly before the Disruption, acknowledged that the Moderates had changed their views in recent years. He affirmed, 'their measures at least have been modified' and, asked if the doctrines of the church as declared in its confessional standards were 'preached in a different manner now by the clergymen of the moderate party, from what they were about 30 years ago', he confirmed that this was the case.[8] In 1843, even the future president of Princeton, James McCosh, then a firebrand editor of the *Dundee Warder* Evangelical newspaper, had to admit that 'there is a section, however, and by no means an inconsiderable one in point of numbers, whom the growing Evangelicalism of the age has not left without impressions of a certain kind, who are, perhaps as far as they can be, Evangelical in their preaching, and a few of them even occasionally somewhat so in their speeches in Church Courts'.[9]

If this is an indication that religious practice and doctrine were ceasing to be primary indicators of party difference – and the evidence from the mouths of opponents is persuasive – then it may follow that more strictly political differences were becoming the major points of division. Returning to the Leslie case, its significance in this context lies in the mortal damage their attitude to Leslie had inflicted on the traditional Moderate image as the champions of toleration and latitude, the heirs and part-creators of what has come to be known as the Scottish Enlightenment. It was now among the 'Orthodox' Evangelicals that more 'new light' (to borrow a phrase current among seceders from the Established Church), had emerged in this argument, and they could aspire to be the party of progress in a new century. In practical terms it also damaged the Moderates' image as a natural and irremovable party of church government.

The Tory Lockhart's identification of Moderatism with his own political allegiance was the common currency of the time. It has been argued persuasively that the party did not wish to become little more than 'the Dundas interest at prayer'.[10] But the realities of a patronage system on which they were dependent drove them inexorably into captivity to one dominant political interest.

Arguably, the roots of this addiction go back to the mid-eighteenth-century heyday of the party. Ideologically, it became progressively difficult for Moderates not to cling to the political establishment in a period when it was evolving in a Tory direction. As it developed in the second half of the eighteenth century, the Moderate party had recoiled from the old Covenanting theocracy, and were content to see its latter-day radical descendants, from Cameronians to less extreme later Seceders, safely outside the fold of the Established Church. Implicitly, the Moderates were becoming ecclesiastical policemen for the civil establishment, and the gap between partnership and dependence was perilously narrow. By the time Robertson retired from active Church politics in 1780, the Assembly reigned supreme, and opposition to 'intrusions' had been worn down by procedural delay. Four years later the Assembly had even ceased to make the ritual protest against the reimposition of crown and private patronage, which it had sustained since 1713.

This process had revived and strengthened the authority of the Assembly, but its management could never be sustained with entire ease, as ministers were sent from their presbyteries in rotation, a practice that both parties generally honoured, at least until the 1840s and particularly in 1842, the eve of the Disruption, when the unwritten practice was set aside. The convention was also applied to the moderatorship of the Assembly. Continuity, and reliability, could come better from the ruling elder 'commissioners' returned by the presbyteries, who did not always rotate their elders; and, especially, from the oligarchic royal burghs and the commissioners of the universities, as, usually, no rotation was applied in either of these constituencies. As ministers without parish charges (in practice, mostly university professors) could sit at this time as ruling elders for presbyteries, burghs and universities, this enabled both parties to return regularly many of their leading men. Indeed, many presbyteries and burghs had the habit of returning the same Assembly elder over a period of years. Many of the latter were Edinburgh lawyers, who were the predominating non-ministerial element in the Assembly, and especially so on the Moderate side of the house.

All this reduced the element of management uncertainty for the both parties, but by the 1820s, with their hegemony among the clerical commissioners eroding steadily in favour of the Popular party, the Moderates were becoming more dependent on the votes of their elders to sustain shrinking majorities when the Assembly divided along party lines. Governments, or at least their Scottish representatives, usually showed some inclination to influence the Assembly, and during the years from 1800 to 1827, in the form of the Dundas of Melville management, they could exercise considerable indirect influence. It could do so on the presbyterial commissioners through the crown patronage, which covered approximately one third of the parishes, and, less directly, through the influence of Tory magnates and lairds who controlled a large segment of the remaining presentations in rural parishes.

In the oligarchic burghs, the government also exercised considerable clout and could ensure easily the return of its own notables. This was to change after the arrival of burgh reform from 1835, with the Evangelicals benefiting initially from the change and the proportion of Moderate Edinburgh lawyers in the Assembly drastically reduced. Another feature of Assembly membership was the regular presence of the law officers (lord advocate and solicitor-general) and, until the dispute with the civil courts became acute, a bench of judges. The solicitor-general in particular, after due ordination as a ruling elder and election as a commissioner to the Assembly by a complaisant presbytery or burgh, was regarded as government's eyes and ears in the Assembly, a trend reinforced in the 1820s when the senior law officer, the lord advocate, Sir William Rae, was excluded from membership by his Episcopalian allegiance.[11]

If the Moderates were increasingly unable to maintain a traditional grip on the Assembly, finally lost in 1834, the post-1800 party was also long enmeshed by this time in a political dependency culture. In 1806 the party chiefs were seriously alarmed when, following the death of William Pitt and moves to impeach the 'manager' of Scotland, Henry Dundas, Lord Melville, the Pittite coalition lost power at Westminster, and the Foxite Whigs, regarded as friends of the Popular/Evangelical party, dominated in a new ministry of 'all the Talents'. This short-lived political revolution coincided with a vacancy in the clerkship of the Assembly, a much sought-after post for which the new government favoured Andrew Duncan, a friend of the Evangelical leader and Whig, Sir Henry Moncreiff. Duncan was, in fact, successfully elected in May 1807.

Scenting a loss of influence, one of the Moderate leadership, the veteran Edinburgh minister, Henry Grieve, wrote in alarm earlier that year to the new home secretary and official controller of the crown patronage in the kirk, Lord Spencer, with an elaborate statement of the party's creed and an implied protest against ministerial interference in what he represented as the established system of church management.

Grieve explained that the ministers of the Church were divided into 'two classes', or parties. His party, he claimed, included two thirds of the Church: by implication, a strong majority whose views should be heeded. The Popular party, unlike his friends, had a 'system of ecclesiastical Conduct [which] lays too much stress upon the Sentiments and Prejudices of the People, and has therefore a tendency to engender a spirit of discontent, not only with all Matters connected with the Government of the Church, but also with the Institutions of Civil Society'. In contrast, his party had 'an immediate tendency to render the established Religion, its Ministers, and the whole Government of the Church independent of the humours and prejudices of the People' and inculcated 'a Spirit of Subordination and Submission to lawful Authority'. It did this by having 'a good correspondence with His Majesty's Ministers', while retaining control of the Church: 'They have not been accustomed . . . either to ask or receive Directions from them respecting their ecclesiastical proceedings, but the particular measures that arise . . . have usually been communicated to some Persons in that respectable situation [and] have uniformly obtained their Approbation and Countenance.'[12]

A Moderate of the previous century such as Grieve liked to think that the churchmen and government negotiated as equals, and the party members were not slaves to the ruling elite. Indeed, as a young man he had written to refute the charge that Moderate defence of the rights of patrons was self-interested. Is it, he had asked rhetorically, 'the good graces of the patrons and the favour of the great that we aim at obtaining? Verily then, we are bubbles of our own craft; we work for thankless masters. The nobility and gentry of this kingdom, heedless of the civil advantages of ecclesiastical order, take no part or concern in these matters.'[13] It has been argued that this, and similar complaints of political interference from other Moderates, free the party from the charge of Erastianism. But, equally, it can be interpreted as special pleading, and one has to wonder if the older Grieve would have addressed, or even felt the need to address, such a strong letter to a member of what he was likely to have seen as the natural party of government – a friend of Lord Melville.

Certainly the early nineteenth-century generation of Moderate leaders were more comfortable in an attitude of mind that reasonably can be called Erastian, as examination of their evidence to the Select Committee on Patronage of

1834, as well as their private correspondence, will readily attest. They were also unequivocal in their Tory allegiance. A telling instance of this can be found in John Inglis, who had retained a vote in his native county of Perthshire. In 1807 he had backed General Sir Thomas Graham, to whom he was heavily indebted for Graham's patronage of a relative. But when Graham stood again in 1812 as a Whig rather than an Independent, and was opposed by a government candidate, Inglis resolved to abstain, thus declining to vote for the somewhat offended General, who pressed him for his reasons. In his defence, Inglis protested that he could not desert his political principles: 'I have been throughout life not only a steady but ardent friend of the principles and measures of those Statesmen whom I consider the present Ministry as representing in the government of the country.' Furthermore, he had the interests of the Church to consider. 'I add that as a professional man I have been honoured on various occasions with their approbation and consent in transacting business connected with the business of the Church.'[14] On the face of it, this was a much closer and more dependent relationship with government than that represented by Grieve to be the ideal.

Other leading Moderates could be quick to emphasise their political loyalism, especially if church patronage showed signs of straying towards their opponents. In 1810 David Ritchie of St Andrew's parish in Edinburgh wrote to chief baron Robert Dundas of Arniston with a message for his kinsman that, 'from a Ministry of which Mr Dundas of Melville forms a part, the Moderate Interest hope for the advantage of Crown Patronage, when it can, without inconvenience, be turned in their favour'.[15] Arniston himself was more proactive, complaining to Melville in 1808 that official support of Moderate candidates was 'essential to the Peace of the Church & by no means immaterial to the support of the Government', as members of the Popular party were better lobbyists and engaged in 'gradually, insensibly but too successfully' converting many former Moderate strongholds into 'Wild Presbyteries'. He was particularly concerned about the strategic Edinburgh presbytery where, he claimed, the maintenance of a Moderate majority was the principle under which 'all administrations acted for half a century'.[16] Another overt example of political lobbying emerges in 1821, when the next Moderatorship of the Assembly appeared to be developing along contested party lines, stimulating Principal Duncan MacFarlan of Glasgow University to write to a Tory peer to remind him that his party were the 'friends of government' while their opponents were identified 'with those who call themselves the Whigs of Scotland'.[17]

It is clear that while the church patronage of Robert Dundas, second Viscount Melville, may have benefited Moderate candidates overall, it was rather more balanced than their lobbyists would have liked. Robert continued to follow his father's policy of making judgements in this area on grounds not based exclusively on church politics. Attempting to judge between two rival candidates for Canongate (Edinburgh) in 1811, he wrote to his parent that 'if Mr Garnock [the Moderate] is preferred, who the parish do not wish for, it ought to be distinctly on the grounds of the other [Evangelical] candidate's improper political opinions'.[18] Some years later Melville showed that he continued not to favour one party exclusively, be it religious or secular. He confided to the duke of Buccleuch that in this area, 'I did not find in the long run that a certain amount of proper (& prudent) liberality towards political opponents was prejudicial to my interest'.[19]

We can see the Melvillian policy in contemporaneous action for a vacant parish charge in Dunfermline. In the context of a large town, while Melville would not countenance any 'indecent proceeding' such as popular election, he felt that he could not ignore the wishes of the 'principal parties interested', the heritors and town councillors, rejecting for these reasons a nominee of the lord advocate and making a choice between two Evangelicals. Confident that both were acceptable locally, he only then applied a political test by recommending Patrick Chalmers, proposed by his namesake Thomas, then regarded as a political friend, against the candidate of the Evangelical leader, Sir Henry Moncreiff, whose opposition politics were 'well known, in State as well as Church affairs'.[20] This trend was to have important consequences for both parties. The Moderate majority was under threat, partly because the perceived Whiggism of Popular/Evangelical ministers was no longer regarded by official dispensers of patronage as a general assumption they had to make.

If this policy was Melville's, its official sponsor was the home secretary, Sir Robert Peel. His rule, following Melville's advice, was 'to adopt the recommendations of the greater heritors of the parish',[21] and, on occasion, Peel did accede to the wishes of political opponents. For instance, for a vacancy in Elgin in 1824, he considered that the claims of the Whig earl of Fife, the chief heritor, should take precedence over the Tory, Grant of Grant.[22] The Melville/Peel policy was commented on favourably by the Whig, Lord Minto, who told his friend Lord Lansdowne, the incoming home secretary in 1827, that his predecessor had found it necessary to 'withdraw his confidence' from the 'servile and intolerant' section of the Moderate party, relying instead on the more flexible Dr John Cook of St Andrews. Cook, nephew of Principal George Hill, to whose influence Cook had fallen heir in 1819, was identified as the person 'a good deal consulted by him' [Minto].[23]

In actuality, Cook, though politically adroit, was in most fundamental respects a very traditional and conservative Moderate. If there were cautiously progressive elements in the party in the 1820s that, on ecclesiastical issues at least, were closer on some issues to the Evangelicals, they may be seen to be represented in John Inglis,[24] who had come to command cross-party respect by his advocacy, ultimately successful, of the state-financed scheme to build new churches in the Highlands (which was not to benefit his own party), and his victory, also with Evangelical backing, over the scheme to establish foreign missions in 1824. Against a passionate plea of the then Evangelical leader, John Erskine, the Moderates had rejected such a proposal in 1796, and some diehard members of the party were still hostile. Significantly, their spokesman was a Tory advocate, John Hope, son of a leading Moderate judge, and associated with the St Andrews leader of the party, Francis Nicoll, who went so far as to write to Melville condemning the mission proposals as a 'preposterous scheme . . . for sending forth missionaries to all quarters of the world' and a 'triumph for the Wild party', and urging him to 'throw cold water' on Inglis' projects.[25] As solicitor-general, Hope had risen to early prominence in kirk politics through the unavoidable absence of his senior, Sir William Rae, from the Assembly. The death of Inglis in the crucial year of 1832 left Hope, seen as an ultra-Moderate, as the single most powerful Edinburgh voice in the party leadership, and he was to use his formidable powers as a lobbyist and political intriguer to promote the most extreme policies of his party.

For the past thirty years the Moderates had been happy to identify their opponents as Whigs and diehard partisans of a near-permanent opposition. When nearly two and a half decades of Tory government came to an end, temporarily in 1827 with a brief coalition of the liberal Tory followers of George Canning and some Whigs, and more decisively with almost ten years of Whig/Liberal administrations following the passage of the Reform Act of 1832, they found themselves in the uncomfortably novel position of having to deal with governments who looked coldly on their track record. Worse, the new administration had turned naturally for advice on Church policy to their rivals, and even when this relationship cooled as government and some leading Evangelicals, particularly Thomas Chalmers, quarrelled with the Melbourne government over church extension issues after 1835, the Whigs continued to sustain popular presentations to crown parishes to Moderate detriment.

The latter party found it could not escape from its ideological inheritance. In the later 1830s, its triumvirate leadership of George Cook of St Andrews, Principal MacFarlan of Glasgow and Duncan Mearns of King's College Aberdeen[26] was increasing referred to as the 'Old Moderates'. They were leaders of what was becoming an ageing and declining group,[27] in dread of a possible demise of lay patronage and the populist campaigning against it. The pressure for popular election of ministers and the accompanying 'agitation' they saw as subverting their influence and offending the landed interest. More than ever, the lairds were becoming their main prop, as they saw much government patronage being exercised in favour of the Evangelicals.

Their traditional skills operating within the old Dundas management system were now obsolete. Psychologically, they were particularly ill-adapted to playing the new politics, seen by Moderates like Cook and MacFarlan as dire harbingers of the downfall of the traditional political and social order. As for patronage, it was the last line of defence. Cook went so far as to tell Lord Melville that by 1839 the current Evangelical 'Ruling Party' were 'instrumental in creating agitation and something approaching even insubordination and rebellion', and without the 'check' of patronage 'a Presbyterian Establishment cannot harmonise well with a Monarchical Government'.[28]

They also had a covertly hostile attitude to the campaign for Church extension being pressed on from 1835 by Thomas Chalmers, seeing the young ministers of the new extension parishes filling the ranks of their rivals. The future seemed to be Evangelical. Asked in 1834 about his attitude to dissent from the Established Church, Principal MacFarlan conceded that it was an 'evil', but added: 'If there is any countervailing advantage it must be this, that men of restless and discontented spirit have the means, without noise or disturbance, of withdrawing themselves from the Establishment.'[29] One can hear in this statement a tacit acceptance of, even some welcome for, a convenient safety valve. When the Evangelical-led Church extension campaign appeared to close this outlet by its internal expansion of the Established Church's parish system and its direct and acrimonious competition with the Presbyterian Seceders, Cook showed reluctance to welcome an expansion of the Church (and its Evangelical element), only complaining that it was 'the creator of much exasperation among those who had previously lived in harmony with one another'.[30]

Given this deep fear of any hint of popular control of government, ecclesiastical or secular, it is evident just how difficult it was for this group to attempt to follow the Evangelicals in their systematic arrangement of mass support through organisation on a parish or regional level, or by means of public meetings. Though the Moderate cause enjoyed the support of a fair number of local or regional newspapers, it was generally as an incidental by-product of their Tory political alignments.[31] The Moderates were also far behind in their inclination or ability to raise funds from their support. It was as late as 1841 before an appeal was circulated, but specifically to cover the legal costs of the presbytery of Strathbogie's Moderate majority, who were facing deposition by the Assembly for their obedience to the judgement of the court of session, which the General Assembly had instructed them to defy. 'They are not prompt, they are indolent,' complained one leading minister supporting the 'Constitutional' case against the Evangelical majority, referring to what he was now calling the 'Old Moderate' leadership.[32]

Just how far by this time were the Moderates a party in serious decline? They appear to have retained regional areas of considerable residual strength, and this is a subject that would repay closer study. Parts of rural Lowland Scotland, and academia, though not as exclusively as in 1800, remained strongholds. But the overall impression is broadly similar to the contemporary Scottish Tories in secular politics: that of a 'country' party, particularly weak in the towns of the industrialising and demographically buoyant central belt, and in Gaelic Scotland, which went overwhelmingly into the Free Church in 1843.

What James McCosh called pejoratively the 'spiritual wastes' of rural and small town Aberdeenshire[33] and the north-east (though he should have excluded from this comment the city of Aberdeen, where the Evangelicals were strong[34]), do appear to have generated some popular support for its Moderate ministers. The normally effective Evangelical propagandist, James Begg, was chased out of Ellon in 1840 by a mob that he complained was put up to it by 'coarse, ignorant and ungodly squirearchy'.[35] In some rural parishes, Moderates, aided by local landlords and their officials, may have organised with similar effectiveness. The great Evangelical journalist Hugh Miller reported on a similar attempted shut-out of Begg and his colleague, Thomas Guthrie, from the Dumfriesshire parish of Thornhill.

> The factor's carriage has driven up to the residence of the baron bailie, the baron bailie has gone to the villagers and all were warned that the 'men who were turning the world upside down were coming there also' and that no house in the village should be given them in which to address the people.[36]

However, such a response appears to have been patchily effective at best. Even from 1840, when the Moderates did begin to organise public meetings to drum up support, the response was limited. They seem to have concentrated on safe county burghs like Haddington and Banff. In 1840 the combative Moderate judge, Lord President Charles Hope, proudly boasted to his Evangelical-supporting colleague Henry Cockburn about two 'prodigious meetings' in these towns. Cockburn was not impressed, describing them to Lord Advocate Andrew Rutherfurd as gatherings of 'Tory lairds and their vassals'.[37]

The party did make some effort to organise in the major cities, but even newspapers like the *Scotsman*, an ally of the presbyterian Seceders and other Dissenters from the Kirk whose hostility to Chalmers and the Evangelicals now made them reasonably sympathetic to the Moderates, were hard put to put a very good gloss on their extent and impact. An Edinburgh meeting by 'Constitutional' Moderates in May 1840 to support Lord Aberdeen's abortive legislative attempt to solve the Church question was described as 'not crowded' though 'well filled by a respectable audience', and the lead was taken by a group of Lothian lairds, backed up by Moderate, many of them identifiably Tory, members of the faculty of advocates. Even in Roxburghshire, a county where Moderate ministers were reasonably strong, a meeting to support the Aberdeen bill had to be described as thinly 'attended'.[38]

By 1842, with the unity of the Evangelical party clearly fracturing and secession from the kirk looming, the old Moderate leadership was reported to be nourishing hopes of a return to ecclesiastical power. The 'extreme folks in the North' led by Dr Duncan Mearns of Aberdeen, were said by the new 'Middle Party' man, Dr William Muir, minister of St Stephen's, Edinburgh, to be far from reluctant to force matters to a disruption. Though classified by McCosh as a Moderate, in reality Muir took a centrist position and had little truck with the traditional Moderate leadership. He was apprehensive at the prospect of their return, and of the rumoured intention to put up Principal MacFarlan against Chalmers in the Assembly of 1843: 'Considering his [MacFarlan's] extreme politics . . . the proposing of him is a handle for saying "You see what is intended to bring back on you" and thus the secession among the people may be increased.'[39]

By this time the new Conservative government of Sir Robert Peel had hardened its resolve not to accept the demands of the Evangelical majority, or to compromise with them on the ever-widening issues in which the latter were at conflict with the civil courts. In doing so they brushed aside the wish of a clear majority of Scottish MPs prior to the threatened secession for legislation to close down the conflict, thus rejecting any claims that this was a national issue on which Scottish voices should be heeded at Westminster. The Assembly of May 1842 had thrown down a nationalist gauntlet, not only demanding the outright abolition of patronage in the Church, but also passing that remarkable and radical constitutional document, the Claim of Right, a declaration of spiritual independence which Chalmers saw as an ultimatum to the London government, whose rejection would result in a severing from the state.[40] The government ministers were also influenced by fears of the effects of major concessions on the principles that they felt ought to govern an Established Church. In reality, this meant any impact on the Church of England, where victory for the presbyterian radicals might encourage the 'Puseyite' high churchmen in that communion to attempt to destabilise the much greater state control exercised over the Anglican Establishment.

This view, taken by the leading Conservatives most involved in the question – Peel, Sir James Graham and Lord Aberdeen – was far from confined to Tories. Though the official Scottish Whig leader, Lord Advocate Andrew Rutherfurd, and many Scots Liberal MPs were strongly supportive of the Evangelicals, the metropolitan Whig/Liberal magnates, with influential Scots Whigs with whom they were associated such as Lord Dunfermline (a former speaker of the Commons), Lord Minto, and the judge, Lord Murray (a former lord advocate), had old scores with the Evangelicals and shared much the same view as Peel and his colleagues.

Before its departure in 1841, the Whig government of Lord Melbourne, politically divided on the issue, had failed to produce healing legislation, and the old association of the Evangelicals with Whiggism could no longer be assumed to be effective. After the Disruption, Lord John Russell wrote to his father-in-law,

Minto, that he had favoured only such 'fair concessions' as would keep the remaining Evangelicals in the Established Church. The furthest Russell wished to go was to remove the taint of Erastianism created by the civil court judgements that had provoked the Disruption by reverting to the pre-Union system of the election of ministers by kirk session elders, who would be subject to 'some control by their congregation'.[41] This was a considerable distance from popular election and not that far removed, despite Russell's belief to the contrary, from the revised proposals of Lord Aberdeen currently under discussion.

It was inevitable, therefore, that a major division in the ranks of the Evangelical party was seen as an opportunity for the government to defeat the radical majority. Sir James Graham, home secretary from 1841, was a self-confident Cumbrian baronet who considered that he had acquired some knowledge of the innards of Scottish Church politics. During Graham's period as lord rector of Glasgow University in particular (1838–40), he had forged contacts with political and ecclesiastical sympathisers in the west of Scotland, and he had a longstanding personal and political friendship with the conservative duke of Hamilton. While wary of the views of ultras like John Hope, Graham had refused to go beyond the compromises laid out in Lord Aberdeen's bill, telling Chalmers that he could not transfer patronage to 'a variable and irresponsible multitude'.[42]

So when Matthew Leishman, minister of Govan, sent him in April 1842 the declaration of the so-called core 'Forty' group opposing any secession, Graham immediately saw its importance. He wrote to Lord Melville that while the Evangelical Non-Intrusionists remained united under an uncompromising leadership,

> legislative interference appeared hopeless . . . But the case assumed a new aspect when we have reason to believe that a Settlement would be received as satisfactory . . . and when a large number of the most respectable of the Ministers pledged to Non-Intrusion declare their willingness to retreat from their present dangerous position, I am disposed to think that it may be prudent on the part of Government . . . to give them every facility consistent with the maintenance of sound Principles.[43]

It is possible that Graham overestimated the strength of the Forty. He was certainly dismayed at the extent of the eventual secession in 1843.[44] However, when he wrote to Melville in April 1842, it was not clear how far the Evangelical coalition had eroded, least of all to Chalmers and the other projectors of a Free Church. Many thought the internal Evangelical split to be even larger than it proved to be in reality. This was the apprehension even to those resolved on secession, if, as was now more than likely, no concessions were forthcoming from a government insistent on obedience to the primacy of statute law.

The calling of a convocation of 465 Evangelical ministers in November 1842 to plan secession was an enormous gamble, and not a few of the foot-soldiers were initially fearful and reluctant to follow the Edinburgh leadership. Some of the leaders were well aware of this feeling. For example, the social reformer Thomas Guthrie recorded his post-convocation relief that fears of the 'Edinburgh clergy or clique' had been overcome.[45] It took all the oratory and persuasion of Chalmers and his lieutenants to secure the immediate adhesion of 354 of the 465 who attended. It may have been sheer eloquence that prevailed with many. One Angus minister, who was later to become prominent in the Free Church, wrote to his wife of his current fears at the 'foolish decision of leaving the Establishment', and his belief that few had come up with the intention to secede, 'but they were fairly overborne by the speeches of the Edin[bu]r[gh] men'.[46]

However, the Evangelical rift was serious enough. By 1843 the Forty had grown to 260 ministers, or a little over a third of those accounted by McCosh as professing (or, so he considered, formerly professing) Evangelical principles.[47] Though departures to the new Free Church of Scotland were proportionally much heavier among younger ministers, probationers, the activist eldership and overseas missionaries, the number remaining was enough to ensure that two thirds of the parish ministry remained in what their Free opponents now called the 'Residuary' Church of Scotland. It was certainly enough to convince the Peel government to reward what they saw as their loyalty to the civil and religious establishment.

The clear objective of Muir and the Middle party leaders, Leishman and Alexander Simpson, minister of Kirknewton, was for government to desist from appeasement of the extreme Moderates, instead enacting a measure on the lines of Lord Aberdeen's bill of 1840, which more radical Evangelicals had then rejected as inadequate. It also helped their case that they were largely Conservative in politics, and Muir in particular was already in the confidence of leading Scottish Tories. But, significantly, they had little time for the judgements of the majority judges in the court of session, which they saw dismantling systematically what remained of the Church's ability to govern and discipline itself without judicial interference: Muir had privately described Lord President Hope's tone and language as 'undignified and violent'.[48]

Legislation to restrain a court of session in which some senior judges were seen as ultra-Moderates was regarded as important to retain waverers among the middlemen: McCosh identified a significant minority of around fifty of the group who had been 'flaming professors' of Non-Intrusion principles.[49] So in the immediate aftermath of the Disruption, Muir urged his conduit to the government, Lord Dalhousie, to promote legislation as soon as possible, and to ignore any objections from Moderates, expressing the fear that:

> If at the instance of the ultra law lords the clauses coinciding with our principles be struck out, and the dicta of cold and extreme *Moderatism* be embodied in the measure; there will be many who will be found to resist the measure thus changed – and in consequence of the change there will be not a few who will join the secession ranks.[50]

In July 1843, when Muir's wishes seem to be nearing achievement, he told Dalhousie that: 'The success [of the new Aberdeen's bill] . . . will appear as so much wrenched out of the hands of those who are viewed as the personifications of ultra-Moderatism.'[51] Despite his hopes, the promised legislation (Aberdeen's Scotch Benefices Act was eventually passed in 1845) did not bring the Free Church back, but it was seen to have served to prevent a feared additional secession and to consolidate the depleted Established Church.

The greatest losers were the Old Moderate leadership, who found themselves in a hollow majority, their old opponents gone but effectively excluded from government favour. Muir wrote at this time that 'rage at not having Government patronage at their disposal' was responsible for the opposition of Cook and MacFarlan to the revived Aberdeen bill, and that he had vetted already thirty vacant parishes for the government.[52] His influence was widely recognised. Lord Murray, who personally preferred the Moderates, wrote that 'Lord A[berdeen] is committed by his former bill and perhaps by assurances given privately . . . and advised by Dr Muir'.[53]

There was no road back to power for the Old Moderates. In the face of ferocious attack from the Free Church, which was resolved to erect a new Establishment to shadow and rival the old, they had little alternative but to close ranks with all who continued to adhere to the depleted Church of Scotland. Muir saw this as a paradoxical effect of the Disruption. 'I think of ultra-Moderatism the dominance is broken for ever.'[54] In a later comment, Lord Bute, lord high commissioner at the immediate post-Disruption General Assemblies, confirmed that the trend was continuing and party strife had largely gone from the Assembly, noting that:

> It is still the fashion to describe parties by the usual Church names of High-men and Moderates, but I do not think that there is much division except the common political division out of the house of those who are disposed to support authority or to support popular opinions.[55]

Perhaps the best epitaph for this ending to the old party system was written by that close observer and sometime participant in the politics of the Kirk, Lord Cockburn, though by entering it in his *Memorials*, in a passage on the decline of the Moderate *ancien régime*, he did call on some hindsight. However, it does fit well if applied to the post-Disruption situation, with one major new Presbyterian Church being created out of the Establishment, and another soon to be born in 1847 out of the heirs of the eighteenth- century secessions. In the new religious geography of Scotland the old party divisions were receding in the face of a reality in which strong and competing denominational loyalties, old and new, had created a situation in which internal division could be seen as self-indulgent and, indeed, irrelevant. 'A new Presbyterian revolution . . . brought out new men, and new dangers, and new popularity, with a necessary elevation of those who shone in it. But about this time the old thing was dead.'[56]

8

The Scottish Young Conservatives: A Local Case Study – Central Ayrshire Constituency, 1950–c.1979

I.G.C. Hutchison

I

One of the most striking features of British politics since 1945 has been the disparity between the performance of the Conservatives in Scotland and in England. In the latter, the Tories briskly recovered from the serious setback of the 1945 general election, and in all but one of the thirteen elections held between 1950 and 1992, they won more seats than Labour. In contrast, the party peaked in Scotland in the 1955 election, when it won a majority of the seats. Thereafter it entered into a steady and apparently irreversible decline, until in 1997 the Conservatives won 36 per cent of the total vote in England, but only 17.5 per cent in Scotland, with not one Tory MP returned for Scotland.

The reasons for the Tories' eclipse in Scotland have naturally attracted much academic analysis. Explanations have fallen into two broad, if slightly overlapping, categories: one stresses policy defaults as the key factor, while a second focuses on changing cultural and social processes.[1] While these aspects undoubtedly have a degree of persuasiveness, one factor not much stressed in these discussions is party organisation. Yet the centrality of the organisational reforms implemented in England after 1945 to the Tories' recovery there has been emphasised by numerous studies. The creation of an efficient, well-funded organisation based on a mass membership, and the democratisation of the social composition of both the grass-roots membership and MPs, were crucial pillars in the Conservative resurgence.[2] The failure to carry out an equivalent root-and-branch modernisation of party machinery in Scotland after 1945 had grave implications for the future of Conservatism there.[3]

One of the main props in the Tories' English revival was the Young Conservatives movement, set up in 1945. Within four years, 160,000 had joined the movement, and it soon became the largest youth political movement in any democratic country. Its contribution to Conservative success in the succeeding quarter-century is held to be threefold. Firstly, it allowed the Tories to project themselves as a rejuvenated party, generating the message that the future lay with the Conservatives, not Labour. Secondly, it afforded the party a cadre of electoral shock troops who campaigned vigorously in most constituencies. Thirdly, it provided an excellent training ground for future MPs and local government councillors. Of the former, Linda Chalker is probably the most prominent example.[4]

This essay looks at the record of the youth movement in Scotland as a means of illustrating the pertinence of organisational factors to the crisis of Scottish Conservatism in the later twentieth century. It will primarily concentrate on the case of Central Ayrshire constituency, but that experience will be related to the general Scottish one.

There are several good reasons for regarding Central Ayrshire as almost custom-built for a successful Young Conservative movement.[5] The constituency was formed in the 1948 constituency redistribution out of three existing seats, namely North Ayrshire & Bute, Ayr Burghs and Kilmarnock. The first two had since at least 1900 been solidly Tory, and the third had usually also been Conservative.[6] The constituency disappeared in the redistribution preceding the 1983 general election.

Central Ayrshire's electoral trajectory between 1950 and 1979 closely reflected that of Scotland as a whole, that is, a steady erosion in support for the Conservatives and the concomitant dominance of Labour. It was initially highly marginal: Labour held it in the 1950 and 1951 elections, but the Conservatives won it in 1955 – the party's only Scottish gain – then Labour recaptured it in 1959, and held it thereafter. In the four elections in the 1950s, the majorities were always under 2,000, but from 1964, when Labour won by well over 5,000 votes, the Tories remorselessly lost ground. In 1979, the last contest for the seat, Labour's lead was a little under 12,000, and the Tories received only 29 per cent of the vote.

The constituency's social composition promised a strong Conservative base. There was a prosperous farming belt centred on Dunlop parish, while Troon was an affluent commuting town for Glasgow business and professional people. Traditional heavy industries present in the constituency included steel, shipbuilding yards, iron founding, textiles and railway workshops. There was, however, virtually no coal mining. Just outside the constituency boundary lay the massive ICI chemical plant at Ardeer, employing 13,000 in the 1950s, a good number of whom travelled from the Irvine and Kilwinning areas.[7]

The adult Conservative constituency association in its heyday in the early 1950s was among the biggest in the west of Scotland, with over 5,000 members (roughly one third of the party's vote). Hence, there were plenty of committed Conservatives who, one might assume, would influence their children's politics. The association was also financially prosperous: it was one of the bigger constituency contributors to central party coffers. Therefore, financial support for the youth wing would not be a problem.

The construction, beginning in 1968, of Scotland's fifth and last New Town at Irvine had a major impact on the constituency. By 1978, the population of the area had grown from 34,000 in 1966 to 58,000, with the expansion mostly occurring in the last five years of that period.[8] Glasgow's working class provided most of the New Town's intake, which might suggest why the seat became a Labour stronghold. But the constituency had shifted irrevocably to Labour by 1966, long before the New Town could have a significant electoral impact. Moreover, the advent of the New Town was at first regarded by the Tories as, politically speaking, an opportunity and not a disaster. The leadership believed that removing Glasgow's skilled workers from the environment of 'Red Clydeside' would dissolve their traditional Labour allegiance, and render them susceptible to the attractions of Conservatism.[9] This assumption was reinforced by the experience of England. At a Young Conservative conference held in 1961 in Largs, coincidentally close to Irvine, a leading English Tory asserted that young voters had helped the party to return an MP in every New Town in England.[10] Naturally, the younger generation, less rooted in the militant political traditions of 'Red Clydeside', was seen as most likely to turn to the Conservatives. Accordingly, local Tories were relaxed about the selection of Stewarton as an overspill town (a smaller version of New Towns) in 1958. They welcomed the advent of 4,000 Glaswegians with enthusiasm, as the burgh would receive the best skilled citizens of that city.[11]

II

The forerunner in interwar Scotland to the Young Conservatives had been the Junior Unionists, who proved to be active and successful.[12] In 1930 there were probably 30,000 members. Junior Unionists participated in election campaigns and carried out propaganda work. Training in political knowledge and skills was offered at weekend schools and public-speaking courses, and in 1938 they held their own conference. Two Junior Unionists won seats on Glasgow City Council in 1936, indicating a high degree of political commitment.[13] Thus, the party had shown itself adroit in securing the involvement of young people, and there was a core of experience at both national and constituency levels to develop the post-1945 youth wing.

In 1946, following up on a resolution carried at the previous year's annual conference, the Central Council of the Scottish Unionist Association (hereafter SUA) agreed to form a youth organisation, open to those aged between seventeen and thirty.[14] The 1948 SUA annual conference passed a motion urging all constituency parties to set up 'Junior Unionist' sections, and also stressing the importance of harnessing 'the enthusiasm and vigour' of the younger generation 'to the full' in preparing for the next general election.[15]

In December 1950, exactly one year after being formed itself, the Central Ayrshire Conservative association began setting up three Young Conservative branches. This commendable show of speed augured well for future support and encouragement by the senior body.[16] At first, growth was rapid: by early 1951 there were seven branches active in the constituency.[17]

Despite the initial afflatus, however, decay rapidly set in, and throughout 1953 branch activity dwindled. By May, three branches were defunct, and soon another branch was struggling.[18] Contrary to natural expectations, the Tories' capture of the seat in the 1955 election did not stimulate a surge in recruits; instead, Beith branch closed by November.[19] Indeed, in 1956 Kilwinning scrapped its policy of holding joint meetings with other branches because most had disbanded. By October 1956, there were only two functioning branches – Kilwinning and Irvine – and elsewhere there was 'only the scantiest contact' between the Young Conservatives and their seniors.[20]

There was no significant improvement until 1959, when at least two branches were relaunched. This renaissance, however, proved to be short-lived, as in June 1961 there were only two branches in existence once again.[21] At the start of 1965, one of these two was experiencing severe difficulties, and only Eglinton – a merger of the Kilwinning and Irvine sections – seemed robust. Six months later, it was intimated that the constituency's Young Conservative organisation had been disbanded.[22] There followed a two-year period of inaction, until February 1968, when two branches were stated to be up and running, and others followed. However, this recovery was yet again transitory, and by 1970 few branches were flourishing. Stewarton was 'in some difficulty', Troon faced problems of low attendance at meetings, and Dalry had a total membership of nine, although the ever-reliable Eglinton branch was functioning effectively. But even this branch soon succumbed to the general malaise, and by the end of 1972 it had fallen to about twenty members.[23]

The mid-1970s represented the nadir for the Young Conservatives. At the constituency association's AGM early in 1976, the party was 'very gloomy' about its youth wing, which was 'at rock bottom', and subsequently it was revealed that there were no active branches in the seat.[24] In October 1976, a brief flutter of life was injected into the movement, when the Irvine branch re-formed. But one year later the constituency association's agent intimated to the SUA headquarters that 'the Young Conservatives here have disintegrated at the moment', optimistically adding that efforts were in hand to revive them.[25] Indeed, in late 1978, Irvine had a 'nucleus' of six members, but in September 1979 there was reported to be very little support outside Irvine and Eglinton, and at the AGM three months later, no member, apart from the executive committee, turned up. On learning this, the senior body resolved that 'the agent would try to find out if the [Young Conservative] Branch was still operating, what programme was being followed and exactly when meetings were supposed to take place'.[26] There are no further references to the Young Conservatives in the parent body's records.

With such a flickering presence, it is no surprise that the membership of the Central Ayrshire Young Tories was never very high. Total numbers are not easy to establish, but in the 1950s the Kilwinning branch usually contained between fifty and sixty members. In the early 1970s, Eglinton had overall numbers in the twenties, and in 1978, Irvine could count on only six members. These figures might be extrapolated to suggest that there were somewhere between 100 and 200 members for the whole constituency in the early 1950s, falling to perhaps between 50 and 100 in the 1970s. This compares poorly with the adult section. In the 1950s, as noted above, Central Ayrshire Tories had over 5,000 members. On a proportional basis, Young Conservative membership should have been around 2,000, rather than the actual total of 200–300.[27] In the 1970s, Troon alone had over 2,000 paid-up senior members, yet the Young Conservative branch existed only intermittently and then struggled to get into double figures.

Moreover, membership did not necessarily mean active involvement. Low attendance at meetings was a recurring theme. Kilwinning complained throughout the 1950s about this, with no more than ten or twelve people (about one fifth of the membership) attending meetings. In the early 1970s Eglinton branch meetings attracted between four and ten people. The draft 1975 annual report for Eglinton noted that there had been 'major disasters because of the general indifference on the part of members, and also the reluctance of YCs in general to pay bills and subscriptions'. That year only the committee members had paid their subscriptions.[28]

Central Ayrshire's long struggle to establish a viable youth wing was replicated across the country. For Scotland as a whole, growth at the outset was rapid; within four years of its inception in 1946 the movement had around 200 branches. But thereafter progress faltered. In 1951 there were 131 branches in western Scotland, yet in 1953 this had fallen to 80. By 1960 there were 116 branches in all of Scotland, half of the 1950 total. Something of a recovery then took place, and by late 1961 the western total had risen from 62 to 75, still 5 below the 1953 tally.[29] Thereafter information on the global branch figure is not readily available, but other indicators suggest there was no substantial growth. For example, a 1972 survey of the six South-western constituencies found low or non-existent membership not just in solidly Labour South Ayrshire, but also in the ultra-safe Tory Galloway and North Ayrshire. In the more marginal Tory Ayr constituency, Prestwick branch (socially as well as physically very close to Troon) had only seventeen members.[30]

In the peak period of the early 1950s, Scottish Young Conservative members numbered about 11,000, but this dropped as branches folded. In 1960, there were 6,500 Young Tories, and a major recruitment campaign drove numbers up to 8,000 in 1962.[31] But these statistics have to be put into a broader perspective. As with Central Ayrshire, these are very low figures when set against the senior movement. In the early 1950s, there were around 150,000 of the latter in the west of Scotland, but instead of the pro rata figure of perhaps 50,000–60,000 Young Conservatives, there were in fact only 5,000–6,000. In 1968, a period of recovery for the party, Glasgow had around 300 members, a remarkably small total in a city with just under one million inhabitants.

Indeed, Glasgow's figure is, proportionately, considerably worse than Central Ayrshire's, whose membership, with a tenth of the city's population, was a quarter of Glasgow's. Further, compared to England and Wales, the Scottish Young Tories appear very weak. A British-wide recruitment campaign in 1956 netted 27,751 new adherents in England and Wales, but in Scotland only 1,588 – just about one half of the proportionate figure.[32] Moreover, historically, these are low figures for Scotland. At the high point of 1950, membership in the west of Scotland was around 5,500 in 112 branches, whereas in 1930 there had been 16,000 members in 144 branches in the same area's Junior Unionists.[33]

Retaining members proved very difficult everywhere: the problem was acknowledged as early as 1953, and the trend persisted. Despite gaining some 1,500 additional members in 1957, by 1959 the overall total was no larger than in 1956. In 1961, 3,200 new recruits signed up, but the net increase for that year was only 1,500.[34] This large turnover suggests that little politicisation of members could occur, and mobilising active engagement in day-to-day politics would be very difficult.

The size of Central Ayrshire branches was broadly in line with the Scottish norm. In the mid-1950s, the average membership in urban branches was put at 59 in the east and 30 in the west, and in rural branches, 30 for both areas. In the 1960s, a branch membership – urban and rural – of between 50 and 60 was regarded as standard. In 1968, a survey of 6 out of Glasgow's 10 branches revealed membership totals between 15 and 68, and averaging 33.[35]

Low participation was not unique to Central Ayrshire. Attendance at meetings everywhere was much lower than nominal membership and quite early on became a topic of concern. A survey in 1953 of 25 western area branches found that only one had an average attendance over 30, 9 had between 20 and 30, and 15 (60 per cent of the sample) between 10 and 20.[36] This, it should be noted, was a period when the Young Conservatives were still quite buoyant. Participation in the various membership campaigns was highly variable: in 1963, some areas, notably Central, Dunbartonshire, Ayrshire and Borders, showed no enthusiasm, and Glasgow was very reluctant. Three years later, Glasgow found it difficult to induce branches to join a new recruitment drive. Efforts to establish a newsletter for the south-west region in 1966–7 had to be abandoned because no branch submitted any material for inclusion.[37]

The party's leadership repeatedly addressed their youth movement's recurrent difficulties. As early as 1952, the SUA managers felt it desirable to revamp the Young Tories, believing that there were too many branches, and in 1954, they discussed the 'considerable drop' in Young Conservative membership from the previous year. They also noted that while better-organised associations had 'small active groups', elsewhere little existed.[38] In 1957, they heard that the youth wing was not as strong as it might be, and in 1963, a substantial input of expertise was made, with seven agents installed in the west of Scotland alone to help the Young Conservatives, who were herded together into groupings of regional federations. This was recognition that small isolated branches needed a wider framework and more effective direction. Yet nearly two years later, they were 'shocked' at the low levels of membership revealed in a survey.[38]

III

It would appear obvious that the primary role of the Young Conservatives was to undertake political work. There were three general areas in which they were expected to contribute: electioneering; acquiring and then widely disseminating a knowledge of Conservative principles; and recruiting future candidates and party activists.

Central Ayrshire Young Tories showed some serious interest in election work. In 1949, a 'commando group' was formed with the object of heckling Labour speakers.[40] In the 1959 election, part of Irvine was canvassed by them, and a special effort was made to identify younger voters, while in the 1970 contest, they worked a specific part of the seat. In one of the 1974 elections, they were again engaged in canvassing the constituency and complained bitterly about the managerial inefficiencies of the campaign. Additionally, they participated in local council election campaigns at various times.[41]

Outwith election periods, however, political commitment operated at low-level intensity, and there was noticeably very little interest in the educational and training elements. Only twelve out of forty-four members went from Kilwinning branch to a Young Conservatives rally at nearby West Kilbride in 1950, a time when enthusiasm for the movement was at its highest. In 1953 the branch agreed to have only one meeting in four dedicated to political matters, and later that year it abandoned even this limited arrangement, all its meetings becoming purely a social or club event, with table tennis, dominoes and cards available. Also in 1953, the branch decided that there was no interest among members in attending the Scottish weekend school at Dunblane. Unsurprisingly, Kilwinning's 1953–4 annual report stated that 'little actual political work has been done this year'.[42] It should be borne in mind that this was the most successful and enduring Young Conservatives branch in the seat.

There was a marked disinclination to take the Conservative case to a wider audience. As early as 1951, Kilwinning branch agreed that heckling was 'more or less a waste of time', despite having formed the 'commando group' two years earlier for that specific purpose, and in that same year no member would undertake any public speaking.[43] Branches were prepared to have debates with other branches of the Young Conservatives but seemed reluctant to go outside their own political confines.[44] This attitude obviously inhibited conversion prospects.

The later 1960s saw a wide range of challenges to orthodoxy, both in domestic and foreign policy. Yet Central Ayrshire Young Conservatives steadfastly ignored such issues. The year 1969 was a year of intense political crises, both at home ('In Place of Strife', Ulster, East African Asian refugees) and abroad (Vietnam, South Africa, Rhodesia/Zimbabwe). At this momentous juncture, the chair of the constituency association gave an address to the party's youth wing. He spoke not on the pressing issues of the moment, but on his collection of snuff-boxes.[45]

In the early 1970s, however, there was a brief flurry of engagement with political issues. When these did emerge they cannot be regarded as extreme, so that it is unlikely that *outré* ideological standpoints caused the problems experienced by the movement. The response to the threat in 1972 to close Glengarnock steelworks, a major local employer, suggested that moderate opinions prevailed. At this point, the Heath government was still fully committed to an unfettered free-market approach, under which 'lame duck' businesses were denied state assistance. Eglinton Young Conservatives protested vigorously against the closure, urging state intervention if necessary to keep the plant open.[46] This moderate stance was underlined the following year, when Eglinton resolved not to elect Enoch Powell as honorary vice-president. At the same time, the branch sent a message to Ted Heath, pledging full support for his economic and industrial policies, which by now were much more pragmatically centrist.[47] There is, then, no sign of support for Thatcherite views, which many have argued lost the Tories ground in Scotland. It is the case that Eglinton decided to press the case for restoring capital punishment on the sitting Labour MP, first testing local opinion through opinion surveys and letters to the local press.[48] But it can be argued that this was not a particularly extreme line to adopt at the time – indeed the majority of the public appeared to agree with the Young Conservatives.

Throughout the quarter-century of its existence, the activities of the Central Ayrshire Young Tories were preponderantly non-political, a pattern established from the outset. The very first committee set up by Kilwinning, the constituency's pioneer Young Conservatives branch, was a catering committee, which was in charge of providing refreshments and, perhaps unsurprisingly, consisted of four female members. Kilwinning's 1950–1 syllabus had two components. First, there was a weekly evening for darts and table tennis. Second, from October to February there were monthly meetings, two of which were political – a talk on the empire, and one on the Young Conservatives' organisation. The remaining events were purely social: a whist drive, a dance, a theatre outing, plus a Christmas social and a coach trip. The main thrust of the minutes of the branch across the 1950s concerns organising dances and other social events, with politics very much a sideshow.[49]

This pattern persisted. In 1961, Troon Young Conservatives inserted a recruiting advertisement in the local press. It began: 'Make the Most of Life. New Friends! New Interests! For Politics and Pleasure there is no finer Organisation.' Under the heading 'Join in the Fun', it advertised forthcoming events, namely a 'Big Walk' at Dunlop, a barn dance at Kilwinning and a grand barbecue on Troon beach.[50] There is virtually no allusion to any political work being undertaken by the branch. The 1966–7 programme for Eglinton had seventeen meetings, of which only two could generously be construed as political: a talk on 'The Art of Public Speaking', and a visit to the Kilmarnock Young Conservatives. The same branch's spring 1972 syllabus was, to put it charitably, light on politics, as it consisted of a film trip to Glasgow, a ten-pin bowling evening, a speaker from the Samaritans, an 'own entertainment' evening, 'Going for a Song', a joint meeting with Kilmarnock Young Tories and a 'Cider Shindig'.[51]

The use of social events to lure new members was tried on several occasions. In 1970, Troon reported a problem of poor attendance, 'but discotheques would be arranged at times when those away at universities and colleges would be able to attend'.[52] In 1972, Eglinton ascribed its success in enlisting twenty new members to holding a 'Miss Eglinton Beauty Queen' competition. The last effort to reinvigorate the Young Tories, in 1976, consisted of a plan to meet every week, with the alternate week being held at a new sports centre, where mixed football teams were mooted.[53]

In all these respects, Central Ayrshire seemed a microcosm of Scotland. Electioneering was widely carried out across the country. In the 1950 general election, eastern area members addressed public meetings, heckled opponents and acted as stewards at party rallies. In the elections of 1959 and 1964, Glasgow Young Tories were apparently very active campaigners in the city contests, and they also did effective work in the 1959 municipal elections.[54]

Interest in political meetings was universally restricted. In 1951, 180 delegates attended the movement's annual conference, but by 1955 this had fallen to 70. As each branch was entitled to send up to six representatives, the notional maximum attendance in 1951 was 1,200, and in 1955, 600, indicating that only about 15 per cent of the possible total turned up. This pattern continued in the 1960s: very few eastern section members attended the 1963 conference, and in 1967 attendance overall was poor. Moreover, only fourteen branches submitted resolutions to the 1968 event.[55] In 1955, the eastern division of the movement reported that there had been very little political activity throughout the region that year.[56] A decade afterwards, the south-western grouping found little support for political discussions, and three years later it was still bemoaning the lack of interest.[57] Glasgow was equally perturbed in 1968 that the monthly political meetings were not popular with members.[58]

Almost from the start, the SUA leadership was concerned to instil both political knowledge and leadership skills into the Young Conservatives. The verdict on the 1949 Young Conservatives' conference was that 'the material of the speeches showed a lack of knowledge of the policy of the Unionist party'. In 1958, concern was expressed at 'deteriorating' debating standards at the conference, while in 1967 the quality of debate was 'extremely low'. In 1964 the complaint was made that the Young Tories were 'far from efficient in their political education and in their ability to obtain political literature'.[59]

Various devices were used to encourage political knowledge. The common ground was that they were not particularly successful, indicating a limited appetite among Young Tories for politics *per se*. Weekend schools were a central pillar in this strategy, and their record is typical. In 1949, the western area meeting in Rothesay drew 160, yet four years later this had slumped to 60. Only eleven members – 0.2 per cent of a total membership of around 5,000 – attended a western area school in 1953, despite the stress placed on its importance for training party speakers. Meanwhile, as early as 1950, the eastern area had to abandon a projected two-day school because of lack of support. The minimal role played by politics in the weekend schools' programme was signposted in 1957, when it was decided not to have any discussion groups at the event.[60] A decade on, little had changed. Glasgow federation decided in 1966 that there was no point in running its own school, as only eight members had attended the previous year's meeting. Two years later, the city party organised a one-day event that was poorly attended, with hardly any branches taking the trouble to submit resolutions.[61]

The lack of support for weekend schools had a further debilitating effect beyond the failure to inculcate Conservative values among members. These courses had a specific objective of giving guidance to branch officials on the discharge of their duties and of fostering leadership qualities among them. In this respect they clearly failed, and there are repeated allusions among the senior party organisations to the need to build a stronger leadership spirit among young Tory office bearers.[62]

Another approach was to hold study groups on topical issues. These were immensely popular in England but failed to take off in Scotland, as the experiences of the federation of Ayrshire Young Conservatives illustrate. In 1961, the federation organised study groups, but two of the five component constituencies – including the safest Tory seat, North Ayrshire – did not participate. A year later, only one association (Kilmarnock) expressed any interest in a second round of study groups. The successor south-western body tried from its inception in 1965 to instigate political discussion, initially selecting the somewhat less than vital topic of 'Tourism in Scotland' for consideration. Yet within fifteen months of this initiative, it was admitted that little political discussion had in fact taken place.[63]

In 1960, SUA headquarters urged constituency agents to discourage Young Conservative branches from accepting invitations to debates with Labour's Young Socialists, and they also warned the youth wing against issuing invitations to organisations with an African interest, as these were often left-wing. In late 1967, with the challenge of Scottish nationalism growing to its first great crescendo, the Young Conservatives' south-western regional executive decided against holding a debate with the Scottish National Party youth wing. One individual voted in favour, while twelve opposed and five abstained.[64] This hardly speaks of a politically confident and motivated movement. Significantly, a report on the 1964 general election contest in Dumfriesshire gloomily commented that whereas the Labour party had sent thirty of its youth wing to attend every Conservative meeting, it was 'doubtful' if the Young Conservatives could have reciprocated.[65]

The ideal of the youth sector as a recruiting ground for a rising generation of Tory politicians on a larger stage did bear fruit, as in England. In Central Ayrshire, the candidate in the 1979 contest had been an active Young Tory earlier in the decade. Elsewhere, similar trends existed: three Young Conservatives stood in the general election of 1950, admittedly in the virtually impregnable Labour fortresses of Maryhill, Govan and Airdrie & Coatbridge. In 1957, three of six Young Conservatives who contested municipal wards in Glasgow were elected as Progressive party councillors, and, somewhat improbably, two members were elected as councillors in Wick that year. Six Young Tories ran in the 1959 general election, and at least ten were chosen to fight in the 1966 election.[66] Several future parliamentary notables were active in the youth movement, for example, Malcolm Rifkind, Allan Stewart, John Corrie and Michael Hirst.

All across Scotland, as in Central Ayrshire, social affairs were given priority over politics. At the end of a recruiting drive in 1954, the attendance of 140 at the final meeting was deemed 'creditable', but it was ruefully noted that another eighty turned up solely for the post-meeting dance, thereby denying themselves the opportunity of listening to an address from Lord Home.[67] A decade later, similar priorities prevailed. In 1963, a Young Conservative requested that the end of conference rally should in future be brought forward, 'to avoid the too early departure of delegates wishing to change for the evening dance'.[68]

Model syllabi produced by the national Young Conservatives' executive in 1965 quite closely followed the Central Ayrshire format. For a small town (presumably akin to Central Ayrshire), there could be a Tramps Ball, a Christmas frolic, debates with the senior association and the Young Farmers, and a study of a local topic. The model for a large town had two political evenings out of eight, alongside items such as a spaghetti-eating contest.[69] In the real world, too, there was convergence with central Ayrshire's pattern. So, about three quarters of the meetings held by Dumbarton Young Tories in 1965 were strictly apolitical.[70] In 1965–6 – an election year – the south-western area federation was preoccupied with organising a Summer Fayre (sic), and branches were absorbed in running golf, tennis and badminton tournaments.[71]

When the Young Tories issued a promotional leaflet, entitled 'What Do We Do?' in 1964, it is significant that the revising committee promoted paragraph three in the draft to the lead position. This paragraph read: 'We hold parties, dances and many social and sporting activities such as barbecues and walks.'[72]

Golf competitions, spring fairs, whist drives and outings seemed to predominate in the minutes of branches of the Young Conservatives at every point in time. Reviewing its activities in 1963, the year before the general election that toppled the party from office, the Ayrshire Young Conservatives Federation admitted that, while 'nothing political had received any great support from the branches', the car treasure hunt and the barbecue had been very successful.[73] In 1964–5, Glasgow Young Tories did canvass during the 1964 general election, but otherwise they were preoccupied with social events: a ramble, a barn dance, a visit to the Edinburgh tattoo and a tennis competition, with a public-speaking contest the sole vaguely political activity.[74] Not for them an agonised post mortem on why the party had lost power after thirteen years in office. It is perhaps typical of this mindset that the only minuted note of dissent in the south-western regional committee's history came in 1967, over a proposal to hire Acker Bilk's band to play at a Young Conservative function at Glasgow's Locarno dance hall.[75] Questions of current politics evoked no irreconcilable divisions of opinion.

The recurring attempts by the parent bodies to redirect the Young Conservatives from social events to more strictly political concerns clearly indicates a mistaken order of priorities. In 1954, the SUA Western area stressed the necessity of having a balanced syllabus 'to ensure that the branch had sufficient political activity, and was not filled up with social functions'.[76] A decade later, progress in this direction seemed minute, as the SUA declared that a major objective was to 'increase the political activity of YC branches' and to 'encourage political leadership'.[77]

IV

The pull of competing attractions was openly acknowledged by insiders as a major reason for the branches' unsuccessful record. Central Ayrshire senior Tories were told that in rural parts Young Farmers Clubs mopped up the energies of young people, while 'in populated industrial areas it was known that evening classes and youth clubs were the outlets for youth activities, and in the residential districts the young people were studying, to the exclusion of political activities'.[78] Nationally, similar arguments were deployed: National Service was charged with taking away branch leaders, while others were said to be too preoccupied with studying for their careers to be active in branches.[79] But these factors are not entirely adequate, given that they equally applied in England but were combated more effectively.

Among possible reasons for the failure of the Young Conservatives in Scotland, at least part lay in the fact that Lord Woolton's English organisational reforms were not adopted in Scotland.[80] Woolton's transformation of England's grass-roots organisation involved the creation of mass, broad-based constituency associations. These were necessitated by the imposition laid on constituencies to remit very high sums of money in order to fulfil HQ quotas, over and above meeting the costs of local expenses, as well as fighting elections. In Scotland, however, this cash-driven impetus to expand membership and to intensify constituency activities did not apply. The payment of quotas to the Scottish HQ were, unlike England, effectively voluntary. Moreover, they were, by English standards, set at extremely low levels. In 1959–60, contributions from the SUA's western area, covering thirty-nine seats, totalled £180.50 and came from only four constituencies, an average of £45 each.[81] By contrast, in England and Wales, as early as around 1950, constituencies had to contribute over a third of a million pounds – around £650 per seat.[82]

An additional complication was the Scottish Tory party's tradition of non-participation in local government politics. Council elections were contested by variously titled front bodies that had been constructed after World War I as a broad anti-Labour alliance.[83] This approach was generally adhered to until the late 1960s, whereafter Conservatives very gradually entered local government elections directly, without fig leaves. This policy meant that the financial pressures on constituencies were heavily reduced. Apart from a general election every four or five years, there was no election expenditure.

The result of these two factors was that in Scotland funding was not an ever-present issue. Constituency associations had little motive to be politically active beyond the quinquennial parliamentary elections, and in particular they lacked any incentive to develop and expand organisational structures. Hence, whist drives, dances and the like, rather than political activity, formed the staple of branch and constituency work. The overriding necessity in England of galvanising all sections of support, most especially the energetic and enthusiastic younger age groups, was never felt in Scotland. It was not until the end of the 1960s that significantly higher quotas were imposed and made mandatory. But even in 1971, Scottish constituency quotas were about one half of the English figure; moreover, just over 50 per cent of the total target was actually met.[84] By this time, however, the local parties, etiolated by twenty years of inactivity, found it difficult to meet these targets, so compounding the electoral and organisational difficulties.

To a considerable degree, this explains the indifference shown by Central Ayrshire senior Tories to the junior wing. In England, Woolton had made the development of the Young Conservatives a matter of high priority, but in Scotland there was no equivalent powerful figure to stir sluggish constituencies into action. In 1955, a leading Scottish Young Tory contended that the crucial difference between the two countries' youth movements was that in Scotland there was never such 'a great force and impetus thrown behind our movement'.[85]

In 1956, 300 Central Ayrshire senior members were asked to submit the names of prospective Young Tory members, and a grand total of six (2 per cent) responded.[86] Likewise, in 1954 Kilwinning Young Conservatives noted that it was difficult to approach senior members in the burgh for assistance in enrolling new members, as many of them were unknown to the youth wing.[87] The lassitude evinced by the senior body is the more remarkable in that it often acknowledged the benefits of a strong youth section. At the association's 1961 AGM, there was admiration at 'so much enthusiasm and ability among the young people'. Yet fifteen years later, the need for closer liaison with the Young Conservatives was deemed essential 'if we are to have young people involved in our political activities'.[88] Also in the mid-1970s, the constituency chair remarked that for too long the Young Tories had been treated as mere electoral fodder and given no reciprocal power.[89]

The same attitude applied in the wider Scottish party. At the inception of the Young Conservatives, the leadership of the senior movement decreed that they should have representation on constituency and area bodies.[90] Yet this policy was rarely adhered to. In 1955, the West of Scotland Young Conservatives' leading office bearer complained that: 'The average Senior branch chairman doesn't bother much about his Juniors; what is more important, the average senior branch member sometimes scarcely seems to know that we exist.'[91] The following year, the SUA Executive urged constituency associations to address the inadequate presence of representatives of the youth wing in senior bodies. In 1958, the Young Tories called for representation at all levels and on committees, as happened in England. In 1960, they were still complaining about the lack of interest shown by the party in them, and the SUA western council minuted that they should be given a full part in constituency as well as central party organisation. But in 1963, the SUA Executive again stressed in striking language the need to encourage young people 'to regard themselves as an integral part of the party.'[92]

An additional complication was that non-involvement in council politics adversely affected the party's appeal to younger people. As the Tories in England – and Labour in Scotland – showed, experience in local government was an invaluable training ground for those with parliamentary aspirations. The Tory youth wing in Central Ayrshire had always been enthusiastic about electioneering, so the lack of opportunities for this kind of activity had a demotivating effect. They were from the start keen to fight council elections: they first pressed the local party in 1952 to contest them,[93] and did so subsequently whenever the anti-Labour parties left wards uncontested. In 1970, the parent association declined to intervene directly in council elections. The Young Conservatives then offered to pay the expenses of one Conservative candidate out of their own funds. If this offer were rejected, they would take no part at all in electoral work. At the 1972 council elections, Eglinton Young Tories reiterated that they would only work for Conservative candidates.[94]

Central Ayrshire Young Tories, like their parent body, presented a quintessential image of the Scottish bourgeoisie. The movement's restricted class identity was explicitly acknowledged in 1970, when Troon branch announced that it would not be active while universities and colleges were in session.[95] At this time, formal higher education was primarily the preserve of the AB social groups. Little that the Central Ayrshire Young Tories did was aimed at social inclusiveness, but rather reinforced distinctively middle-class manners and pursuits. Furthermore, from the middle 1960s these were becoming ever more archaic, even to the younger members of that class.

The sporting and leisure activities of the Young Conservatives were geared overwhelmingly to the tastes of the solid middle classes. Tennis and badminton tournaments were regularly held, but virtually no football was played until 1976. Significantly, this occurred in Irvine, where the influence of the New Town's population may have been greater than elsewhere. Social occasions were exclusively middle-class in form. Car treasure hunts in the later 1950s and early 1960s were only possible for that class, as widespread working-class car ownership did not occur until a decade or so later. Functions like the barbecue held on Troon beach in 1965, and wine and cheese parties, were at the time the embodiment of specifically middle-class leisure habits. Dances were often quite formal affairs. The women's section of the constituency association deprecated the 10/– (50p) ticket price for the Young Conservatives' ball in 1951, arguing that for many young people this was 'too expensive', and that 'no section of the community could feel excluded by the cost involved' from any Tory party social function.[96]

Central Ayrshire simply mirrored the whole Scottish movement. Socially, the membership was similarly restricted. In late 1964, the Young Conservatives organiser delivered a scathing review of the movement. She noted that branches were 'almost entirely' middle-class, and quite failed to attract 'the top and bottom of society'. This critique was substantiated by an observation in 1963 that the Glasgow Kelvingrove branch members were almost entirely drawn from one or two neighbouring streets that had much in common. The model syllabus for a small town drawn up by the national executive as late as 1965 suggested debates with the Young Farmers Club – the rural middle class meeting their urban counterparts.[97] Dinner dances featured prominently everywhere, as did whist drives, and both were unlikely to attract working-class young people. Glasgow decided in 1954 to hold lunchtime meetings to boost support. These were held in the city centre, effectively drawing on business and professional people who worked nearby, but out of reach of young factory workers in the city's industrial areas.[98] Supper clubs, a kindred venture tried afterwards, once again were targeted at financially comfortable middle-class people.[99]

This starchy middle-class lifestyle became increasingly unattractive from the middle 1960s, when the so-called 'counterculture' emerged among the young. This expressed itself, among other ways, in informality of dress and manners, sexual permissiveness and an interest in British and American rock music. In this changing climate, which affected all classes, the Young Tories must have seemed dinosaurs. It was only in 1967 that they agreed to abolish the formal dress (dinner jacket, etc.) rule for conference dances, but with the proviso that casual wear was not permitted. Also in 1967, compulsory church attendance at south-west regional weekend schools was ended. But a follow-up resolution to scrap 'morality patrols' at the schools was rejected.[100] They were also slow to identify with the new cultural icons, rather clinging to older, more sedate ones. Glasgow Young Conservatives drew up a list of entertainers who might be asked to open their 1967 spring fair, among them the Alexander brothers, Andy Stewart and Kenneth Mackellar.[101] The choice of these epitomes of Scottish cultural kitsch, already the objects of derision for most younger Scots, suggests why the movement struggled to recruit.

9

Thatcherism, Civil Society and the Road to Home Rule: Scotland 1980–1997

RICHARD J. FINLAY

The Scots MPs
Danderin ae day a wuid alowe
Wi purslane-pink an hyacinthine blue
Seein the springtime gar the gowans grow
An mak the grumly face o Scotland new,
I heard wee Abi say, in her bairny wye,
'If you're in the country of a wolf or tod,
You musn't dress like a rabbit'. 'Aye.
Ye may weel say that again, by God!'
I thocht, 'The She-wolf rages ower this land,
Gars crunch hail industries atween her teeth,
Lays waste wir touns an fields an ilka hand,
Maks devastation frae Kintyre tae Leith
An tae scare her frae our bounds, our people keep
A puckle rabbits dressed tae look like sheep.'
Stanley Fisher

It might be assumed that because an event in the present can be said to be of historic importance that the same event has long-established roots in history. This would appear to be common sense. Surely an event of great importance could not suddenly transpire as if from nowhere without first having built up the necessary historical momentum to burst upon the present. The creation of Scotland's parliament in 1998 is a case in point. According to Winnie Ewing, the 'Mother of the House': 'The Scottish Parliament closed in 1707, is hereby reconvened.'[1] Implicit in this statement was the assumption that the intervening period between 1707 and 1997 was not the norm, and that the resumption of the Scottish parliament was a reassertion of the continuity of pre-1707 Scottish history. Yet, as Iain Hutchison reminds us, the demand for home rule was not as dominant a feature of the political history of twentieth-century Scotland as has sometimes been suggested.[2] Unlike Ireland, where nationalism has been the predominant historical theme for most of the modern era, Scotland does not have a strong vein of nationalist historiography to mine in order to explain why it achieved a large measure of self-government by the late twentieth century.[3] In short, contemporary Scotland's political destination seems to be at odds with much of the prevailing direction of Scottish history since 1707. For historians who like to stress the continuity of historical change, the dramatic shift in direction towards self-government in the latter part of the twentieth century presents a number of problems. First, it is always difficult to subject the recent past to the full rigour of historical inquiry. Trends and development have not yet run their full course and deprive the historian of the vantage point of distance in time, which makes them more apparent. Second, there is the difficulty of assessing the enormity of social and economic change in the last two decades of the twentieth century. The period was one that witnessed the wholesale transformation of the economy from one that had a high proportion of heavy industry and manufacturing to one that was increasingly centred on the service sector.[4] Indeed, it could almost be said that the Scotland of 1950 had more in common with the Scotland of 1850 than the Scotland of 2000. Analysing the political consequences of such changes in the 1980s and 1990s is difficult to assess because much of the source material, such as census returns, was subject to reclassification that made it difficult to chart social and economic change over time with both consistency and accuracy. Third, there is the difficulty of marrying the political interpretations of the 1980s and 1990s with the evidence of social and economic change. Although the popular representation of the 'Thatcher years' in Scotland is one that is dominated by images of mass unemployment and poverty, the period was one in which the social and economic profile of the nation increasingly converged with that of England.[5] Finally, there is the problem of 'myths', which can be described as contemporary explanations that are constructed in response to the immediate circumstances. History is littered with many such myths that arise in response to the need to provide immediate explanations for complex contemporary events. The 'Strange Death of Liberal England' followed World War I, the myth of the blitz was constructed during the war, the 'Guilty Men' of appeasement appeared after 1945 and the advent of the post-war 'New Jerusalem' became embedded in popular memory in the 1960s. While each of these explanations of historical change or historical events held more than a kernel of truth, subsequent investigation by historians demonstrated that the reality was much more complex and multi-faceted. Yet such myths maintain a powerful grip on the popular imagination, and historians find them difficult to dislodge.[6]

Regarding the impetus to create the Scottish parliament, a powerful 'myth' has emerged: that of 'civic Scotland'. Propounded in the main by sociologists and political scientists, the notion of civic society has crossed into the mainstream of cultural and political commentators in the media.[7] In essence, the idea behind civic Scotland could be propounded as follows. The advent of

Thatcherism initiated a political reaction in Scotland. The emphasis on the free market, individualism and the withdrawal of the state from the leading role in social and economic development, which garnered much support in the Tory heartlands of the south-east, was rejected by the Scots. Scottish national identity had continued to exist within the union on account of the degree of autonomy accorded to civil society and its institutions. The Scottish political vision was friendlier towards state involvement, had less trust in the market and believed that the well-being of society was more important than the well-being of the individual. The often-quoted statement that 'society does not exist' found no resonance in Scotland. The repeated rejection of Thatcherism at the polls had little impact, as the Conservatives could rely on an electoral hegemony that was based on the party's massive support in the south-east, which meant that no matter what way the Scots voted the Tories were always returned. The divergence of Scottish and English political behaviour, both north and south of the border, was increasingly explained within a national frame of reference. Yet commentators in Scotland eschewed ethnic or racial definitions of the nation's rejection of Thatcherism. Instead, the concept of civic nationalism was posited as an explanation for Scottish society's dismissal of free-market individualism.[8] Unlike the destructive ethnic nationalism that caused such havoc and bloodshed in the 1990s in the former Yugoslavia, for example, commentators were keen to stress that the conception of Scotland as a political nation was one that was inclusive and based around institutions, values and ideas that were independent of race or ethnicity. In short, it was argued that anyone resident in Scotland was able to be included under the broad heading of civic nationalism. In many respects this was a useful political ploy. At a time when there was a fear that the Scottish National party (SNP) might rise to power on the growing sense of frustration that Scottish voters felt at their obvious impotence to affect the electoral outcome of the United Kingdom as a whole, the concept of civic nationalism or society was sufficiently toned down from full-blown nationalism to be used by Labour and Liberal politicians to justify the Scottish sense of grievance but, it was hoped, mild enough not to give succour to their nationalist opponents.

Home rule emerged as a key policy to redress the constitutional imbalance of the United Kingdom electoral system in which the wishes of the anti-Conservative electorate of Scotland were swamped by the pro-Conservative electorate of the south. Devolution would preserve the constitutional integrity of the union but would allow the Scots considerable self-government in domestic issues, which was the arena where most of the unpopular Conservative policies manifested themselves. Evidence of the power of civic Scotland manifested itself in the formation of the Scottish Constitutional Convention and its publication of A Claim of Right for Scotland in 1988. It brought together the main opposition parties – with the exception of the SNP – the churches, local government, trade unions and various civic forums to press a united claim on behalf of the nation for home rule.[9] The convention based its legitimacy upon the premise that, as it had the support of a majority of Scottish MPs and the backing of many of the most influential civic organisations within Scottish society, it could justly be said, within the confines of the existing political system, to represent the democratic will of the people. It was this belief that there was a mobilisation of the Scottish people in favour of home rule through the available civic institutions and forums that was the most important kernel of truth in the myth of civic Scotland. Also, the appearance of groups protesting against the poll tax and Trident among other things, added weight to the argument that there was a strong sense of civic identity in Scotland that was democratic, leftist and politically active. Yet this image of a politically aware, populist, left-of-centre populace was not accepted by everyone. In particular, the right-wing Scotsman newspaper dismissed the claims as being the product of the 'blethering classes'; a euphemism for the middle-class chattering class that depended on the state for its well-being.[10] Tory politicians were likewise sceptical of the claims of the convention to represent the nation, and believed the only thing that mattered was a democratic mandate from the Scottish electorate, which they cleverly polarised between a vote for independence and the SNP on one hand, and a vote for unionist parties, which would have to stick by the majority decision of the United Kingdom electorate. The advent of a majority Labour government in 1997 that was committed to devolution (subject to a referendum) was the critical factor in securing a Scottish parliament. Yet the activities of the convention prior to 1997 and its endorsement by a popular vote in the referendum lent weight to the idea of the creation of a Scottish parliament as a manifestation of the will of civic Scotland.

Yet this version of history is one that does not take into cognisance the enormity of social and economic change as the prime motivator of historical change. The easy accessibility of tracts, the propensity of protagonists to emphasise their own importance and the long-held notion that civic leaders play an important role in society have conspired to produce a reading of the creation of the Scottish parliament in which these actors play centre stage. Another factor reinforcing this trend is that these sources can be easily packaged into a coherent account of a political movement. Often there is an almost implicit assumption that ideas and pronouncements have led public opinion and moulded it into an acceptance of home rule as a viable political future for the Scottish nation.[11] It is the objective of this essay to take issue with many of these assumptions and instead argue for the primacy of social and economic forces as the key factor in explaining the widespread acceptance of home rule as the 'settled will of the Scottish people'. Also, it should be borne in mind that the idea of civil society was one that was hardly used by the home rule movement, and was only used in the latter stages of the campaign.

The 1980s brought back many memories of the hungry thirties. Time and time again, politicians, political and economic commentators, and trade union leaders harked back to the time of the 'devil's decade' to make the point that the social and economic deterioration of the Scottish nation was at its lowest point in the post-war era. According to one up-and-coming political commentator, the Labour MP Gordon Brown, 'For the first time since the war, not only are the numbers of the poor rising dramatically, but, also, government legislation is ensuring that the poor cannot enjoy the increased prosperity that may come to the nation.'[12] This had a special resonance in the fact that by 1985 over a fifth of the Scottish population was over the age of sixty-five and would have had first-hand memories of the period. Furthermore, much of the dominant Scottish political ethos in the post-war period was based on the fact that there would never be a repetition of the poverty and unemployment that had scared Scottish society between the wars. Not surprisingly, the use of the metaphor of the thirties as a tool to quantify the extent of Scottish social and economic problems struck a resonant chord among many Scottish voters. Time and time again trade union leaders drew attention to the fact that the manufacturing capacity of the Scottish nation was being undermined.

> The Ravages of the recession have torn at Scotland's industrial guts. The core industries on which our future depends – coal, steel, railways, heavy engineering and shipbuilding – have been pared down to such an extent that the stricken Scottish whisky industry, once regarded as a lucrative national sideline, is now on a par in employment terms with the once great industries of central Scotland.[13]

An important aspect in such claims was the belief that Scotland could not exist without producing goods that could be sold in the international market. The inability to 'make things', it was believed, would lead to bankruptcy, and the nation would be unable to sustain itself. Such views of what might be called popular political economy, while bearing no relation to conventional economic theory, were important in explaining the reaction of ordinary Scots to the experience of de-industrialisation. For many, there was an ingrained faith in the Scottish economy of the heavy industries, which had, while perhaps not having provided prosperity, been part of the fabric of Scottish culture and its way of life that spanned the generations. According to the novelist William McIlvanney, 'The most nourishing roots of the Scottish identity, the roots that offer potential for continuing growth, have their soil not in the historically romanticised past but in the more recent industrial history of the nineteenth and twentieth centuries.'[14] It is important to emphasise the generational dimension of Scottish employment in the period after World War II. Shipbuilding, heavy engineering, mining and scores of local industries had provided employment for fathers and sons. Added to the strongly localised nature of industry in Scotland, de-industrialisation had a truly communal impact, with many areas lacking the economic diversity to withstand the closure of local industry. In Bathgate, following the closure of Linwood, almost 60 per cent of school leavers went straight into the Youth Training Scheme (YTS), as there was little in the way of employment opportunities in the area.[15] Furthermore, it was those very industries that tended to recruit their labour over the generations that were most vulnerable to closure. The closure of industrial giants such as Caterpillar at Uddingston and British Steel at Ravenscraig were typical of the closures that adversely effected communities.

With hindsight it can be said that the Scottish economy was undergoing major structural change and at the end of the process it would emerge much stronger and healthier.[16] As has been noted, in the late 1980s and early 1990s, the Scottish economy increasingly began to match that of England and the major structural differences between the two societies had all but disappeared by the mid-1990s. The service sector, clustering around insurance and banking, the petro-chemical industry, light engineering and tourism displaced the old traditional industries and by the mid-1990s, Scotland was reckoned to be the second most prosperous part of the United Kingdom outside the south-east triangle.[17] Such structural changes in the economy, however, were not reflected in Scottish politics. The Conservative party was repeatedly rejected by the Scottish electorate in successive general elections, in stark contrast to England and this political divergence at a time of economic convergence has led some to conclude that a Scottish civic political culture that rejected the individualism of Thatcherism was responsible for the decline in Scottish Conservative fortunes. According to an analysis by Radical Scotland this trend was evident in the 1987 general election:

> At the more personal level there seems to be a simple egalitarianism emerging, wherein people won't just vote Tory because they themselves would be better off . . . they don't want to be better off if it's at the expense of someone else living in poverty . . . and it may be that this egalitarianism is now becoming a positive national characteristic . . . the extent of this national factor in voting patterns can be graphically shown by looking at specific constituencies. A constituency like North East Fife – prosperous, with a farming and university make up – would surely have returned a huge Tory majority anywhere in the South, yet in Scotland was taken from the Tories by the Liberals. The farming and fishing communities of Banff and Buchan would have sent back a Tory seat almost anywhere in England, yet here it was the

> SNP that took the seat. And in East Kilbride – a new town with unemployment under 10 per cent – would seem tailor made for large support from the new type of British Tory voter, yet here the Labour majority increased from 4,300 to 12,600.[18]

The widespread adoption of tactical voting in which the primary objective was the defeat of the Tory candidate seemed to further confirm that civic nationalism was the driving force behind anti-Conservatism in Scotland.

The Tories were singled out for condemnation of a number of reasons. The policy of the free market was interpreted as an attack on the corporate foundations of the Scottish economy. Hostility to the state sector was seen as a further anti-Scottish policy as it was proportionally a bigger employer north of the border.[19] The Thatcherite message of individualism, property ownership and profit was culturally out of kilter with a Scottish sense of public service, communitarianism and social obligation. The Conservative party's celebration of economic liberalism, conspicuous consumption and social mobility that was based on wealth creation did not strike a chord in a Scottish society that was in many respects more traditional, disapproved of show-offs and arguably had much more rigid class barriers. Scottish notions of social mobility tended to be centred on working class boys who had done well at school, gone into university and entered the professions. The self-made businessman was a comparative rarity north of the border. To begin with, such policies as were pursued by the Conservative party were criticised in the main for the adverse effect they had on the Scottish economy, rather than being anti-Scottish policies. In the mid-1980s when the full impact of a global recession coupled with Conservative economic policy resulted in a rash of industrial closures and mounting unemployment, few of Scotland's non-Conservative civic leaders advocated anything other than a return to the old corporate forms of government economic intervention and state subsidy.

While the impact of Conservative economic policy could be interpreted as having a 'national' dimension in that it had an adverse effect on the Scottish economy, many politicians pointed out that the old industrial heartlands of the north of England suffered to a similar extent.[20] It was the dramatic reversal of Conservative electoral fortunes in the 1987 general election when tactical voting reduced the Tory party to ten seats and increased Labour to fifty that injected the debate with a national dimension in Scotland. The critical factor here was the emphatic rejection of the Conservative party, coupled with overwhelming support for Labour, although this was due more to the first past the post system than an upsurge in support for the party. On the surface, it seemed to indicate a clear divergence between Scottish and English politics and it was perhaps inevitable that the debate became infused with the language of civic nationalism. For Labour politicians the situation was fraught with difficulties. A failure to acknowledge the divergence between Scotland and England would play into the hands of the SNP, while too much focus would likewise inject into the debate a dose of Scottish nationalism that could have the potential to backfire. Civic nationalism was a way of acknowledging the bonds within Scottish society that rejected the individualism of Thatcherism, but stopped short of providing an endorsement for the separatist claims of the SNP.

Yet, was it civic nationalism and its endorsement of the bonds of civic society against the individualism of Thatcherism that best explains the Scots' rejection of the Conservative party at the ballot box? Certainly the idea of a strong Scottish civic identity provided a suitable explanation of the divergent political behaviour. The emergence of 'alternative' political forums was cited as evidence of the strong sense of civic identity in Scotland and ranged from anti-poll tax organisations, the involvement of local government and churches in politics and the anti-nuclear weapons lobby. Yet, it can be argued that the emergence of alternative politics was a response to the failure of conventional party politics in this period. The key development in Scottish politics from the late 1980s to the mid-1990s was the collapse of the Conservative party and the voters' ability to use tactical voting to oust sitting Tory MPs. This one simple fact accounts for the success of the Labour party in this period as it was best placed to win under the first-past-the-post system and the Liberal Democrats, likewise, experienced a boost from the electoral vagaries of the first-past-the-post system coupled with anti-Conservatism.

The key to understanding the rise of anti-Conservatism in Scotland and its transformation into support for home rule is the economic trauma of the early 1980s. The extent of the depression in Scotland following a global economic downturn, coupled with a withdrawal of state intervention meant that unemployment levels in Scotland soon returned to record levels and had the greatest impact on those areas associated with traditional industries. Yet, arguably it was the fear of unemployment that had the most dramatic political effect. Well into the early 1990s after the worst of the economic dislocation had passed and employment levels had risen to acceptable levels, opinion poll evidence found that fear of job losses was a consistent concern of the electorate (see below). Furthermore, the rash of industrial closures may have attracted the greatest amount of press attention, but it is worth pointing out that rural employment decreased at a much higher rate than urban employment and that it was in the rural constituencies that the Conservatives were most vulnerable. Low-paid and part-time employment in the 1980s was another consequence of the economic shift towards the service sector as many were forced to work longer hours in low skilled jobs. Even middle management was not safe from the economic onslaught as companies downsized and rationalised. The closure of company headquarters and relocation affected many who would have regarded their occupational status as safe. This was a factor that differentiated the experience of the middle class north and south of the border. A survey of Scottish graduates in the 1980s showed that about 30 per cent had to leave to find work and that the proportion for those working in scientific, technical and industrial management was higher. Furthermore, the Scottish share of the UK graduate market declined from 9.4 per cent to 7 per cent at a time when the market was growing. The fact that the public sector was the most important job market for Scottish graduates undoubtedly helped to reinforce the middle-class alienation from the Conservative party, as a result of its repeated attacks on the 'nanny state'.[21] The broad trends of Scottish economic development in the period from 1980 to 1995 appear to show a successful transition from an economy that was over-dependent on old industries and manufacturing to one that was dominated by the newer service sector. Yet, such a broad overview masks a massive social turbulence that occurred under the surface. Contemporary estimates in the mid-1980s from a variety of sources claimed that as many as one in three Scots were adversely affected by the Thatcher revolution. Yet, it was the speed of the change and the fear that it would not stop that helped to harbour lingering suspicions as to the future impact of Conservative policy. In short no one felt safe nor could predict where the economic juggernaut would strike next.

While it is comparatively easy to identify those areas and constituencies that were most affected by mass unemployment (usually safe Labour seats in any case), the massive youth unemployment of the early 1980s was one that had a much wider geographical and social impact. In 1983, youth unemployment accounted for half of the total unemployed women and a third of men, as the number of job vacancies dried up in a shrinking economy. Whereas industrial closure tended to hit specific types of industries in particular areas, youth unemployment was much more diverse and diffuse. Contractions in key industries meant that the young were no longer able to follow the paths of their fathers. The cost of youth unemployment was one borne by many families in the 1980s as many young people were forced into a state of dependency that ate away at family income. Given the average age of marriage was over twenty-five for both men and women there was little opportunity for the young to escape the family home, although it is worth pointing out that the period witnessed the rise of the single mother and many hostile commentators, particularly in the tabloid press, attributed this rise as a result of becoming pregnant was the best way to secure a council house. The problem was further compounded by the widespread introduction of the Youth Training Scheme, in which the young were provided with marginally more money than unemployment benefit but had to work while receiving 'training' from a particular company. In reality, most were used as free labour provided at government expense. The middle-aged were also adversely hit by unemployment, particularly those who had worked in manufacturing or the building industry. For those in their fifties, retraining was not regarded as much of an option, and many were put on incapacity benefit as a means of disguising the true extent of the unemployment total. Yet perhaps the most dramatic consequence of the impact of industrial closures in the early 1980s was the widespread tendency for families to compensate by taking lower-paid jobs and working longer hours. The number of mothers entering the job market in the 1980s showed a substantial increase, mainly in part-time work. Of the 200,000 increase in the number of people in employment between 1985 and 1989, 134,000 were women. In the period from 1989 to 1994, the total in employment increased by only 9,000, yet the number of women in the workforce increased by 43,000 showing that women's employment was covering up a shrinking male labour force. In the same period, the proportion of women workers who were part-time was some 40 per cent. This picture of women who were doing part-time work to help make ends meet was reinforced by a survey in 2000 which showed that almost a quarter of a million Scottish workers, the majority of them women, believed that they were under-employed. On the surface, the growth in employment masked a wider aspect of social change that many believed left them no better off.[22]

Housing was one of the key political issues of Scottish politics in the post-war era. The commitment to public-sector housing was arguably the most important determinant affecting Scottish elections as both Tories and Labour promised to build more and better houses. The Thatcherite policy to focus on the free-market and private sector brought an end to this central plank of the post-war welfare state, and undoubtedly suffered from the political fallout. On one level, the 'right to buy' scheme and the growth of the private sector in housing might have created more Tory voters, as members of the propertied class were usually identified as potential Conservative voters. Before 1979, two thirds of Scotland's housing stock was held by the public sector, but by the end of the century that had dwindled to a third.[23] Tenants using the 'right to buy' scheme between 1981 and 1994 bought 218,000 homes. Furthermore, between 1980 and 1991, 168,000 private homes were built and came onto the market, all of which should have created a fairly substantial reservoir of potential Tory voters.[24] In short, two thirds of Scottish families now owned their homes. On the face of it, there seems to be a substantial hypocrisy on the part of Scots, as they rejected the Conservative party at the polls but at the same time took advantage of Tory policies to own their homes. Indeed, the largest increase in the 'right to buy' took place in the two years following the 1987 general election, when the Tories were trounced in Scotland.[25]

Yet the issue of housing in Scotland did not fit into the rather black-and-white assumption of Conservative strategists that homeowners were likely to become Tory voters. First, although the numbers of people buying private housing in the 1980s increased, there was an element of compulsion about this. Public-sector housing building dwindled in the 1980s. Whereas almost 100,000 dwellings were completed in the public sector between 1974 and 1979, this dropped to 35,000 between 1980 and 1985, and 24,000 between 1986 and 1991.[26] Further, the housing stock decreased as a result of the 'right to buy' scheme. Not only that, it was the best housing that was bought first. Between 1980 and 1985, of the 74,000 homes that were bought by council tenants 63,700 were houses as opposed to apartments, and in the period after this date sales of houses as compared to apartments were of the magnitude of two to one. Not only was it more difficult to get council housing, it was increasingly difficult to get decent council housing.[27] The changes in the housing market coincided with major structural upheaval in the Scottish economy. Up until 1987, when unemployment began to decline, there was considerable job insecurity, and fear of unemployment lingered on well after this date (it was still the most important issue in opinion polls in 1990).[28] Culturally, many Scots were attuned to the notion that decent affordable council housing was the norm, yet it was now denied to them, and taking out a mortgage was the only option open to obtain a decent house. As well as uncertainty in the job market, mortgages ate up more of a typical monthly income than rent. So although many bought private housing, it was done at considerable cost, compared to their parents' generation. This was a cultural shift in Scottish attitudes to housing, but one that was not necessarily going to bring any benefits to the Conservative party.

One factor in encouraging people to buy their council houses was the fact that rents were increased as the grant to council housing from central government was decreased.[29] By the time that many bought their houses, it was almost as expensive to pay rent as it was to pay a mortgage, and as such their decision was motivated as much by simple financial pragmatism as an ideological commitment to property ownership. The fact that the real upsurge in ownership took place after 1988, once the economy began to stabilise, shows that job insecurity was a real deterrent to home ownership. By the end of 1987, only 5 per cent of council housing stock had been sold off compared to England, where it was 15 per cent.[30] Although it may be argued that there was more of a culture of home ownership in England, which can explain the readiness of council tenants to buy south of the border, the importance of economic factors cannot be left out of the equation. In 1984, Scotland had a total employment rate of 64 per cent, compared to the United Kingdom average of 68 per cent, and by 1986 the Scottish total had risen marginally, but that of the United Kingdom was now 70 per cent.[31] Further, a gap in average earnings opened up between Scotland and England in 1986.[32] By and large, it was the better-off skilled workers living in better areas who bought their council houses. Again, this should have seen a target group for the Conservatives, given that it was the same group of skilled workers in England who so decisively tipped the electoral balance in favour of Thatcherism.[33] Yet home ownership was not enough to win their loyalty.

There has been a tendency for opinion pollsters to concentrate on individuals when measuring voter intention and how this relates to the key issues of the day. But in order to reconstruct the social experience of the 1980s it is perhaps more instructive to look at family life and how that could possibly affect attitudes towards government policy.[34] While there were skilled workers lucky enough to hold onto their jobs during the economic upheaval of the first half of the 1980s and fortunate to have bought their own houses, the situation did not always look that rosy. For parents there was the continued problem of youth unemployment. A survey in 1987 showed that 48 per cent of 16-year-old school leavers expected to go into a Youth Training Scheme, while a further 24 per cent were unemployed, and only 27 per cent had found a job.[35] Undoubtedly the prevalence of low-paid and low-skilled YTS workers and unemployed youth added a strain to family life. Though the figures are not available to quantify this, the additional resources required to maintain children until they found their feet was another burden on Scottish society added by the Thatcher revolution. Indeed, it is worth speculating that the Scottish electorate's tendency to place unemployment at the top of its political concerns was more to do with the impact of unemployment on the immediate family rather than the individual polled.[36] Further, in a world that no longer had easily accessible and decent council housing for the young, it must have seemed to many parents that with few decent jobs and housing beyond their reach, their offspring would be with them for the duration.

It was not just the young who were adversely affected by government policy in the 1980s – the old in Scotland were also hit hard. The over-65s came to occupy a larger part of Scottish society in the 1980s, and most of these were brought with the idea of a welfare state that would look after them from 'the cradle to the grave'. Most had believed that the state old-age pension would be adequate for their means upon retirement, and few had a private pension. The removal of the link with average earnings meant that the pension declined in terms of its relative value throughout the 1980s, and together with an increase in the costs of living, many were consigned to poverty. The introduction of more complex means-tested benefits was shunned by many, too proud to take handouts from the state.[37] Also, the lottery of council housing meant that many stayed in over-large family homes that were more expensive to maintain and heat, unwilling to give them up in case they were moved to a bad neighbourhood. The increased burden on the welfare state occasioned by high unemployment put increased pressure on limited resources. Likewise, while local government had its block grant from central government cut, social services had to tackle new problems caused by single-parent homes, drug abuse, juvenile crime and other difficulties associated with the newly emerging 'welfare culture'.[38] As with the burdens associated with youth, many found that they had to provide additional care for elderly parents.

Not surprisingly, at times of economic upheaval there was also considerable social upheaval, and Scottish family life was drastically altered in the 1980s. While it is important to state that there was an increase in the rates of divorce before the 1980s and that changing cultural attitudes had their part to play, there can be no denying that the strain that exogenous social and economic factors brought to bear on relationships in the 1980s played their part in breaking up the family. The divorce rate in the 1980s shot up to almost a third, with many claiming that financial pressure had played a major part in causing separation. Further, it was shown statistically that those who married young and had children were most likely to separate, which 'raises questions as to the capacity of young men to deal adequately with responsibility of marriage and a family'.[39] The growth of single-parent families was another feature associated with social change in the 1980s. By 1987, over 100,000 households were single parents, and unmarried mothers headed 20,000 families. By 2001, a quarter of all families with children were headed by a single parent.[40] Reports from social services throughout the 1980s showed that there was a strong correlation between domestic abuse, suicide, child abuse and domestic violence among the low-paid and the unemployed.[41] By the mid-1980s the 'sink estates' had become clearly identifiable, in which whole communities tended to be unemployed, dependent on state benefits, and prone to living in single-parent households as well as suffering from alcoholism and drug abuse.

The efforts to create a more just and fair society were rolled back in the 1980s. The extensive redistribution of wealth that had taken place in the era after 1945 was reversed with savage speed. In 1985 the top 10 per cent of earners took home more money than the bottom 50 per cent, and the richest 10 per cent owned 80 per cent of the nation's wealth.[42] The gap between rich and poor was growing at an unprecedented rate. Coupled with the development of generational poverty in 'sink estates', for all that commentators talked about a strong sense of Scottish civic society, the reality was that Scottish society was fragmenting and losing its cohesion. Even when the economy steadied in the period after 1985, significant problems remained. The much-vaunted tourism and electronics industries were dependent on low wages and foreign investment, and did not involve high levels of skill. The electronics industry was built around low-skilled assembly work and was dependent on the ebb and flow of the world market.[43] Government strategy of seeking inward investment meant that much of the sector was vulnerable to the tendency of international corporations to take flight to areas that had cheaper labour. Tourism, likewise, was mainly low-paid and unskilled, and by adding all sorts of sundry business that could make money from passing tourist trade, the size of the sector was artificially inflated to make it seem a more important growth industry than it actually was. In 1989, the Scottish Low Pay Unit recorded the fact that half of the labour force was earning less than £144 per week and, as such, was classified as low-paid.[44] Further, official statistics showed that 850,000 Scots were dependent on incomes that were below or at the level of income support, and that a further 600,000 were just marginally above that level.[45] The financial sector, petrochemicals and light engineering led the way in economic recovery towards the 1990s.

The fragmentation of Scottish society in the 1980s was reflected in its politics. After 1987, there was a marked decline in the Conservative party's fortunes, which has been attributed largely to tactical voting. The existence of a four-party system in Scotland, in contrast to England and Wales, helped exacerbate the effect of this in the sense that reduced swings were necessary to achieve a result under the first-past-the-post electoral system. Anti-Conservative sentiment was the key driver behind political change. The Liberal Democrats were the principal beneficiaries of the Scottish electorate's aversion to the Tory party, and in spite of evidence of increasing prosperity the Scottish upwardly mobile held true to their faith that the welfare state was responsible for allowing their achievements. Yet it should also be remembered that the breakdown of the share of the vote in Scotland after 1987 demonstrated that there was little political cohesion. The Scottish National party and the Liberal Democrats each held just under a fifth of the vote, the Conservatives a quarter, and the Labour party held just over a third. While it is true to say that there was a persistent anti-Conservative bloc in Scottish electoral politics, it is equally true to say that there were also consistent anti-Labour, anti-Liberal Democrat and anti-SNP blocs. The fact that the Conservatives were in office and the so-called 'Doomsday scenario', in which the ruling government of Scotland failed to attract a credible number of Scottish votes, has attracted attention away from this issue of the fracture of Scottish politics in the 1980s. Had Labour come to power in 1992, it could equally have been argued that more than 60 per cent of the Scottish electorate had not voted for them.

The fragmentation of Scottish politics was also reflected in the growth of extra parliamentary pressure groups. This was the result of the failure of conventional party politics in the 1980s and early 1990s. The rejection of the Conservative party at the polls in Scotland did little to stop the imposition of unpopular policies by a British government whose majority was based on English votes. The spectacular victory of fifty Labour MPs in the general election of 1987 did little to stem the tide of unpopular legislation, including the introduction of the poll tax a year ahead of the rest of the United Kingdom in 1989. The Conservative reaction to the electoral meltdown in 1987 was a hardening of attitudes to Scotland and, in particular, its 'subsidy junkie' culture. The perception of Scottish ingratitude from a Conservative government that paid out higher per capita public expenditure north of the border, coupled with the fact that Scotland was unlikely to provide any electoral dividends, meant that increasing attention was paid towards the fiscal imbalance of the

United Kingdom. Also, Conservatives were well aware that under the existing constitutional arrangement (which neither Labour or the Liberal Democrats wished to overtly challenge), there was little that the opposition could do to question the legitimacy of the Tory government's rights to impose policies on Scotland, no matter how unpopular they might be. Indeed, Conservatives were quite happy to goad Liberal Democrats and Labour towards tacit support of the nationalist position in order to undermine their credibility. The poll tax, the basing of Trident nuclear missile submarines on the Clyde, the privatisation of public utilities such as water and the growing unease about the constitutional issue led to the creation of specific action groups that were determined to take direct action and bypass the parliamentary political process altogether. The existence of such groups was not necessarily evidence of civil society flexing its muscles against a cold and indifferent central government whose policies were far removed from the wishes of the Scottish people; rather it was the result of the frustration felt by diverse groups and the failure of conventional politics to represent their interests.

It was this failure in conventional politics that led to the creation of the cross-party Scottish convention in 1988 and the espousal of home rule as a mechanism to defend the nation from hostile policies that emanated south of the border. In short, it was a negative reaction to the failure of the British political system to adequately deal with a divergence of political opinion north and south of the border. At the time, little was said about the potential positive benefits of home rule; rather it was mainly about stopping unpopular policies. The key advocates in the debate for devolution were those who had politically lost out as a result of the Thatcher revolution. The Scottish Trades Union Congress (STUC), whose membership was in decline as a result of anti-trade union legislation and the sweeping economic reforms of the 1980s; the churches, whose moral authority had been in decline for many years as membership plummeted; and local government, which found its autonomy under threat from new legislation and a squeezing of finance as a result of cuts in the money that came direct from central government, all found common cause to halt the tide of Conservative government policy by endorsing home rule. For the Liberal Democrats and Labour, home rule seemed to offer a road out of sterile and futile opposition and formed a policy that could circumvent the Doomsday scenario. While there is no denying the fact that a great many were long-time advocates of home rule, the critical factor in coalescing anti-Thatcherite forces around the banner of home rule was the desire to shore up and protect their declining authority in Scottish society. After all the STUC, the churches and local government had not been particularly worried about ideas of democratic accountability in the past. Most had been used to the corporate state of the post-1945 era, in which little account was taken of local democratic process or consultation. In mitigation, it may be said that Thatcher brought such issues into sharp relief, but self-preservation was undoubtedly an important factor in the desire to establish a devolved Scottish parliament.

The idea of civic society would become very important to this project. After all, civil society was, to a large extent, in meltdown. As was mentioned earlier, the gulf between rich and poor was increasing; society was becoming atomised and more individualistic; relations between Edinburgh and Glasgow remained poor; political loyalties remained hard and fast in traditional party mode; the growth of sink estates continued unabated, with their culture rooted in benefits; and traditional authorities of respect no longer commanded the same deference. Reports of attacks on firemen, hospital staff and police were not indicative of a strong civic society. Voluntary services came under increasing strain in the 1980s as society opted for greater individual freedom and people spent less time in community activity. Membership of churches, youth organisations, charities, clubs and other communal activities declined at a terrific speed. If Scotland had a strong sense of civic society during the 1980s, the evidence shows that it experienced the same growth of individualism and atomisation as other societies in the modern Western world. Indeed, it was not particularly different to England; the only difference was that the electorate would not forgive the Conservative party for unleashing a barrage of policies that brought about widespread disruption, hardship and uncertainty throughout the 1980s. The idea of civic society was necessary to glue the disparate anti-Thatcherite elements of Scottish society into a coherent political grouping.

The idea rather than the reality of civil society was seized upon by political commentators and pundits to explain Scottish antipathy towards Thatcherism. The argument was that the Scots had a greater sense of social responsibility than the English and were more amenable to the public service. The rampant individualism of Thatcherism was alien to Scottish society and was rejected by the Scottish electorate as an imposition. The argument ran that the Scots were keener on the mixed economy, did not mind paying higher taxes for better public services and regarded the unbridled free market with suspicion. While some of this may well have been true, there is little empirical evidence to show that this was primarily motivated by a belief in the virtues of civil society. Rather, the reasons for the Scottish belief in greater state involvement and hostility to the free market were grounded in practical reasons of self-interest. The state sector had a bigger share of employment – especially middle-class employment – there was little in the way of small business, and political culture was grounded in notions of the corporate state, where it was accepted that government had a duty to look after the welfare of its citizens. Even after the creation of the Scottish parliament, there was little enthusiasm to use the tax-varying powers to pay for better public services. The notion of civil society was used to replace the notion of corporatism that had died under an onslaught of government policy. By slightly adjusting the intellectual parameters, the quest of civic Scotland to attain home rule could encompass most of the elements that had made up the corporate state. Paradoxically, the interest groups that had been such a mainstay of corporate society had most to lose from the democratic process of a Scottish parliament. After all, trade union and local government power in the corporate state was not dependent on democratic accountability. A left-of-centre Scottish parliament, however, was thought to offer better prospects for survival than the ideological onslaught from the south. The notion of civil society was also useful in that it was designed to distance the campaign for a Scottish parliament from nationalism. By emphasising inclusiveness and eschewing notions of ethnicity, it was possible to put the case for separate Scottish treatment without surrendering too much to the nationalist case for independence.

Although espoused by well-meaning and committed people, the idea of civil society acted as ideological glue for a range of disparate interests groups that had seen their political, economic and social position decline as a result of the policies of the Conservative governments. The concept of civil society was used to provide an intellectual vindication of anti-Conservatism in Scottish society that was more positive than the typical recourse that Scots could not stand that 'bloody woman'. Three critical factors are responsible for its widespread dissemination throughout Scottish political culture. First, the idea of civil society gained increased intellectual currency as the reality of civil society collapsed under the weight of socio-economic change. Second, the idea of civil society acted as an important source of intellectual common ground for the diverse anti-Conservative elements in Scottish society. Third, civil society enabled the movement to espouse a quasi-nationalist cause without an overt endorsement of nationalism that would have played directly into the hands of the Scottish National party.

By the late 1980s and early 1990s, many of the standard assumptions of the old corporatist state were coming under increasing pressure from modernisers in the Labour party, who believed that the party's surge to the left had been electorally damaging. This trend was further reinforced after the 1992 general election when the party increasingly moved towards a more market-friendly and less state-interventionist policy. While Gordon Brown condemned the greed of Thatcherite Britain in 1989, he was careful to avoid outright criticism of the market, and hinted at a fundamental policy shift. He claimed that 'only by combining public with private intervention, not to suppress the market or dictate to it for reasons of dogma but to ensure that its forces serve public objectives, can we succeed'. As one commentator shrewdly noted, this was very close to the concept of the social market and the use of Thatcherite economics towards social-democratic ends.[46] George Kerevan, likewise, began to think the unthinkable and looked to the market for economic regeneration.[47] Labour in Scotland was more traditional rather than left wing, and avoided the excesses of the 'loony left' that were a staple of tabloid newspapers in England. With the party shifting towards a more moderate and centrist position, many began to question the ability of a future Labour government to live up to the expectation of the Scottish electorate. It was soon becoming apparent that there would be no return to the old policies of massive state intervention in the economy. The adoption of devolution would shift the emphasis away from expectation of the central government in London to the one in Edinburgh. Further, with the intellectual discrediting of corporatism, the notion of civil society was an excellent replacement for the foundation stone of a left-of-centre policy in Scotland. Indeed, as the division between rich and poor grew and unemployment blackspots became ingrained, the greater was the recourse to the notion of civil society as an explanation for the rejection of Conservative policies. Yet in itself, the idea of civil society did not specifically address the issue of how to reverse the growing gaps between the haves and the have-nots, nor did it necessarily espouse greater state intervention. Rather, the idea of civil society was an aspiration. It was how the Scots would like their society to be rather than how their society really was.

The idea of civil society was vague enough to enable disparate groups to adhere to it. It was a form of consensus based on anti-Conservatism; but although it was the supposed consensual nature of Scottish society that rejected Conservative policy, what that consensus was never received any serious elucidation. Rather, the steering committee of the Scottish Constitutional Convention was self-appointed.

> The members of the steering committee can't be elected, because no system of election could be devised. They can't be delegated by organisations or authorities, because that would take too long and be subject to too many power-broking hassles. And the members of a committee so constructed would be too beholden to the bodies nominating them. Some appropriate body – and again the campaign for a national assembly comes to mind – must screw up its courage to approach and gather together a group of people of recognised ability and known commitment to a Scottish assembly, who reflect fully in their persons and connections all of the interests and strands of Scottish opinion seeking an Assembly, and who accept that there is an overwhelming case for a body such as I have described.[48]

Indeed, the somewhat pragmatic underpinning of the convention can be illustrated by the extensive horse-trading that went on. Concessions on proportional representation, increased equality of gender representation, and the like were largely the result of the fact that the coalition needed unity, rather than consensus. Although the Liberal Democrats were the minority political party, they won most of the issues, especially on proportional representation.[49] Further, it is difficult not to conclude that as the intellectual mainstream moved away from ideas of state intervention as a means of socio-economic regeneration, the vague concept of increased Scottish self-government was mooted with increased gusto because it avoided tackling those thorny issues.

Finally, the concept of civil society avoided the vexed issue of nationalism. It also left enough common ground for the possibility of cooperation with the SNP, as the nationalists were always seen as belonging to the anti-Conservative political movement and were promoters of constitutional change. While formal political hostilities did not cease, especially between Labour and the SNP, many in the political community recognised the significant area of common ground between them.[50] Civil society tried to square the circle of making the claim for a separate Scottish parliament, but without framing it within a nationalist context. Also, by leaving it to the Scottish Constitutional Convention, the political parties were able to maintain a degree of distance and insurance should the project fail. In part, it was an endeavour to make nationalism sound less threatening and hostile, but it was also necessary to maintain ideas of preserving the union within the context of a devolved political structure. Indeed, much of the Claim of Right was directed at the imperfections of the British constitution and the imbalance between power and checks in the British government. It even went on to claim that the establishment of a Scottish parliament would be the first process in the reform of British government into a more democratically accountable form. By forming around the convention, and even following the defeat in the 1992 general election, the idea of civil society manifested in the convention enabled the opposition parties to posit an alternative to the SNP and contain the nationalist threat.

Undoubtedly the groundswell of public opinion against the Conservative government paved the way for the establishment of a Scottish parliament in 1998. There can also be no doubt that the ideals and actions of those in the convention were equally important. What is less clear, however, is the extent to which these two quite separate forces were linked. It is one thing to say that Scots by the 1990s believed that the existing constitutional arrangement was unpopular and in need of change, but quite another to claim that it was motivated by a belief in civil society. Indeed, opinion poll evidence shows that the Scots were increasingly conflating their national identity with class identity, and that the experience of Conservative government was the single most important determinant in convincing the majority to vote for a Scottish parliament in the 1997 referendum.[51] The evidence from the pollsters shows it was a sense of grievance over Scotland not being treated fairly that was a key motivation in conditioning support for constitutional change. Surely the socio-economic upheaval of the 1980s was paramount in this development? The idea of civil society has acted as a convenient intellectual bridge that has enabled the leaders of civic Scotland to claim that they had popular support in the 1990s for a very particular form of constitutional change. It should be remembered that opinion poll evidence has since found that far from being the 'settled will of the Scottish people', the devolution settlement 'may prove to have been a very important watershed in Scottish politics but by no means a defining moment in Scotland's constitutional status'.[52] Old-fashioned Scottish nationalism has shown no signs of going away.

Notes

Chapter 1: Scotching the Beggars

1 *The Complaynt of Scotland by Robert Wedderburn (c.1550)*, ed. Stewart, A.M. (Edinburgh 1979), p. 120.
2 Ferguson, William, *Scotland's Relations With England: A Survey to 1707* (Edinburgh, 1977), p. 32.
3 Lyndsay, Sir David, *Ane Satyre of the Thrie Estaitis*, ed. Lyall, Roderick (Edinburgh, 1989).
4 *Ane Satyre*, p. x; Edington, Carol, *Court and Culture in Renaissance Scotland. Sir David Lindsay of the Mount (1486–1555)* (East Linton, 1994), p. 71. While Dr Edington is correct to stress that *Ane Satyre* 'is an allegorical and not a mimetic drama', it seems to me that Lindsay relied heavily upon the essentially Renaissance concept of 'experience', a humanist notion which he shared with his contemporary, John Mair. Experience is a character in Lindsay's poem 'The Monarche'. Also, most commentators, Edington included, do not hesitate to detect Lindsay's personal experience and autobiographical detail in most of his other works; to deny that element in *Ane Satyre* is unconvincing.
5 See Rankin, David, *Celts and the Classical World* (London, 1987), *passim*; Cowan, Edward J., 'Back Home and the Backcountry' contribution to 'Culture Wars: David Hackett Fischer's *Albion's Seed; Four British Folkways in America*' (Oxford, 1989) in *Appalachian Journal*, 19, no. 2 (1992), pp. 166–72. For some further discussion of these matters see Cowan, Edward J., 'The Discovery of the Gaidhealtachd in Sixteenth Century Scotland', *Transactions of the Gaelic Society of Inverness*, lx 1997–8 (2000), pp. 259–84.
6 Scottish Burgh Records Society *Extracts from the Records of the Burgh of Edinburgh 1528–1557* (Edinburgh, 1875), pp. 89–91.
7 *Ane Satyre*, p. ix.
8 The line appears in Lindsay's poem 'The Dreme', discussed below.
9 Thomson, T. and Innes, C. (eds), *Acts of the Parliaments of Scotland*, 12 vols (London 1814–75), vol. I, p. 324; vol. II, pp. 8, 36, 242, 251, 347–8, 374; vol.

III, 86–9; vol. IV, 287; vol. VI, 893; vol. X, 62. See also vol. XII, Index, under subjects 'Poor' and 'Vagrant'.

10 All numbers are those conferred in Child, F.J., *English and Scottish Popular Ballads*, 3rd edn, 5 vols (Boston and New York, 1882–98).

11 Ramsay, Allan, *The Tea-table Miscellany: A Collection of Choice Songs Scots & English*, 2 vols (Glasgow 1876), vol. I, pp. 80–82.

12 Hamer, Douglas (ed.), *The Works of Sir David Lindsay of the Mount 1490–1555*, 4 vols (Edinburgh, 1931–6), vol. I.

13 Ramsay, Allan, *The Ever Green. A Collection of Scots Poems Wrote by the Ingenious before 1600* 2 vols 1724 (Glasgow, 1874), pp. 231–3, most recently anthologised in Gifford, Douglas and Riach, Alan (eds), *Scotland's Poets and the Nation* (Manchester and Edinburgh, 2004), pp. 32–4.

14 *The Sempill Ballates. A Series of Historical, Political, and Satirical Poems ascribed to Robert Sempill mdlxvii–mdcx to which are added poems by Sir James Semple of Beltrees mdxcviii–mdcx now for the first time printed* (Edinburgh, 1872), pp. 22–7.

15 *Sempill Ballates*, pp. 81–4.

16 Calderwood, David, *History of the Kirk of Scotland by Mr David Calderwood*, ed. Thomson, T. and Laing, D., 8 vols (Edinburgh,1842–9), vol. 5, pp. 655–668.

17 For the most recent re-evaluation of Buchanan's tract see Mason, Roger A. and Smith, Martin S., *A Dialogue on the Law of Kingship among the Scots: A Critical Edition and Translation of George Buchanan's De Iure Regni apud Scotos Dialogus* (Aldershot, 2004).

18 John of Fordun, *Chronicle of the Scottish Nation*, ed. Skene, W.F. (Edinburgh 1872), pp. 321–32; Andrew of Wyntoun, *The Orygynale Cronykil of Scotland*, ed. Laing, D., 3 vols (Edinburgh, 1872), vol. II, pp. 339–49.

19 Watt, D.E.R. (ed.), *Scotichronicon* by Walter Bower, 9 vols (Aberdeen and Edinburgh, 1989–8), vol. II, p. 95.

20 Buchanan, George, *The History of Scotland*, trans. Aikman, J., 4 vols (Glasgow, 1827), vol. II, pp. 406–7.

21 Brunsden, George M., 'Aspects of Scotland's Social, Political, and Cultural Scene in the Late 17th and Early 18th Centuries, as Mirrored in the Wallace and Bruce Traditions' in Cowan, Edward J. and Gifford, Douglas (eds), *The Polar Twins: Scottish History and Scottish Literature* (Edinburgh, 1999), pp. 75–113.

22 Schofield, W.H., *Mythical Bards and the Life of William Wallace* (Cambridge, 1920), p. 195.

23 On Wallace see Cowan, Edward J., 'The Wallace Factor in Scottish History' in Jackson, Robin and Wood, Sydney (eds), *Images of Scotland. The Journal of Scottish Education*, Occasional Paper, Number One (Dundee, 1997), pp. 5–18, and *'For Freedom Alone' The Declaration of Arbroath, 1320* (East Linton, 2003), pp. 20–7, 72–6.

24 Cowan, *'Freedom Alone'*, pp. 62–82.

25 Nicholson, Ranald, *Scotland: The Later Middle Ages* (Edinburgh, 1974), p. 109.

26 John Barbour, *The Bruce*, ed. Duncan, A.A.M. (Edinburgh, 1997), p. 57.
27 Brown, Michael, *James I* (East Linton, 1996), Chapters 6 and 9.
28 *The Complaynt of Scotland*, pp. 97–110, 123, 131.
29 Cody, E.G. and Murison, W. (eds), *The Historie of Scotland wrytten first in Latin by the most reverend and worthy Jhone Leslie Bishop of Rosse and translated in Scottish by Father James Dalrymple*, 2 vols (Edinburgh, 1895), vol. II, p.261.
30 Buchanan, *History*, vol. II, p. 324.
31 Dickinson, William Croft (ed.), *John Knox's History of the Reformation in Scotland*, 2 vols (Edinburgh, 1949), vol. I, p.40.
32 Edington, *Court and Culture*, p. 135.
33 Donaldson, Gordon, *Scotland James V to James VII* (Edinburgh, 1965), p. 56.
34 Edington, *Court and Culture*, p. 33 and note.
35 Scott, Sir Walter, *Tales of a Grandfather, being stories taken from Scottish History* 3 vols (London and Glasgow, 1923), vol. I, p. 287. See too Cameron, Jamie, *James V The Personal Rule 1528–1542* (East Linton, 1998), pp. 2–3.
36 Edington, *Court and Culture*, p. 6.
37 Cody and Murison (eds), *Historie of Scotland*, vol. II, pp. 220–1; Buchanan, *History*, vol. II, pp. 304–5.
38 Edington, *Court and Culture*, pp. 196–204.
39 Laing, D. (ed.), *The Works of John Knox*, 6 vols (Edinburgh, 1895), vol. IV, pp. 528–9.
40 *Miscellany of the Wodrow Society: Containing tracts and original letters chiefly relating to the ecclesiastical affairs of Scotland during the sixteenth and seventeenth centuries* (Edinburgh 1844), vol. I, pp. 57–8.
41 *Calendar of State Papers Relating to Scotland*, vol. I, p. 144. Harrison was also concerned about the poor labourers of the ground 'whos commonwelth is mischeffe, and libertie mor servitude then was the children of Israell in Egipte', p. 143.
42 Dickinson, *John Knox's History*, vol. II, app. V and notes. See also vol. I, p. xcviii.
43 McPherson, J.M., *The Kirk's Care of the Poor* (Aberdeen, n.d.), p. 7. See too Cowan, Ian B., *The Scottish Reformation Church and Society in Sixteenth Century Scotland* (London, 1982), pp. 194–6.
44 *Jack Upland Friar Daw's Reply and Upland's Rejoinder*, ed. Heyworth, P.L. (Oxford, 1968), pp. 61, 63, 66–71.
45 Walter Bower, *Scotichronicon*, ed. Watt, D.E.R., 9 vols (Aberdeen and Edinburgh, 1989–98) see Index under 'friars' and 'Lollards'.
46 See now Milligan, Tony, '"To Ding Thir Mony Kingis Doun": Jock Upaland and the Scottish Labourer Stereotype', *Scottish Literary Journal*, vol. 25, no.1 (May 1998), pp. 26–36.
47 *The Praier and Complaynte of the Ploweman unto Christe*, ed. Parker, Douglas H. (Toronto, 1997), p. 22.

48 Contrary to what might have been anticipated, however, there is no evidence that Fish, Simon, *A Supplicacyon for the Beggars* (London, 1529) had any influence on 'The Beggars' Summons'. For text see *A Supplicacyon for the Beggars written about the year 1529 by Simon Fish now re-edited by Frederick J. Furnivall* (London, 1871), pp. 19–58.

CHAPTER 2: PAPER MONUMENTS

1 Rivers, Isabel, 'Biographical Dictionaries and Their Uses from Bayle to Chalmers' in Rivers, Isabel (ed.), *Books and their Readers in Eighteenth-Century England* (London, 2001), pp. 135–69.
2 Ipsos MORI poll for University of Stirling and the Scottish National Portrait Gallery, 2006; polls to identify the 10 best and 12 worst Scots, *Scotland on Sunday*, 1 and 8 January 2006.
3 Ferguson, William, *The Identity of the Scottish Nation: An Historic Quest* (Edinburgh, 1998); Pittock, M.H., *The Invention of Scotland* (London, 1991); Kidd, C., *Subverting Scotland's Past* (Cambridge, 1993); Mackenzie, John M., 'Empire and National Identities: The Case of Scotland', *Transactions of the Royal Historical Society*, 6th series, VIII (1998).
4 Sturges, P., 'Collective Biography in the 1980s', *Biography*, VI, 4 (1983), 316–32.
5 Lawrence Stone's jibe against collectors of biographical information is quoted in Sturges, 'Collective Biography', p. 316.
6 Myers, Robin, Harris, Michael and Mandelbrote, Giles (eds), *Lives in Print: Biography and the Book Trade from the Middle Ages to the 21st Century* (New Castle, Delaware and London, 2002).
7 Thomas, Keith, *Changing Conceptions of National Biography: The Oxford DNB in Historical Perspective* (Cambridge, 2005).
8 Thomas, *Changing Conceptions*, p. 9.
9 *Ibid.*, pp. 14–15.
10 Mackenzie, 'Empire and National Identities', p. 217; Finlay, R.J., 'Caledonia or North Britain? Scottish Identity in the Eighteenth Century' in Broun, D., Finlay, R.J. and Lynch, M. (eds), *Images and Identity: The Making and Re-making of Scotland through the Ages* (Edinburgh, 1998), pp. 143–4.
11 Chambers, R., *Lives of Illustrious and Distinguished Scotsmen* (1835), vol. I, Preface.
12 Moret, Ulrike, 'An early Scottish national biography: Thomas Dempster's *Historia ecclesiastica gentis Scotorum* (1627)' in Houwen, L.A.J.R., MacDonald, A.A. and Mapstone, S.L. (eds.), *A Palace in the Wild: Essays on Vernacular Culture and Humanism in Late-Medieval and Renaissance Scotland* (Leuven, 2000), pp. 249–69.
13 Thomas, *Changing Conceptions*, p. 10.

14 Nicolson, William, *The Scottish Historical Library: . . . Down to the Union of the Two Kingdoms in K. James the VI* (London, 1702), p. 134.
15 NLS, Adv Ms 33.3.19, f.32; Adv MS 33.5.17, materials for bibliotheca Scotica; cf. Nicolson, William, *The Scottish Historical Library*. p. 250.
16 NLS, Adv Ms 33.3.19, f.37r
17 Sibbald, Robert, *Scotia Illustrata sive Prodromus Historiae* (Edinburgh, 1684), Part 2, Book 3, Section I, Chapter 2, pp. 2–4, and plate x.
18 NLS, Adv Ms 33.3.19, f.37r.
19 *Ibid*; NLS Wodrow Quarto 52.
20 Bodl Ms Smith 65, f.257r, Dr Thomas Smith to William Smith, 16 Sept 1707.
21 Dick, O.L. (ed.), *Aubrey's Brief Lives* (London, 1949); Wood, Anthony A., *Athenae Oxonienses* (London, 1691–2).
22 *Proposals for Printing the Lives and Characters of the Most Eminent Writers of the Scots Nation, &c. by George Mackenzie M.D.* (Edinburgh,1706); Nicolson, William, *Scottish Historical Library*, 2, quoted in Allan, David, *Virtue, Learning and the Scottish Enlightenment* (Edinburgh, 1993), p. 29.
23 Mackenzie, George, *Lives and Characters of the Most Eminent Writers of the Scots Nation* (Edinburgh, 1708), vol. I, pp. i–iii; (Edinburgh, 1711), vol. II; (Edinburgh, 1722), vol. III.
24 Maidment, James, *Analecta Scotica* (1834), vol. I, p. 69, quoting Wodrow's 'Analecta'.
25 Irving, David, *The Lives of the Scottish Poets*, 2 vols (Edinburgh, 1810).
26 Wodrow, Robert, *History of the Sufferings of the Church of Scotland from the Restoration to the Revolution*, 2 vols (Edinburgh, 1721–2).
27 Calamy, Edmund, *Account of the Ministers . . . ejected by the Act for Uniformity* (1702).
28 *Collections upon the Lives of the Reformers and Most Eminent Ministers of the Church of Scotland* (1834–48); *Analecta: or Material for a History of Remarkable Providences; Mostly Relating to Scotch Ministers and Christians*, 4 vols (1848).
29 Quoted in Thomas, *Changing Conceptions*, p. 18; Cameron, N.M. de S. (ed.), *Dictionary of Scottish Church History and Theology* (Edinburgh, 1993), pp. 414–5.
30 *Disruption Worthies: A Memorial of 1843* (Edinburgh, 1876); *Disruption Worthies of the Highlands: Another Memorial of 1843* (Edinburgh, 1877); Ewing, W., *Annals of the Free Church*, 2 vols (1941).
31 Scott, H., *Fasti Ecclesiae Scoticanae*, 7 vols (1915–28).
32 *Ibid.* (1915), vol. I, pp. xv–xvi.
33 Crawfurd, George, *Peerage* (1716), p. iv.
34 Crawfurd, G., *Genealogy of the Royal and Illustrious Family of Stewart* (1710).

35 Allan, David, '"What's in a Name": Pedigree and Propaganda in Seventeenth Century Scotland' in Cowan, Edward J. and Finlay, Richard (eds), *Scottish History: The Power of the Past* (Edinburgh, 2002), p. 153.
36 Keith, Robert, *History of the Affairs of Church and State in Scotland* (1734).
37 Superseded by Dowden, John, *The Bishops of Scotland*, ed. Thomson, J. Maitland (Glasgow, 1912).
38 Dalrymple, David, Lord Hailes, *Catalogue of the Lords of Session* (1767), 'Advertisement'.
39 Sturges, 'Collective Biography'. Mr James Foulis of Collingtoun, clerk-register (d. 1549), was said to have been the son of a skinner in Edinburgh; NLS Adv Ms 37.2.6, ff. 173–4, notes by Lord Woodhouselee on his copy of Hailes' *Catalogue*. The posthumous edition (1798) contained the same note unaltered.
40 *Maidment Analecta Scotica* (1834), vol. I, pp. 164–5, discussing Douglas's *Peerage* (1764).
41 Wood, J.P., *The Antient and Modern State of the Parish of Cramond* (Edinburgh, 1794)
42 NLS, Adv MSS 37.2.1–10, lives of lord presidents, lords of session, lord advocates, barons of exchequer, justice clerks, lords of justiciary, jury court judges, clerks of session, solicitors, writers to signet and advocates.
43 NLS, MS 1878, ff. 28–9, printing the text in Adv Ms 37.2.1, pp.1–19
44 NLS, MS 332, ff. 87–8, Thomas Thomson to J P Wood, 1 January 1817, printed in Constable, Thomas, *Archibald Constable and his Literary Correspondents* (1873), vol. II, pp. 169–171.
45 NLS, MS 9402, f. 12r, Joseph Robertson to John Hill Burton [Nov 1830].
46 Brunton, George and Haig, David, *An Historical Account of the Senators of the College of Justice from its Institution in M.D.XXXII* (Edinburgh, 1836), p. vi.
47 Grant, Francis, *The Faculty of Advocates in Scotland, 1532–1943* (Edinburgh, 1944).
48 *A History of the Society of Writers to Her Majesty's Signet with a List of the Members of the Society from 1594 to 1890* (Edinburgh, 1890); *Register of Writers to Her Majesty's Signet* (Edinburgh, 1983).
49 E.g., Innes-Smith, R.W., *English-Speaking Students of Medicine at the University of Leyden* (Edinburgh, 1932).
50 Thomas, *Changing Conceptions*, pp. 4–5.
51 Bernard, J.P., Birch, T. and Lockman, J., *A General Dictionary, Historical and Critical*, 10 vols (1734–41), *passim*, including entries on the Gregories: (1737), vol. V, pp. 550–7, and the Keills: (1738), vol. VI, pp. 506–9.
52 Rivers, 'Biographical Dictionaries', p. 158; Thomas, *Changing Conceptions*, p. 13.
53 *Biographia Britannica* (1747), vol. I, pp. 575–93; (1760), vol. V, pp. 3385–97.
54 Fifteen of the 26 Scottish lives occur under 'A' to 'C': *Biographica Britannica* (1747–8), vols I–II, *passim*.
55 *Biographica Britannica* (1750), vol. III.

56 Thomas Birch, compiler of much of the *General Dictionary*, and Andrew Kippis, second editor of the *Biographia Britannica*, were both dissenters: Thomas, *Changing Conceptions of National Biography*, pp. 12, 18–19.

57 *Biographica Britannica* (1748), vol. II , pp. 1139–42; (1757), vol. IV, pp. 2251–4.

58 Rivers, 'Biographical Dictionaries', brilliantly explores aspects of the *Biographia Britannica* and the universal dictionaries modelled on Bayle, but not their national or patriotic character.

59 Kafker, F.A., 'The Achievement of Andrew Bell and Colin Macfarquhar', *British Journal for Eighteenth Century Studies*, 18.2 (1995), pp. 143.

60 *Encyclopaedia Britannica* (1778), vol. II, p. 1489; (1783), vol. X, p. 8774; cf. the lengthier treatment of David, James and John Gregory: *Encyclopaedia Britannica* (1780), vol. V, pp. 3406–8.

61 Simpson, Grant G., 'Studies of Scottish Historians: (3) Lord Hailes – Judgement on Scottish History', unpublished Presidential Address to the Scottish History Society, 9 December 1995.

62 Lives of Boyd, Hamilton and Barclay were published by 1784: NLS, MS 25304, ff.4–19, letters to Hailes (1784).

63 Hailes, *Catalogue* (1798), p. 37, notes on his bibliography.

64 Hailes, *Sketch of the Life of Mark Alexander Boyd*, supplementary sheet.

65 NLS, MS 25372, f. 54, unpublished life of Mark Duncan.

66 Hailes, *Sketch of . . . Mark Alexander Boyd*, supplementary sheet. Hailes suggested John Napier, the Keills and 'the numerous and worthy Gregories'.

67 NLS, MS 25298, f. 99, Bishop of Worcester to Hailes, 9 Sept 1784.

68 NLS, MS 25304, f. 10, Gilbert Stuart to Hailes, 4 Nov 1784.

69 Erskine, D.S., earl of Buchan and Minto, Walter, *An Account of the Life, Writings and Inventions of John Napier, of Merchiston* (Perth, 1787), pp. v–vi.

70 James Steuart Denham (d.1780), George Heriot, earl of Mar (d.1634) and William Drummond of Hawthornden: *The Anonymous and Fugitive Essays of the Earl of Buchan Collected from Various Periodical Works* (1812), vol. I, pp. 264–328.

71 Kidd, *Subverting Scotland*, p. 214; Erskine, D.S., earl of Buchan, *Essays on the Life and Writings of Fletcher of Saltoun and the Poet Thomson* (London, 1792).

72 Cant, Ronald G., 'David Steuart Erskine, 11th Earl of Buchan' in Bell, A.S. (ed.), *The Scottish Antiquarian Tradition* (Edinburgh, 1981), pp. 17–18.

73 Earl of Buchan, '"Memoir" of Sir James Steuart Denham', *Transactions of the Society of Antiquaries of Scotland* (1792), vol. I, pp. 129–139; James Short: *ibid.*, pp. 251–6; Cardinal John Geddes: *ibid.* (1818), vol. II, part 1, pp. 129–133; no biography: (1823), vol. II, part 2; William Hamilton of Bangour, poet: (1831) vol. III, pp. 255–66.

74 Stewart, Dugald, 'Account of the life and writings of Adam Smith', *Transactions of the Royal Society of Edinburgh* (1794), vol. 3, part 1, pp. 55–137, reprinted, with lives of Thomas Reid and William Robertson in Stewart, Dugald, *Biographical Memoirs* (Edinburgh, 1811). John Playfair's life of James Hutton, and Adam Ferguson's of Joseph Black are in *Transactions of Royal Society of Edinburgh* (1805), vol. V.
75 Hailes, *Sketch of the Life of John Barclay* (*c.*1784), supplementary sheet.
76 *Sketch of the Life of Mark Alexander Boyd* (1784); *Sketch of the Life of Sir James Ramsay* (1787).
77 Buchan and Minto, *Account of John Napier*, p. vii.
78 Thomas, *Changing Conceptions*, p. 48.
79 *The Edinburgh Magazine and Review* (1773–6); ex inf. Dr Bill Zachs.
80 Granger, J., *A Biographical History of England from Egbert the Great to the Revolution* (1769).
81 Kay, John, *A Series of Original Portraits and Etchings . . . with Biographical Sketches and Illustrative Anecdotes*, 2 vols (Edinburgh, 1837).
82 Kerr, Robert (ed.), *Memoirs of the Life, Writings and Correspondence of William Smellie*, 2 vols (1811), 1996 edition, vol. II, p. 436; cf. Brown, Stephen, 'William Smellie and the Culture of the Edinburgh Book Trade, 1752–1795' in Wood, Paul (ed), *The Culture of the Book in the Scottish Enlightenment* (Toronto, 2000), pp. 72–3.
83 Brown, 'William Smellie', p. 73.
84 Kerr, Robert (ed.), *Memoirs of the Life, Writings and Correspondence of William Smellie*, 2 vols (1811), 1996 edition, vol. II, pp. 415–22; Smellie, William, *Literary and Characteristical Lives* (1800).
85 NLS, MS25298, ff. 69–70, Bishop of Worcester to Hailes, 2 July 1791.
86 Stark, J., *Biographia Scotica* (1805), unpaginated, portraits of John Napier, George Drummond, Duncan Forbes, George Heriot and Alexander Runciman.
87 Kidd, *Subverting Scotland's Past*, p. 271.
88 Stark, *Biographia Scotica*, unpaginated.
89 *Oxford DNB* (2004), vol. 4, pp. 566–8.
90 Scoto-Britannicus, *The Scottish Biographical Dictionary* (Edinburgh, 1822); Anderson, William, *The Popular Scottish Biography* (Edinburgh, 1842); Irving, Joseph, *The Book of Scotsmen* (Paisley, 1881); Geddes, John, *Great Scots: A Condensed Biographical Dictionary of 1450 Notable Scots* (Ilfracombe, 1974), and an expanded version with 1,626 lives, *Ye Ken Noo!* (Durham, 1993); Kirkpatrick, Betty, *The Concise Dictionary of Great Scots* (Edinburgh, 2005).
91 Ash, Marinell, *The Strange Death of Scottish History* (Edinburgh, 1980), pp. 99–100.
92 Tytler, P.F., *An Account of the Life and Writings of Sir Thomas Craig of Riccarton: Including Biographical Sketches of the Most Eminent Legal Characters since the Institution of the Court of Session* (Edinburgh, 1823).

93 Alexander III, John Barbour, Andrew Wynton, John de Fordun; Robert Henrysoun, William Dunbar, Gavin Douglas, David Lindsay and Michael Scott: Tytler, P.F., *Lives of Scottish Worthies*, 3 vols (London, 1831–3; reissued 1838–40 and 1855).
94 Ash, *Strange Death*, pp. 100–17; 134–5, 137.
95 Chambers, R., *Biographical Dictionary of Eminent Scotsmen* (1870), vol. I, p. v.
96 *Ibid.*
97 Chambers, R., *Lives of Illustrious and Distinguished Scotsmen* (1832), vol. I, part I, cover. NLS copy.
98 NLS, Dep 231/66–72, manuscript entries, 'Abercromby' to 'Mallet'.
99 Chambers, *Lives* (1835), vol. I, p. vi.
100 Anne Halket, Elizabeth Blackwell, Elspeth Buchan, Mary Brunton and Mary, Queen of Scots: Chambers, *Lives,* vols I–IV, *passim.*
101 David I, William the Lion, John and Edward Baliol, Robert I, Alexander I–III, James I, James IV – VI, Charles I: Chambers, *Lives,* vols I–IV, *passim.*
102 Chalmers, Alexander, *General Biographical Dictionary*, 32 vols (1812–17); Irving, David, *The Lives of the Scottish Poets*, 2 vols (Edinburgh, 1810).
103 Chambers, *Biographical Dictionary* (1864), vol. I, p. vi.
104 Chambers, *Lives* (1835), vol. I, pp. 336–7, 339.
105 *Monthly Review* (1835), vol. I, p. 316.
106 Chambers, *Lives* (1835), vol. IV, pp. 314–5. Thomson later inserted a sterner account, stressing Mary's intention to subvert the Reformation: Chambers, *Biographical Dictionary* (1870), vol. III, pp. 425–6.
107 Chambers, *Lives* (1835), vol. I, p. 436.
108 Beavan, Iain, 'Advertising Judiciously: Scottish Nineteenth-Century Publishers and the British Market' in Isaac, Peter and McKay, Barry (eds), *The Mighty Engine: The Printing Press and its Impact* (Winchester and Oak Knoll, 2000), pp. 72–3.
109 Thomas, *Changing Conceptions*, p. 15.
110 Chambers, *Biographical Dictionary* (1870), vol. III, p. 604.
111 *Ibid.*, vol. I, pp. vi–vii. The joint articles on Blackwell and Foulis are counted as two each, and the entry for the Dundases of Arniston is counted as five substantive entries.
112 Webb, Alfred, *A Compendium of Irish Biography: Comprising Sketches of Distinguished Irishmen, and of Eminent Persons connected with Ireland by Office or by their Writings* (Dublin, 1878).
113 Chambers, *Biographical Dictionary* (1870), vol. I, p. vii.
114 Alexander Bethune, J D Carrick; Robert Mudie, David Scot, James Wilson: Chambers, *Biographical Dictionary*, vols I and III, *passim.*
115 Chambers, *Biographical Dictionary*, vol. II, p. 255.
116 Chambers, *Biographical Dictionary*, vol. III, p. 605.

117 Of clergy who died after 1834 and were added from 1855 to 1875, twelve out of forty-two were Free Churchmen, fifteen were post-1834 established ministers, and fifteen represented all the other denominations. Six pre-1834 Church of Scotland ministers were added. The Free Churchmen were Robert Buchanan, R.S. Candlish, Thomas Chalmers, William Cunningham, Patrick Fairbairn, John Fleming, Robert Gordon, Thomas Guthrie, David Landsborough, John Macdonald, Thomas Thomson, David Welsh: Chambers, *Biographical Dictionary*, vols I–III, *passim*.

118 Cf. Robert the Bruce (18½ pages), James Graham, Marquis of Montrose (18), David Hume (13), Robert Burns (11) and Mary, Queen of Scots (5½): Chambers, *Biographical Dictionary*, (1875), vols I–III, *passim*.

119 Chambers, *Biographical Dictionary*, vol. III, pp. 404–9; Lynch, Michael (ed.), *The Oxford Companion to Scottish History* (Oxford, 2001), p. 307.

120 Chambers, *Biographical Dictionary* (1875), vol. I, p. vi.

121 Chambers, *Biographical Dictionary*, vol. III, pp. 32–42, 424–30.

122 E.g., Lord Clyde: Chambers, *Biographical Dictionary*, vol. I, pp. 287–92; Col Alexander Seton: Chambers, *Biographical Dictionary*, vol. III, pp. 337–40.

123 Allan, Stuart and Carswell, Allan, *The Thin Red Line: War, Empire and Visions of Scotland* (Edinburgh, 2004), pp. 27–30.

124 E.g., Sir Andrew Agnew, Hanoverian, replaced Chambers' long article on John Erskine, Earl of Mar: Chambers, *Lives* (1835), vol. II, pp. 244–58; Chambers, *Biographical Dictionary* (1870), vol. I, pp. 21–3.

125 Chambers, *Lives* (1835), vol. I, pp. 477–8.

126 Joanna Baillie, Susan Ferrier, Anne Grant, Christian Johnstone, Caroline Nairn, Catherine Sinclair: Chambers, *Biographical Dictionary* (1875), vol. I, *passim*; Mary Somerville: *Op. cit.*, vol. III, pp. 661–3. Chambers omitted Anne Barnard and Alice Cockburn in 1835.

127 Ryan, Richard, *Biographia Hibernica. A Biographical Dictionary of the Worthies of Ireland from the Earliest Period to the Present Time*, 2 vols (Dublin, 1821–2). Eighteen of the 305 lives were of women, mostly authors.

128 *Monthly Review* (1835), vol. I, p. 315.

129 Kidd, Colin, '*The Strange Death of Scottish History* Revisited: Constructions of the Past in Scotland, *c.*1790–1914', *Scottish Historical Review*, LXXVI, I (1997), pp. 90, 95.

130 Kidd, Colin, *Subverting Scotland's Past* (Cambridge, 1993), p. 215.

131 E.g., Chalmers, A., *General Biographical Dictionary*, 32 vols (London, 1812–17).

132 E.g., Cochrane, Robert, *The Treasury of Modern Biography: A Gallery of Literary Sketches of Eminent Men and Women of the Nineteenth Century* (London, 1878), and works in Nimmo's Library of Biography series, 1870–80s; ex inf. Dr William Ferguson.

133 MacDiarmid, John, *Lives of British Statesmen*, 2 vols (London, 2nd edn, 1820).

134 Hanham, H.J., *Scottish Nationalism* (London, 1969), p. 81.

135 Cunningham, George Godfrey, *A History of England in the Lives of Englishmen*, 8 vols (1850–1); *The English Nation; or A History of England in the Lives of Englishmen*, 5 vols (*c.*1867).

136 Cunningham, G.G., *Lives of Eminent and Illustrious Englishmen* (1837), vol. VI, pp. 721–846 *passim*.

137 Anderson, W., *Scottish Nation* (1864), vol. I, p. vii.

138 Anderson, *Scottish Nation* (1864), vol. I, p. viii.

139 For example, see 'Achaius' in Anderson, *Scottish Nation* (2nd edn, 1882), vol. I, p. 17.

140 Irving, Joseph, *The Book of Scotsmen Eminent for Achievements in Arms and Arts, Church and State, Law, Legislation, and Literature, Commerce, Science, Travel and Philanthropy* (Paisley, 1881).

141 Quoted in Horden, John, 'A Dictionary of Scottish Biography' in Horden, John (ed.), *Bibliographia: Lectures 1975–1988* (London, 1992), p. 67.

142 Matthew, Colin, 'The *New DNB* and Scotland', unpublished talk to Edinburgh Bibliographical Society, 9 Dec. 1996.

143 Horden, 'Dictionary of Scottish Biography', pp. 67–8; Nichols, C.S. (ed.), *The DNB Missing Persons* (Oxford, 1993), pp. 435–6, 609–10.

144 *Dictionary of Welsh Biography down to 1940* (1959), first published in Welsh in 1953, with a supplement for 1941–70 (1997), translated in 2001.

145 Horden, 'Dictionary of Scottish Biography', pp. 67, 71–2, 76.

146 Boase, Frederick, *Modern English Biography*, 6 vols (London, 1892–1921).

147 Thomas, Keith, 'How it Strikes a Contemporary', *Times Literary Supplement*, 16 Dec. 2005, p. 6

148 Cf. the investigations into searchable text by the National Biographies Research Unit, University of Glasgow: Sturges, 'Collective Biography in the 1980s', *Biography*, VI, 4 (1983), p. 329.

149 Horden, 'Dictionary of Scottish Biography', p. 81.

150 Goring, Rosemary (ed.), *Chambers Scottish Biographical Dictionary*, (Edinburgh, 1992).

151 Roy, Kenneth (ed.), *Dictionary of Scottish Biography vol. 1, 1971–75* (Carrick, 1999).

152 Approximate mean figure of 5,106 Scots by birth and 6,276 articles referring to Scotland: raw figures courtesy of Dr Henry Summerson, OUP, 2006.

153 Alexander, Jack, *McCrae's Battalion: The Story of the 16th Royal Scots* (Edinburgh, 2003).

154 For example, Conolly, M.F., *Biographical Dictionary of Eminent Men of Fife* (Cupar, 1866).

155 Slaven, A. and Checkland, S. (eds), *Dictionary of Scottish Business Biography 1860–1960*, 2 vols (Aberdeen, 1986); Knox, W. (ed.), *Scottish Labour Leaders 1918–193: A Biographical Dictionary* (Edinburgh, 1984); Watt, D.E.R., *A Biographical Dictionary of Scottish Graduates to A.D. 1410* (Oxford, 1977).

156 Ewan, Elizabeth, Innes, Sue, Reynolds, Sían and Pipes, Rose (eds), *Biographical Dictionary of Scottish Women* (Edinburgh, 2006), pp. xxviii–ix.
157 Project led by Professor David Walker, St Andrews University; website: www.scottisharchitects.org.uk.

Chapter 3: The Legacy of the Revolution

1 See Kidd, Colin, *British Identities Before Nationalism* (1999), Chapter 6; and Kidd, Colin, 'Teutonist Ethnology and Scottish Nationalist Inhibition, 1780–1880', *Scottish Historical Review*, LXXIV (1995), pp. 45–68.
2 See note 4, below.
3 Although see the bold Marxist attempt to re-examine its legacy in Davidson, Neil, *Discovering the Scottish Revolution 1692–1746* (2003). There will also be more to come from Dr Derek J. Patrick, based on his 2002 University of St Andrews' PhD, 'People and Parliament in Scotland, 1689–1702'. See his essay, 'Unconventional Procedure: Scottish Electoral Politics after the Revolution' in Brown, Keith M. and Mann, Alastair J. (eds.), *Parliament and Politics in Scotland, 1567–1707* (2005).
4 Dundas, Henry, *Substance of the Speech of the Right Hon. Henry Dundas in the House of Commons, Thursday Feb 7, 1799, on the Subject of the Legislative Union with Ireland* (1799). There were four editions published in London in addition to the Dublin edition, all published in 1799.
5 For the unionist tradition in modern Scotland, see Macdonald, Catriona M.M. (ed.), *Unionist Scotland 1800–1997* (1998).
6 An exception is Harris, Tim, *Revolution: the Great Crisis of the British Monarchy, 1685–1720* (2006). I am very grateful to him for allowing me to read Chapter 9, 'The Glorious Revolution in Scotland', in advance of publication.
7 See Lynch, Michael, *Scotland: A New History* (2nd edn, 1992), Chapter 18; Brown, Keith M., 'Reformation to Union, 1560–1707' in Houston, R.A. and Knox, W.W.J., *The New Penguin History of Scotland* (2001), pp. 259–66.
8Ferguson, William, *Scotland: 1689 to the Present* (1968); Halliday, James, 'The Club and the Revolution in Scotland 1689–90', *SHR*, 45 (1966). For a critical introduction to the Irish parliamentary 'nationalism' of 1760–1800 see Smyth, Jim, *The Making of the United Kingdom 1660–1800* (2001), pp. 143–4.
9 See Bartlett, Thomas, 'Ireland: From Legislative Independence to Legislative Union, 1782–1800' in Dickinson, H.T. and Lynch, Michael (eds), *The Challenge to Westminster: Sovereignty, Devolution and Independence* (2000), pp. 61–70.
10 Murdoch, Alex [Alexander], 'Scottish Sovereignty in the Eighteenth Century' in Dickinson, H.T. and Lynch, Michael (eds), *The Challenge to Westminster: Sovereignty, Devolution and Independence* (2002), pp. 42–9. I am grateful to Professor Daniel Szechi for his comments on this point. He notes that there were significant changes in the position of the Church of England as well after 1688.

11 Harris, Tim, 'The People, The Law and the Constitution in Scotland and England: A Comparative Approach to the Glorious Revolution', *Journal of British Studies*, 38 (1999), pp. 28–58.
12 Clarke, Tristram, 'The Williamite Episcopalians and the Glorious Revolution in Scotland', *Records of the Scottish Church History Society*, 24 (1990–2), p. 46.
13 Kidd, Colin, 'Integration: Patriotism and Nationalism' in Dickinson, H.T. (ed.), *A Companion to Eighteenth-Century Britain* (2002), pp. 369–80; and Kidd, Colin, 'Conditional Britons: The Scots Covenanting Tradition and the Eighteenth-century British State', *English Historical Review*, 117 (2002), pp. 1147–76.
14 Quoted in Kidd, Colin, *Subverting Scotland's Past: Scottish Whig Historians and the Creation of an Anglo-British Identity, 1689–c.1830* (1993), p. 245.
15 Macpherson, James (ed.), *Original Papers; Containing the Secret History of Great Britain from the Restoration to the Accession of the House of Hanover*, 2 vols (1775), vol. II, p.360.
16 Riley, P.W.J., *The Union of England and Scotland* (1978); Riley, P.W.J., *King William and the Scottish Politicians* (1979). Manchester University Press, publishers of *The Union of England and Scotland*, refused to publish the chapters that became *King William and the Scottish Politicians*, which could only find a publisher in Scotland as a separate book.
17 Riley, *Union*, p. 314.
18 Goldie, Mark, 'Divergence and Union: Scotland and England, 1660–1707' in Bradshaw, Brendan and Morrill, John (eds), *The British Problem c.1534–1707* (1996), pp. 220–45.
19 Gibson, A.J.S. and Smout, T.C., *Prices, Food and Wages in Scotland 1550–1780* (1995), pp. 170–1. Of course, the 'ill years' did not affect Scotland alone, but were part of the result of harsh climactic conditions affecting all of northern Europe during this period.
20 See Mijiers, Esther, 'Scotland and the United Provinces, c.1680–1730', PhD Thesis, St Andrews University, 2002; Catterall, Douglas, *Community without Borders: Scots Migrants and the Changing Face of Power in the Dutch Republic, c.1600–*1700 (Leiden, 2002); Gardner, Ginny, *The Scottish Exile Community in the Netherlands 1660–1690* (2004); and Mijiers, Esther and Stiubhart, Domhnall Uilleam, 'Special Issue: Papers from the "Williamite Scotland and the United Provinces" Symposium', Institute for Advanced Studies in the Humanities (IASH), University of Edinburgh, June 2004; *Dutch Crossing: A Journal of Low Countries Studies*, 29, no. 1 (Summer 2005). Also see Dunthorne, Hugh, '"An Inseparable Alliance"? Scotland and Holland in the Age of Improvement', *Documentatieblad Werkgroep Achttiende Eeuw*, 19 (1987), pp. 157–70.
21 Lenman, Bruce, *The Jacobite Risings in Britain 1689–1746* (1980, reissued 1995), p. 153.
22 Riley, *Union*, p. 180.

23 Robertson, John, 'Andrew Fletcher's Vision of Union' in Mason, Roger A. (ed.), *Scotland and England 1286–1815* (1987), p. 204.
24 Robertson, John, 'The Union Debate in Scotland 1698–1707' in Robertson (ed.), *A Union for Empire? Political Thought and the Union of 1707* (1995), p. 212.
25 Ferguson, William, *Scotland's Relations with England* (1977, reissued 1994), pp. 172, 209, 217; Young, John R., 'The Scottish Parliament and the Covenanting Heritage of Constitutional Reform' in Macinnes, Allan I. and Ohlmeyer, Jane (eds), *The Stuart Kingdom in the Seventeenth Century* (2002), pp. 226–50.
26 Szechi, Daniel, *George Lockhart of Carnwath 1689–1727* (2002), pp. 66–7; Riley, *Union*, pp. 150, 177. I am grateful to Professor Szechi for making clear to me the extent of his scepticism regarding any connection the duke of Hamilton might have had with the concept of principled politics.
27 For the Scottish context, see Allan, David, *Philosophy and Politics in Later Stuart Scotland* (2000); and Allan, David, *Virtue, Learning and the Scottish Enlightenment* (1993).
28 Clarke, 'The Williamite Episcopalians and the Glorious Revolution in Scotland', pp. 33–52.
29 Drummond, Andrew and Bulloch, James, *The Scottish Church, 1688–1843* (1973), p. 29, draws on the full but dated account in the relevant chapters in Grub, George, *An Ecclesiastical History of Scotland*, vol. IV (1861). White, Gavin, *The Scottish Episcopal Church: A New History* (1998) is able to only touch on the subject. There is a need for more research on episcopalianism in eighteenth-century Scotland. Also see Brown, Callum G., *Religion and Society in Scotland since 1707* (1997), pp. 33–6.
30 McCormick, Joseph (ed.), *State-Papers and Letters, Addressed to William Carstares, Confidential Secretary to K. William during the Whole of his Reign* (1774).
31 Sher, Richard B., *Church and University in the Scottish Enlightenment* (1985), pp. 289–90; Campbell, Thorbjörn, *Standing Witnesses: An Illustrated Guide to the Scottish Covenanters* (1996), p. 166.
32 Sher, Richard B., '1688 and 1788: William Robertson on Revolution in Britain and France' in Dukes, Paul and Dunkley, John (eds), *Culture and Revolution* (1990), p. 99.
33 *Ibid.*, pp. 99 and 108 (reference 3).
34 *Ibid.*, p. 102.
35 Sankey, Margaret and Szechi, Daniel, 'Elite Culture and the Decline of Scottish Jacobitism 1716–1745', *Past and Present*, no. 173 (2001), pp. 90–128, which discusses the reasons for 'the incontestable fact that Scottish Jacobitism was virtually moribund by 1750' (p. 102).
36 Colley, Linda, *Britons: Forging the Nation 1707–1837* (1992), Chapter 3.
37 Murdoch, Alexander, 'Lord Bute, James Stuart Mackenzie and the government of Scotland' in Schweizer, Karl W. (ed.), *Lord Bute: Essays in Re-interpretation* (1988), pp. 117–46.

38 Colley, *Britons*, pp. 117–32; Mackillop, Andrew, *'More Fruitful than the Soil': Army, Empire and the Scottish Highlands, 1715–1815* (2000); and Harris, Bob, *Politics and the Nation: Britain in the Mid-Eighteenth Century* (2002), Chapter 4.

39 Findlay, David and Murdoch, Alexander, 'Revolution to Reform: Eighteenth-Century Politics, *c.*1690–1800' in E. Patricia Dennison, et al. (eds), *Aberdeen Before 1800: A New History* (2002), pp. 267–77.

40 Landsman, Ned C., 'The Provinces and the Empire: Scotland, the American Colonies and the Development of British Provincial Identity' in Stone, Lawrence (ed.), *An Imperial State at War: Britain from 1689 to 1815* (1994), pp. 258–87. I am grateful to Daniel Szechi for pointing out to me 'the continuous stream of anxiety about the vulnerability of the Kirk because of its indirect association with the Church of England'.

41 Smollett to John Moore, 2 Jan. 1758, Letter 48 in *The Letters of Tobias Smollett*, ed. Knapp, Lewis M. (1970), pp. 64–65.

42 Wilkinson, David, 'Sir James Smollett' in *The History of Parliament: The House of Commons 1690–1715*, ed. Cruickshanks, Eveline, et al. (2002), vol. V, p. 515.

43 See Sher, Richard B., *Church and University in the Scottish Enlightenment* (1985). Also see the short and balanced summary in Allan, David, *Scotland in the Eighteenth Century* (2002), pp. 63–86: 'Moderatism: Toleration and Civility'.

44 For example, see Fontana, Biancamaria, *Rethinking the Politics of Commercial Society: The Edinburgh Review 1802–1832* (1985).

45 Hopkins, Paul, *Glencoe and the End of the Highland War* (1986, revised reprint 1998).

46 Kidd, Colin, 'The Rehabilitation of Scottish Jacobitism', *SHR*, 77 (1998), pp. 58–76.

47 Murdoch, Alexander, *The People Above: Politics and Administration in Mid-Eighteenth-Century Scotland* (1980), p.99; Murdoch, Alexander, 'Scotland and the Union' in Dickinson, H.T. (ed), *Companion to Eighteenth-Century Britain* (2002), pp. 386–7; and Harris, *Politics and the Nation*, pp. 148–91, which achieves a genuinely 'British' perspective on the phenomenon.

48 Although Forbes was more than 'a Presbyterian Whig'. See Gurses Tarbuck, Derya, 'Duncan Forbes of Culloden (1685–1747): A Presbyterian Whig and a Hutchinsonian', *Eighteenth-Century Thought*, 3 (2005).

49 See Pittock, Murray G.H., 'Lord George Murray'; Birkeland, Marianna, 'James Murray, second duke of Atholl'; and Henderson, T.F., revised by Clyde, Robert, 'John Murray, third duke of Atholl', all in the *Oxford Dictionary of National Biography*.

50 Lenman, Bruce, *The Jacobite Clans of the Great Glen 1650–1784* (1984, reissued 1995), p. 108; Lenman, Bruce, 'From the Union of 1707 to the Franchise Reform of 1832' in Houston, R.A. and Knox, W.W.J. (eds), *The New Penguin History of Scotland* (2001), pp. 277, 352.

51 Published in Mackay, David N. (ed.), *Trial of James Stewart (The Appin Murder)* (1907), pp. 290–1. See Hunter, James, *Culloden and the Last Clansman* (2001) for a very different perspective from that valorised in Argyll's speech. Daniel Szechi has noted to me that earlier the second duke of Argyll had been accused of intrigue with the Jacobite court as part of his problematic relationship with Sir Robert Walpole's government.
52 Sankey and Szechi, 'Elite Culture and the Decline of Jacobitism'.
53 Duffy, Christopher, *The '45* (2003). John Home, who was a participant in Whig resistance to the Jacobites during the rebellion, produced an extraordinary *History of the Rebellion in 1745* (1802), in which Scottish Jacobites were portrayed as noble followers of a lost cause; Sher, *Church and University in the Scottish Enlightenment*, p. 40.
54 Phillipson, Nicholas, 'Propriety, Property and Prudence: David Hume and the Defence of the Revolution' in Phillipson, Nicholas and Skinner, Quentin (eds), *Political Discourse in Early Modern Britain* (1993), pp. 302–20.
55 Kidd, *Subverting Scotland's Past*, pp. 101–7.
56 Szechi, Daniel, *The Jacobites: Britain and Europe, 1688–1788* (1994).
57 Szechi, *George Lockhart*, p. 196.
58 Hutton, Ronald, *Charles the Second: King of England, Scotland, and Ireland* (1989), caption to illustration 2 between pp. 274 and 275.
59 Phillipson, Nicholas, *Hume* (1989) and Phillipson, 'Propriety, Property and Prudence'.
60 Dunthorne, Hugh, 'The Dutch Republic' in Fitzpatrick, Martin, et al. (eds), *The Enlightenment World* (2004); and Smyth, J., *Making of the United Kingdom*, pp. 136–44.
61 Cairns, John W., 'Scottish Law and the Status of the Union' in Robertson, John (ed.), *A Union for Empire* (1995), emphasises that the Union brought Scots lawyers into fuller engagement with the English legal tradition.
62 Murdoch, 'Sovereignty' in Dickinson and Lynch (eds), *Challenge to Westminster*, p. 46; Robertson, John, 'Empire and Union: Two Concepts of the Early Modern European Political Order' in Robertson (ed), *Union for Empire*, p. 34.
63 There is a flawed but challenging discussion of this issue in Davidson, Neil, *The Origins of Scottish Nationhood* (2000).
64 Murdoch, Alexander, 'The Squadrone', thematic article in the online edition of the *Oxford Dictionary of National Biography* released October 2005.
65 Murdoch, Alexander, 'John Campbell, second duke of Argyll' and 'Archibald Campbell, third duke of Argyll' in the *Oxford Dictionary of National Biography* (2004).
66 Owen, J.B., *The Rise of the Pelhams* (1957), pp. 295–301; and see Bricke, Margaret S., 'The Pelhams vs. Argyll: A Struggle for the Mastery of Scotland 1747–1748', *SHR*, 61 (1982), pp. 157–65.

67 Sankey and Szechi, 'Elite Culture and the Decline of Jacobitism'.
68 Simpson, John M. 'Who Steered the Gravy Train, 1707–1766?' in Phillipson, N.T. and Mitchison, Rosalind (eds), *Scotland in the Age of Improvement* (1970, reissued with a new introduction 1996), especially pp. 57–61 and 64–9.
69 Andrew Mitchell to Duncan Forbes, 22 May 1747, in Warrand, Duncan (ed.), *More Culloden Papers*, 5 vols (1922–30), vol. 5, pp. 182–3.
70 *Ibid.*
71 *Ibid.*
72 Fontana, *Rethinking the Politics of Commercial Society*; McFarland, E.W., *Ireland and Scotland in the Age of Revolution* (1994); Brims, John D., 'The Scottish Democratic Movement in the Age of the French Revolution', PhD Thesis, University of Edinburgh, 1983; Pentland, Gordon, 'Patriotism, Universalism and the Scottish Convention, 1792–1794', *History*, 89 (2004), pp. 340–60.
73 Historical Manuscripts Commission, *Report on the Manuscripts of the Right Honourable Lord Polwarth*, vol. 5, ed. Paton, H. (1961), no. 346, 26 January 1747/8.
74 Colley, *Britons*, pp. 127–32.
75 Murdoch, Alexander J., 'Politics and the People in the Burgh of Dumfries, 1758–1760', *SHR*, 70 (1991), especially pp. 158, 162 and 168.
76 Quoted in Brims, John, 'The Scottish Democratic Movement in the Age of the French Revolution', p. 414.
77 Pentland, Gordon, The Debate on Scottish Parliamentary Reform, 1830–1832', *SHR*, vol. LXXXV, no. 219 (April 2006).
78 Brown, Stewart J., *Thomas Chalmers and the Godly Commonwealth* (1982), pp. 328–9.

CHAPTER 4: THE NOTORIOUS CAPTAIN JOHN PORTEOUS

1 Logue, Kenneth J, *Popular Disturbances in Scotland, 1780–1815* (Edinburgh, 1979 and 2003).
2 For example, Rudé, George, *The Crowd in the French Revolution* (Oxford, 1959); *The Crowd in History: A Study of Popular Disturbances in England and France, 1730–1848* (New York, 1964).
3 Cobb, Richard, *The Police and the People: French Popular Protest, 1784–1820* (Oxford, 1970).
4 Thompson, Edward, esp. 'The Moral Economy of the English Crowd in the Eighteenth Century', *Past & Present*, l, 1971, and his more recent 'The Moral Economy Reviewed' in Thompson, E., *Customs in Common* (London, 1991).
5 Quinault, R. and Stevenson, J. (eds), *Popular Protest and Public Order* (London, 1974).
6 'The Tayside Meal Mobs, 1772–1773', *SHR*, XLVI (1967).

7 Whatley, Christopher A., esp. his chapter on 'Stability and Protest' in his *Scottish Society, 1707–1830: Beyond Jacobitism, towards Industrialisation* (Manchester, 2000).
8 'How tame were the Scottish Lowlanders during the Eighteenth Century?' in Devine, T.M. (ed.), *Conflict and Stability in Scottish Society, 1700–1850* (Edinburgh,1990).
9 Whatley, Christopher A., 'Royal Day, People's Day: The Monarch's Birthday in Scotland, *c.*1660–1860", in Mason, Roger and MacDougall, Norman (eds), *People and Power in Scotland* (Edinburgh, 1982).
10 Fraser, W.H., 'Patterns of Protest' in Devine and Mitchison (eds), *People and Society in Scotland*, vol. 1 (Edinburgh, 1988); and also in his *Conflict and Class: Scottish Workers 1700–1838* (Edinburgh, 1988), *passim*.
11 Houston, R.A., 'Popular Protest', in his *Social Change in the Age of Enlightenment: Edinburgh 1660–1760* (Oxford, 1994).
12 Houston, R.A., 'Popular Politics in the Reign of George II: The Edinburgh Cordiners', *SHR* (1993).
13 Thompson, E., especially 'The Moral Economy of the English Crowd in the Eighteen Century', *Past and Present*, 1 (1971).
14 Thompson, E., esp. 'The Moral Economy Reviewed', in Thompson, E., *Customs in Common* (London, 1991), pp. 259–351.
15 *Ibid.*, p. 260.
16 See especially pp. 272–5.
17 *Wealth of Nations*, Chapter 5, *passim*.
18 Thompson, E., *Customs in Common*, (London, 1991), p. 275.
19 The two other studies of the riot and its aftermath, undertaken by Logue, K.J. and Dickinson, H.T., are: 'The Porteous Riot: A Study of the Breakdown in Law and Order in Edinburgh, 1736–1737', *Journal of the Scottish Labour History Society*, x (1976), and 'The Porteous Riot', *History Today* (1972).
20 Roughhead, William (ed.), *The Trial of Captain Porteous* (Edinburgh, 1909), p. 3.
21 Anon, *The Life and Death of John Porteous* (1737), pp. 11–12.
22 *Ibid., passim.*
23 *Ibid.*, p. 7.
24 See Logue, *Popular Disturbances*, p. 5.
25 The sources for the events described hereafter are contemporary pamphlets such as *The Life and Death of Captain Porteous* (Edinburgh, 1737) and *A Memorial for the People of Scotland* (Dublin, 1737, both of which can be found in the Edinburgh Central Library's 'Porteous Mob Pamphlets I' collection along with other papers. The very full *The Trial of Captain Porteous*, ed. Roughhead, William (Edinburgh, 1909) also publishes much original material. The Morton Papers (GD 150/3480) in the National Archives of Scotland, and the Saltoun Papers (MS. 17509) in the National Library of Scotland provide important contemporary material. Other accounts and sources include Dick-

inson and Logue, 'The Porteous Riot' (1972); Dickinson and Logue, 'The Porteous Riot' (1976); Lever, Sir Tresham, 'Sir Walter Scott and the Murder of Porteous', *Blackwood's Magazine*, cccx, (1971), pp. 212–224 (but see also his short article in the *Scotsman*, 6 January 1973, and response from Dickinson and Logue, *ibid.*, 12 January, 1973); Omond, G.W.T, 'The Porteous Riot', *The Scottish Review*, xx (1892), pp. 52–67; and McNeill, Robert, *The Porteous Riot* (Edinburgh, n.d.).

26 See, for instance, *HMC*, VIII (1881), Report and Appendix (1), p. 10, letter from Alexander Wilson, Lord Provost of Edinburgh to Patrick Lindsay, MP, 15 April 1736.

27 See Roughhead, *op. cit.*, pp. 145–216.

28 Scott's account in *Heart of Midlothian* paints a relatively accurate description of events that night.

29 Houston, R.A., 'Popular Politics in the Reign of George II: The Edinburgh Cordiners', *SHR* (1993).

30 *Ibid.*

31 James Douglas to [the earl of Morton], n.d. but clearly 1737, SRO GD 150/3480/28.

32 Edinburgh City Archives, Town Council Minutes, lvi , p.125 and lvii, p.56.

33 Whatley, C.A., *Scottish Society 1707–1830* (Manchester, 2000), p.153. Houston, 'Popular Protest', p. 318, agrees with this 'social cohesion' interpretation.

34 Town Council Minutes, lvii, p. 77.

35 NLS, Saltoun MSS, Box 32.

36 Cobbett's *Parliamentary History of England*, vol. X, pp. 187–319.

37 *Ibid.*, p. 246.

38 *Ibid.*, p. 294.

39 Horace Walpole's Memoirs of the Reign of King George II, ed. Lord Holland (London, 1846), vol. I, pp. 42–3, and 59.

40 Cobbett's *Parliamentary History of England*, vol. X, 317.

CHAPTER 5: THE KING'S MEN OR GLENGARRY'S?

(Note by the editor: important research relevant to the general context of this essay published since its composition include Cookson, J.E., *The British Armed Nation 1793–1815* (1997) and Mackillop, Andrew, *'More Fruitful Than the Soil': Army, Empire and the Scottish Highlands 1715–1815* (2000) – my thanks for Dr Andrew Mackillop for his comments on this paper.)

1 National Archives of Scotland (NAS), GD248/190/3/7, James Grant, factor at Castle Grant, to the Rev. James Grant, Urquart, 24 Feb. 1793; GD248/683/2, Col. Alex. Murray Macgregor to Sir James Grant, 12 Mar.

1793; GD248/683/2, Lt Col. A.P. Cumming of Altyre to Sir James Grant, 3 Mar. 1793.

2 GD248/683/2, Alexander Macdonell of Glengarry to Sir James Grant, 4 Mar. 1793.

3 GD248/683/2, Capt. Macdonell of Glengarry to Col. Sir James Grant, 27 Mar. 1793. 'A State of the Grant Fencible Regiment', May 1793, shows that Glengarry's contingent numbered eighty men – only one other captain could claim to have fifty men of his own recruitment.

4 GD248/684/2, Lt Col. A.P. Cumming to Col. Sir James Grant, 19 Jul. 1793.

5 GD248/684/3, Lt Col. A.P. Cumming to Col. Sir James Grant, 27 Aug. 1793.

6 GD248/684/4, Major John Grant to Col. Sir James Grant, 18 Sep. 1793.

7 GD248/684/5, Lt Col. A.P. Cumming to Col. Sir James Grant, 4 Oct. 1793.

8 Formal recruiting for the 97th Highlanders commenced in January 1794.

9 GD248/685/1, Memorandum, Oct. 1793.

10 GD248/684/5, Major John Grant to Col. Sir James Grant, 29 Oct. 1793.

11 GD248/685/1, General Lord Adam Gordon to Col. Sir James Grant, 16 Nov. 1793.

12 GD248/684/6, Lt Col. A.P. Cumming to Col. Sir James Grant, 4 Nov. 1793.

13 GD248/684/6, Lt Col. A.P. Cumming to Col. Sir James Grant, Nov. 1793.

14 GD248/684/6, Capt. Macdonell of Glengarry to Col. Sir James Grant, 10 Nov. 1793.

15 GD248/683/2, Capt. Macdonell to Col. Sir James Grant, 4 Mar. 1793.

16 GD248/685/1, Lt Col. Cumming to Col. Sir James Grant, undated but Dec. 1793.

17 GD248/685/1, Lt Col. A.P. Cumming to Col. Sir James Grant, 14 Dec. 1793.

18 Another soldier discharged to Seaforth's Regiment is described by Colonel Cumming as 'the wicked Campbell from the Light Company . . . one of the worst and most unprincipled men in the Regt.'.

19 Lieut. John Grant of Auchterblair was a tacksman on the Grant estate and a half-pay lieutenant of an established corps.

20 GD248/684/6, Lt Col. A.P. Cumming to Col. Sir James Grant, Dec. 1793.

21 GD248/685/1, Lt Col. A P. Cumming to Col. Sir James Grant, 18 Dec. 1793.

22 GD248/685/1, Capt. Macdonell to Col. Sir James Grant, 23 Dec. 1793.

23 GD248/685/1, Lt Col. A.P. Cumming to Col. Sir James Grant, 18 Dec. 1793.

24 GD248/685/1, Capt. Macdonell to Lt. Col. Cumming, 19 Dec .1793.

25 GD248/685/3, Lt Col. A.P. Cumming to Col. Sir James Grant, 3 Jan. 1794.
26 GD248/685/3/52, Lt Col. A.P. Cumming to Col. Sir James Grant, 12 Jan. 1794.
27 GD248/685/5, Lt Col. A.P. Cumming to Sir James Grant, 31 Mar. 1794.
28 GD248/686/1, Lady Grant to Col. Sir James Grant, 26 Mar. 1794.
29 GD248/685/5, Lt Col. A.P. Cumming to Col. Sir James Grant, 31 Mar. 1794.
30 GD248/684/6, Capt. Macdonell to Lieut. John Grant, 23 Dec. 1793.
31 GD248/684/6, Lieut. John Grant of Auchterblair to Capt. Macdonell of Glengarry, undated.
32 GD248/685/1, Lt Col. A.P. Cumming to Col. Sir James Grant, 24 Dec. 1793.
33 GD248/685/3/31, Lt Col. A.P.Cumming to Col. Sir James Grant, 1 Jan. 1794.
34 *Ibid.*
35 GD248/685/5, Lt Col. A.P. Cumming, to Col. Sir James Grant, 31 Mar. 1794.
36 GD248/685/3, Lt Col. A.P. Cumming to Col. Sir James Grant, 14 Jan. 1794.
37 GD248/685/3, Lt Col. A.P. Cumming to Col. Sir James Grant, 2 Feb. 1794.
38 GD248/686/3, Messrs Ainslie & Fraser, Regimental Agents, to Col. Sir James Grant, 23 May 1794.
39 GD248/687/2, Lt Col. A.P. Cumming to Col. Sir James Grant, 4 Jul. 1794.
40 NAS, GD51/1/839, Melville Castle Papers, Col. Macdonell of Glengarry to the Rt Hon. Henry Dundas, 20 Oct. 1794.
41 NAS, GD51/1/844/1, Col. A. Macdonell of Glengarry to the Rt Hon. Henry Dundas, 27 Oct. 1794.
42 GD248/688/1, Capt. John Grant to Col. Sir James Grant, 28 Oct. 1794.
43 GD248/688/2, Capt. Allan Grant to Col. Sir James Grant, 4 Nov. 1794.
44 GD248/688/2, Capt. Simon Fraser to Major John Grant, 6 Nov. 1794.
45 *Ibid.*
46 GD248/688/2, Capt. S. Fraser to Col. Sir James Grant, 13 Nov. 1794.
47 GD248/688/2, Col. A. Macdonell to Col. Sir James Grant, 7 Nov. 1794.
48 GD248/688/2, The Rt.Hon. Henry Dundas to Col. Sir James Grant, 3 Nov. 1794.
49 GD248/688/2, Col. Alex. Mackay, DAG, to Col. Sir James Grant, 7 Nov. 1794.
50 GD248/688/2, Col. Sir James Grant to Major John Grant, 20 Nov. 1794.
51 GD248/688/3, Major John Grant to Col. Sir James Grant, 3 Dec. 1794.

52 GD248/688/2, Lt Col. A.P. Cumming to Col. Sir James Grant, 27 Nov. 1794.
53 GD248/688/3, Major John Grant to Col. Sir James Grant, 12 Dec. 1794.
54 *Ibid.*
55 GD248/688/3, Col. A. Macdonell to Col. Sir James Grant, 17 Dec. 1794.
56 NAS, GD51/1/864 Melville Castle papers, Col. A. Macdonell to Henry Dundas, 1 Mar. 1795.
57 The National Archives, Kew (hereafter NA), W.O.17/237 x/1 9610, Monthly Return of H.M. McDonell, Loyal Fencible Regt, 1 Apr. 1795.
58 NA, W.O. 17/237 x/1 9610, Monthly Return, 1 Jun .1795.
59 United Services Museum, Edinburgh Castle, Fraser Fencibles Order Book 356.486.261 FRA, 'Establishments in Ireland'.
60 GD248/697/4/11, General Sir R. Abercromby to Col. Sir James Grant, 13 Mar. 1799.
61 GD248/688/3, Lt Col. A.P. Cumming to Col. Sir James Grant, 25 Dec. 1794.
62 GD248/688/3, Major John Grant of Achindoun to Lady Grant, 14 Dec. 1794.

Chapter 6: The Ministry of All the Talents

1 For Melville's view of the Pittite exclusion, see National Library of Scotland (NLS), Melville, Ms 19579, ff. 19–28, Melville to his son Robert, 3 Feb. 1806.
2 For the English Pittites see National Archives of Scotland (NAS), Melville, GD51/1/90/3, William Huskisson to Melville, 9 Feb. 1806. Melville was also aware of a prospect of Grenville's turning to the Pittites: *ibid.*, GD51/1/195/13, Melville to his son Robert, 12 Feb. 1806 (copy).
3 NLS, Melville, Ms 19579, ff. 11–16, letters of Melville to his son Robert, 31 Jan. [1806] and to Charles Hope lord justice-clerk, 31 Jan. 1806 (copies).
4 NLS, Melville, Ms 9370, ff. 93–8, Charles Hope to Melville, 24 Jan. 1806; *ibid.*, Ms 19579, ff. 13–16, Melville to Hope, 31 Jan. 1806 (copy).
5 NAS, Melville, GD51/1/195/5, Robert S. Dundas to Melville, 3 Feb. [1806].
6 NLS, Melville, Ms 19581, f. 22, Col. A. Cochrane Johnstone MP to Melville, Thursday (endorsed 20 Feb. 1806, but almost certainly 6 Feb.).
7 NLS, Melville, Ms 19579, ff. 29–30, Melville to his son Robert, 4 Feb. [1806] (copy).
8 NAS, Melville, GD51/1/195/7, Melville to his son Robert, 5 Feb. 1806 (copy).
9 NLS, Melville, Ms 19579, ff. 37–40, Melville to his son Robert, 6 Feb. 1806.
10 NLS, Melville, Ms 19579, ff. 49–52, Melville to his son Robert, 8 Feb. [1806], with enclosure.
11 There is a clear statement of the plans of the English Pittites at NAS, Melville, GD51/1/90/4, William Huskisson to Melville, 10 Feb. 1806.

12 NAS, Melville, GD51/1/195/13, Melville to his son Robert, 13 Feb. 1806 (copy).

13 NLS, Melville, Ms 19579, ff. 41–2, Melville to his son Robert, 6 Feb. 1806: 'For if the body of Mr Pitt[']s friends are resolved to keep together and without either avowedly opposing or supporting government[,] act systematically on the principle of doing what they feel he would have done if he had been alive, I should certainly wave every other consideration to throw all the weight I could into that scale. I know of no other way in which they who revered him, can show a just regard for his memory.'

14 On 28 February, Melville would write a long denunciation of the mischief and danger threatened to the country by party politics: NLS, Melville, Ms 19579, ff. 82–93, Melville to his son Robert, 28 Feb. 1806.

15 NLS, Melville, Ms 19579, ff. 94–7, Melville to his son Robert, 28 Feb. 1806.

16 Melville was always prepared to boast about the strength of the alliance around him and did it again in the letter cited in note 14 above. It is fair to say that not all his associates were so confident.

17 NAS, Melville, GD51/1/195/10, Robert S. Dundas to Moira, 10 Feb. 1806 (copy).

18 NAS, Melville, GD51/1/195/12, Moira to Robert S. Dundas, 11 Feb. 1806 (copy); NLS, Melville, Ms 19581, ff. 16–17, Moira to Robert S. Dundas, 13 Feb. 1806.

19 NAS, Melville, GD51/1/195/9, Robert S. Dundas to Melville, 11 Feb. 1806 (copy); NLS, Melville, Ms 19579, ff. 57–62, letters of Melville to his son Robert, 13 and 14 Feb. 1806.

20 NAS, Melville, GD51/1/195/8, Robert S. Dundas to Melville, 6 Feb. 1806. This shows that Moira overset plans to dismiss Gordon from the Keepership of the Great Seal. He claimed to have stopped other removals: NAS, Melville, GD51/1/195/12, Moira to Robert S. Dundas, 11 Feb. 1806 (copy).

21 NLS, Melville, Ms 19581, ff. 18–19, Charles Hope to Robert S. Dundas, 15 Feb. 1806, records the disappointment of Hope, Buccleuch, Dalkeith, Hopetoun and Haddington at the turn of events. Hope was still moaning days later: Hopetoun House, Hopetoun muniments, NRA(S) Survey 888, bundle 1237, letter of Hope to Earl of Hopetoun, [25 Feb. 1806]. The lord chief baron was equally unsure of his uncle's actions: NAS, Melville, GD51/1/90/5, Robert Dundas, chief baron to Melville, 17 Feb. 1806.

22 This was partly the consequence of the principal interested parties being in three separate locations (London, Bath and Edinburgh), trying to cope with the time lags in postal deliveries. Melville could be almost as easily foxed by rumours as any other observer: see for instance NLS, Melville, Ms 19579, ff. 78–81, Melville to his son Robert, 23 and 26 Feb. [1806].

23 NAS, Melville, GD51/1/195/11, Robert S. Dundas to Melville, 12 Feb. [1806]; *ibid.*, GD51/1/195/14, same to same, 13 Feb. 1806.
24 BL, Dropmore, Add. Mss 59379, ff. 154–5, William Dundas to Grenville [18 Feb. 1806].
25 NAS, Melville, GD51/1/195/18, Robert S. Dundas to Melville, 26 Feb. 1806.
26 NAS, Melville, GD51/1/195/19, Robert S. Dundas to Melville, 10 Mar. [1806]; Aspinall, A. (ed.), *The Later Correspondence of George III*, 5 vols (Cambridge, 1966–1970), vol. IV, pp. xxviii–ix, quoting Lord Minto; See also Sack, James J., *The Grenvillites 1801–29: Party Politics and Factionalism in the Age of Pitt and Liverpool* (Illinois, 1979), p. 96. It has to be said that this was the result Melville had forecast as early as mid February, when he wrote that Grenville and Spencer never would 'abandon the charge of one half of the island' to Moira or Lauderdale: NLS, Melville, Ms 19579, ff. 60–2, Melville to his son Robert, 14 Feb. 1806. At that stage, however, very few Scots politicians would have agreed with his diagnosis.
27 NAS, Melville, GD51/1/195/18, Robert S. Dundas to Melville, 26 Feb. 1806; NLS, Melville, Ms 19579, ff. 82–93, Melville to his son Robert, 28 Feb. 1806.
28 There is a good summary of the negotiations and of the attitudes of the Scots and English Tories in Hopetoun House, Hopetoun muniments, NRA(S) Survey 888, bundle 1237, Brigadier General Alexander Hope MP to Hopetoun, 19 Feb. 1806.
29 BL, Dropmore, Add. Mss 59241, ff. 11–12, Lauderdale to Grenville, 12 Mar. 1806. The lists themselves can be seen at BL, Holland House, Add. Mss 51471, A and B. There is a further copy in the Althorp papers also in the British Library.
30 For this committee and its deliberations see BL, Dropmore, Add Mss, 58885, ff. 52–3, Thomas Grenville to Lord Grenville, [6 March 1806]; *ibid.*, Add. Mss 59263, ff. 79–80, Marquis of Douglas to Grenville, 25 June 1806; Thorne, Roland G. (ed.), *The History of Parliament: The House of Commons, 1790–1820* (5 vols, London, 1985) (hereafter *Hist. Parlia.*), I, p.87.
31 See, e.g., BL, Dropmore, Add. Mss 59380, ff. 23–4, Duke of Gordon to Grenville, 27 Feb. 1806; *ibid.*, ff. 119–120, Henry Mackenzie to William Dundas, 13 Mar. 1806; *ibid.*, ff. 129–130, Brig. Gen. Alexander Hope to Grenville, 14 Mar. 1806; *ibid.*, Add. Mss 59382, ff. 18–19, George Buchan to same, 27 Apr. 1806.
32 Aspinall, *Correspondence of George III*, vol. IV, p. 360, quoting a letter of Spencer to Grenville, late February 1806.
33 *Ibid.*, vol. IV, pp. 451–2, quoting a letter of Lord Justice-Clerk Hope to Spencer, 7 March 1806.
34 Meville's preferred candidate was David Home, and he was heavily ironic

about Hay's qualities: NLS, Melville, Ms 19579, ff. 41–2, Melville to his son Robert, 6 Feb. 1806.

35 NLS, Melville, Ms 19581, ff. 27–30, Charles Hope, justice-clerk to Robert S. Dundas, 11 April 1806. It had also been planned to appoint Lord Sempill as chamberlain of Ettrick Forest in place of a friend of Buccleuch's.

36 BL, Althorp, G/64, Minute of Lauderdale and Grenville conversation, 16 July 1806. When I first read through the Althorp papers in the 1990s, they still awaited their subsequent cataloguing and rearrangement. I cite them here with the box numbers used at the time of my research.

37 BL, Dropmore, Add. Mss 58941, ff. 39–40, Lauderdale to Grenville, 18 April 1806; *ibid.*, f. 41 Grenville to Lauderdale, same date (copy).

38 *Hist. Parlia.*, I. p. 89 talks of a Grenville party in Scotland. Charles Long wrote to Melville, 1 Dec. 1806: 'You say in Scotland the name of Grenville is hardly known & the interest opposed to yours is that of the Foxites – it is very much so in Ireland.' (NAS, Melville, GD51/1/108/1). What was seen in Scotland was a tension between the ministerial policies of Grenville and the pent-up frustrations of the Foxites. Grenville's attitudes in effect acted as a harness on the Foxites rather than as an obstruction. For Cassillis, see BL, Dropmore, Add. Mss 58983, ff. 56–7 and 67–70, letters of Cassillis to Grenville, 3 Feb. and 17 Nov. 1806. Lord Fife was similarly a Grenvillite and clearly ill at ease with Fox: *ibid.*, Add. Mss 58987, ff. 109–10, Fife to Grenville, 16 Sep. 1806. In time, and particularly after Fox's death, some Scots felt able to support government where previously they had stood aloof and they might perhaps be called Grenvillites. This categorisation should not be pushed too far, however. The most obvious example was Sir Hew Dalrymple Hamilton: NAS, Melville, GD51/1/104, Sir Hew to Melville, 25 Oct. 1806. Late in the year, the earl of Kellie, long a Melville supporter, tried to parlay an old association with Grenville into a chance to get the lord lieutenancy of Fife: BL, Dropmore, Add. Mss 58994, f. 87, Kellie to Sir John Anstruther, 7 Dec. 1806.

39 NAS, Melville, GD51/1/198/28/6, Lord Garlies to Melville, 17 Sep. 1806; BL, Dropmore, Add. Mss 59389, f. 166–7, Galloway to Grenville, 19 Oct. 1806.

40 BL, Dropmore, Add. Mss 59263, ff. 22–4, Lord Archibald Hamilton to Henry Erskine, Lord Advocate, 20 Sep. [1806].

41 BL, Dropmore, Add. Mss 59263, ff. 12–15, Henry Erskine to [?Grenville], 19 Aug. 1806.

42 NLS, Melville, Ms 19581, ff. 5–7, Charles Hope, justice-clerk to Robert S. Dundas, 10 Feb. 1806.

43 BL, Huskisson, Add. Mss 38737, ff. 135–42, letters of Robert Dundas, lord chief baron to Huskisson, 12–22 July 1806.

44 NAS, Melville, GD51/1/195/16, Melville to his son Robert, 16 Feb. [1806]. Melville felt that his nephew's excuse, that he was preserving his Sutherland seat,

was inadequate, not least because the Stafford family, under an earlier agreement, were bound to continue it to him regardless of his politics.

45 BL, Dropmore, Add. Mss 58941, f. 46, Grenville to Lauderdale, 18 April 1806 (copy).

46 NAS, Treasury Out letter books, Scotland, RH2/4/495, pp. 9–10, copy of warrant by King George III for appointing Cunynghame, 6 May 1806.

47 Furber, Holden, *Henry Dundas, First Viscount Melville* (Oxford, 1931), pp. 159–62. Furber used a transcript of shorthand notes of the committee's sittings.

48 NLS, Melville, Ms 19579, ff. 66–73, Melville to his son Robert, 17 Feb. 1806.

49 For this, see Hopetoun House, Hopetoun muniments, NRA(S) Survey 888, bundle 1236, Melville to Hopetoun, 15 July 1805.

50 Glasgow City Archives (GCA), Campbell of Succoth papers, TD219/6/369, Lord Dunsinnan to Ilay Campbell, lord president, 24 April 1805; Thompson, H.W. (ed.), *The Anecdotes and Egotisms of Henry Mackenzie 1745–1831* (Oxford, 1927), p. 145. It is worth recalling that Pitt himself was an utter incompetent in handling his private finances.

51 NLS, Melville, Ms 19579, ff. 43–6, Melville to his son Robert, 7 Feb. 1806.

52 NLS, Melville, Ms 19579, ff. 17–18, Melville to his son Robert, 2 Feb. 1806.

53 NAS, Melville, GD51/1/195/19, Robert S. Dundas to Melville, 10 Mar. 1806. See also Sack, *The Grenvillites*, p.83.

54 For accounts of the trial and its background, see Matheson, Cyril, *Henry Dundas, First Viscount Melville* (London, 1933), pp. 366–72; Fry, Michael, *The Dundas Despotism* (Edinburgh, 1992), pp. 261–76; Furber, *Henry Dundas*, pp. 163–5; and Fulford, Roger, *Samuel Whitbread 1764–1815: A Study in Opposition* (London, 1967), pp. 128–39.

55 Edinburgh University Library (EUL), Laing Mss, Div. II, 461/2, Lord Kellie to Lord Napier, 17 May 1806.

56 *Ibid.*, 461/2, letters of Kellie to Lord Napier, 29 and 31 May, and 3 June 1806.

57 These were the second and third charges. Matheson, *op. cit.*, p. 371 prints the voting totals.

58 NAS, Melville, GD51/1/198/12/12, Robert Dundas, chief baron to Melville, 19 June 1806.

59 NAS, Melville, GD51/1/198/12/6 and 11, lettters of Robert Dundas to Melville, 16 and 24 June 1806. Melville received hundreds of letters congratulating him on his acquittal. A sample can be seen at NAS, Bonar, Mackenzie and Kermack, W.S., GD235/10/8.

60 NAS, Melville, GD51/1/195/5, Robert S. Dundas to Melville, 3 Feb. [1806];

NAS, Dundas of Arniston, RH4/15/6, letterbook 8, no. 42B, Robert Dundas, chief baron to his wife Elizabeth, 26 June 1806.

61 NAS, Leith Hall papers, GD225/34/25/21, William Maule to Alexander Hay, 21 June 1806: 'I, with some others have written letters to the Advocate (at his own desire) pressing the necessity of removing all the Melvillites immediately.'

62 *Ibid.*, GD225/34/25/22, James Mansfield to Alexander Hay, 28 June 1806.

63 BL, Dropmore, Add. Mss 59263, ff. 79–80, Marquis of Douglas to Grenville, 25 June 1806.

64 *Ibid.*, Add. Mss 59263, ff. 84–5, Grenville to Marquis of Douglas, 27 June 1806 (copy).

65 *Ibid.*, Add. Mss 58933, ff. 21–2, Spencer to Grenville, [27 June 1806].

66 *Ibid.*, Add. Mss 59385, ff. 91–2, Grenville to Gordon, 27 July 1806 (copy). Lauderdale's commission was dated 25 July.

67 Thorne, *Hist. Parlia.*, vol. I, p. 87, using BL, Althorp, G/256, correspondence of Lauderdale and Spencer, 22–26 Jul. 1806; *ibid.*, G/64, memo of conversation, 16 July 1806.

68 BL, Dropmore, Add. Mss 59263, ff. 1–3, Henry Erskine, lord advocate to [Grenville], 6 Aug. 1806, with enclosure.

69 BL, Althorp, G/256/Book C, pp. 4–5, Spencer to Henry Erskine, lord advocate, 12 Aug. 1806 (copy).

70 BL, Dropmore, Add. Mss 59391, ff. 3–6, Mackenzie to [?Grenville or Spencer], 31 Oct. 1806.

71 BL, Althorp, G/253, Thomas Grenville to Spencer, 7 Aug. 1806, enclosing Colin Mackenzie to Lady Stafford, 23 Jul. 1806.

72 Brown, David J, 'Henry Dundas and the Government of Scotland', PhD Thesis, University of Edinburgh, 1989, pp. 374–5.

73 NAS, Melville, GD51/1/198/12/14, Robert Dundas, chief baron to [Melville], 22 June 1806.

74 For the few nuggets on this issue, see Saville, Richard, *Bank of Scotland: A History, 1695–1995* (Edinburgh, 1996), p. 179, and Brown, Thesis, p. 17.

75 BL, Althorp, G/256, 50, Lauderdale to Spencer, 24 Feb. 1807.

76 BL, Althorp, G/256, Letters between Spencer and Kellie, 24 Feb., and 4 and 10 Mar. 1807; *Ibid.*, G/66, J Beckett to Spencer, 7 Mar. 1807.

77 BL, Dropmore, Add. Mss 59263, ff. 4–11, Henry Erskine, lord advocate to [Spencer], 18 Aug. 1806.

78 *Ibid.*, Add. Mss 58933, f. 50, Grenville to Spencer, 5 Sep. 1806 (copy); *Ibid.*, ff. 51–2, Spencer to Grenville [8 Sep. 1806]; BL, Althorp, G/251, correspondence between Henry Erskine, lord advocate and Spencer, 24–28 Sep. 1806.

79 BL, Dropmore, Add. Mss 59263, ff. 26–9, Henry Erskine, lord advocate to Spencer, 6 Oct. 1806.

80 *Ibid.*, Add. Mss 58994, ff.85–6, Sir John Anstruther to Grenville, [13 Dec. 1806].
81 NLS, Melville, Ms 9370, ff. 93–4, Melville to Portland, 19 Oct. 1806 (copy).
82 BL, Dropmore, Add. Mss 59263, ff. 93–4, Henry Erskine, lord advocate to Adam Gillies, 20 Oct. 1806 (copy).
83 Counties contested: Aberdeenshire, Banffshire, Dumfriesshire, Fife, Lanarkshire and West Lothian. Burgh group seats contested: Aberdeen, Dumfries, Glasgow, Linlithgow, Stirling and Tain.
84 There is a full account of the contest by Patrick, John, 'The 1806 Election in Aberdeenshire', *Northern Scotland*, vol. I (1973), pp. 151–76. For government's support for Hay, see BL, Dropmore, Add. Mss 58941, f. 70, Grenville to Lauderdale, 16 June 1806 (copy).
85 Thorne, *Hist. Parlia.*, vol. II, p. 522; BL, Dropmore, Add. Mss 58953, f. 150, D. MacDowall Grant to Henry Erskine, 16 Sep. 1806.
86 NAS, Melville, GD51/1/195/11, Robert S. Dundas to Melville, 12 Feb. [1806]; NLS, Melville, Ms 18579, ff. 57–9, Melville to his son Robert, 13 Feb. 1806.
87 Thorne, *Hist. Parlia.*, vol. II, p. 538–9.
88 *Ibid.*, vol. II, pp. 555–6, 610–11; BL, Dropmore, Add. Mss 59263, ff. 20–1, Henry Erskine, Lord Advocate to [?Grenville], 27 Sep. 1806; *ibid.*, ff. 22–4, Lord Archibald Hamilton to Erskine, 20 Sep. [1806]; *ibid.*, Add. Mss 58953, ff. 157–8, Erskine to Grenville, 19 Oct. 1806.
89 NLS, Melville, Ms 19581, ff. 27–30, Charles Hope, justice-clerk to Robert S. Dundas, 11 April 1806; BL, Dropmore, Add. Mss 59263, ff. 26–9, Henry Erskine, Lord Advocate to [Spencer], 6 Oct. 1806.
90 Dirom's stance is described in NAS, Melville, GD51/1/198/7/16, Dirom to [Melville], 11 June 1806 and in NAS, Buccleuch, GD224/519/2/8, Buccleuch to Queensberry, 6 November 1806 (copy). Buccleuch papers cited with kind permission of his Grace the duke of Buccleuch and Queensberry, KT.
91 NAS, Buccleuch, GD224/519/2/5, Queensberry to Henry Erskine, lord advocate, 1 Nov. 1806 (copy).
92 *Ibid.*, GD224/519/2/8, Buccleuch to Queensberry, 6 Nov. 1806 (copy).
93 NAS, Melville, GD51/1/198/7/15, William Johnstone Hope to [Melville], 6 May 1806; NAS, Buccleuch, GD224/519/2/4, Queensberry to William Johnstone Hope, 15 April 1806 (copy).
94 BL, Dropmore, Add. Mss 58941, f. 178, Grenville to Lauderdale, 25 Oct. 1806 (copy).
95 Thorne, *Hist. Parlia.*, vol. II, pp. 591, 603–4, 617, 620–1.
96 NAS, Buccleuch, GD224/668/12/11–13, Melville to Buccleuch, 4 April 1806.

97 NAS, Leith Hall papers, GD225/34/25/57, James Mansfield to Alexander Hay, 29 July 1806.
98 NAS, Melville, GD51/1/195/9, 18, letters of Robert S. Dundas to Melville 11 and 26 Feb. 1806; NAS, Buccleuch, GD224/668/12/7, same to Buccleuch, 12 Mar. 1806.
99 The story can be followed in Thorne, *Hist. Parlia.*, vol. II, pp. 547–8, and in NAS, Melville, GD51/1/198/12/5-27.
100 NLS, Melville, Ms 19579, ff. 80–1, letters of Melville to his son Robert, 26 Feb. [1806]; NAS, Melville, GD51/5/432, Lord Dunsinnan to Melville, 10 Mar. 1806.
101 Thorne, *Hist. Parlia.*, vol. I, p. 90, examines Adam's calculations, now in the Grey Mss, Durham University.
102 BL, Dropmore, Add. Mss 59263, ff. 26–9, Henry Erskine, lord advocate to [Spencer], 6 Oct. 1806.
103 NAS, Leven and Melville, GD26/13/198/5/1-2, Lord Spencer to earl of Leven, 29 Oct. 1806, lists the government candidates: Erroll, Elgin, Leven, Selkirk, Northesk, Balcarres, Stair, Glasgow, Forbes, Cathcart, Sempill, Elphinstone, Somerville, Blantyre, Reay and Kinnaird. The crude manner in which the government list was touted around was so much of a break from Melville's own past methods that Abercorn contemplated complaining in parliament about government interference: NLS, Melville, Ms 1041, ff. 99–100, Lord Aberdeen to Melville, 21 Dec. 1806.
104 NAS, Leven and Melville, GD26/13/198/8, Lord Spencer to earl of Leven, 15 Nov. 1806.
105 BL, Dropmore, Add. Mss 58941, ff. 200–1, Lauderdale to Grenville, 4 Nov. [*rectius* Dec.] 1806 alludes to Kinnaird's late re-emergence as a candidate.
106 They were: Elgin, Northesk, Balcarres, Stair, Glasgow, Cathcart, Elphinstone and Somerville.
107 EUL, Laing Mss, Div. II, 461/2, Melville to Lord Napier, 6 Nov. 1806. His candidates were Strathmore, Kellie, Haddington, Elgin, Dalhousie, Balcarres, Aboyne, Aberdeen, Glasgow, Forbes, Cathcart, Somerville and Napier.
108 This insistence can be seen in EUL, Laing Mss, Div. II, 461/2, Spencer to Lord Napier, 27 Oct. 1806 and NAS, Leven and Melville, GD26/13/198/9, Same to Earl of Leven, 17 Nov. 1806.
109 NAS, Buccleuch, GD224/579/2/35, 37, letters of Napier to Buccleuch, 14 and 15 Nov. 1806 discuss the operation of the government restriction. Of Melville's friends, Forbes – on both the government's and Melville's lists – was much embarrassed in adhering to government's strictures: *ibid.*, GD224/579/2/47, Melville to Buccleuch, 23 Nov. 1806.
110 Kirkcudbright's conduct was in this vein: NLS, Melville, Ms 9370, ff. 104–5, Kirkcudbright to Melville, 11 Nov. 1806.
111 EUL, Laing Mss, Div. II, 461/3, Melville to Lord Napier, 16 Nov. 1806.

This letter is also printed in Furber, *Henry Dundas*, pp. 279–80. The problem was also detailed to Buccleuch: NAS, Buccleuch, GD224/579/2/34, Melville to Buccleuch, 13 Nov. [1806].

112 EUL, Laing Mss, Div. II, 461/2, Melville to Lord Napier, 21 Nov. 1806, in which Melville confesses himself 'puzled' as to the possible result.

113 For Sempill, see EUL, Laing Mss, Div. II, 461/3, Melville to Lord Napier, 16 Nov. 1806, and BL, Dropmore, Add. Mss 58941, ff. 202–4, Lauderdale to Grenville, 5 Dec. 1806.

114 There is a brief report on the election in BL, Dropmore, Add. Mss 58941, ff. 200–1, Lauderdale to Grenville, 4 Nov. [*rectius* Dec.] 1806.

115 Aspinall, *Correspondence of George III*, vol. IV, pp. xxxvi–vii.

116 NAS, Melville, GD51/1/106/1, Lady Abercorn to Melville, 12 Nov. 1806.

117 NAS, Melville, GD51/1/195/20, Melville to his son Robert, 7 Jan. 1807; NLS, Melville, Ms 19579, ff. 114–5, same to same, 10 Jan. 1807.

118 NAS, Melville, GD51/1/195/21, Robert S. Dundas to Melville, 24 Jan. 1807.

119 NAS, Melville, GD51/1/112/1, Spencer Perceval to Melville, 19 Jan. 1807.

120 NLS, Melville, Ms 19579, ff. 128–33, Melville to his son Robert, 25 Jan. 1807; NAS, Melville, GD51/1/112/2, Melville to Spencer Perceval, 27 Jan. 1807 (copy).

121 NLS, Melville, Ms 19579, ff. 128–33, Melville to his son Robert, 25 Jan. 1807; NAS, Melville, GD51/1/986, Charles Hope, lord justice-clerk to Lord Cathcart, 27 Sep. 1806 (copy); *ibid.*, GD51/1/987, John Hamilton of Sundrum to Melville, 30 Dec. 1806.

122 BL, Dropmore, Add. Mss 59385, ff. 143–4, Dr John Burns, Dunse, to Grenville, 19 Jul. 1806; *ibid.*, 59263, ff. 62–3, Malcolm Laing to Francis Horner, 27 Feb. [1807].

123 BL, Dropmore, Add. Mss 59396, f. 96, Grenville to Lord Archibald Hamilton, 13 Mar. 1807 (copy). Earl's move north was known in December 1806: BL, Dropmore, Add. Mss 59393, ff. 67–8, William Porthouse to Grenville, 18 Dec. 1806; for Reid's resignation, see *ibid.*, Add. Mss 59395, ff. 47–8, Reid to same, 3 Feb. 1807.

124 NAS, Melville, GD51/5/364/15/47, David Reid to Robert S. Dundas, 16 Feb. 1808; *ibid.*, GD51/5/364/15/22, David Reid to Melville, 23 Mar. 1808; *ibid.*, GD51/5/364/15/24, George Cuninghame, inspector general of customs to Reid, 25–27 Mar. 1808; *ibid.*, GD51/5/364/15/63, David Reid to Melville, 2 Apr. 1808.

125 Caithness and Sutherland were divided into separate sheriffdoms in September. In December, Kinross and Clackmannan, split from Fife and Stirlingshire respectively, were united under one sheriff.

126 There is a full account of the bill and its progress in Phillipson, N.T., *The Scottish Whigs and the Reform of the Court of Session, 1785–1830* (Edinburgh, 1990), pp. 85–110; NLS, Melville, Ms 12, ff. 125–130, 'Notes on the Scotch Judicature Bill' (undated, but ?Mar. 1807).
127 BL, Dropmore, Add. Mss 59259, ff. 4–5, Lord Armadale to Grenville, 26 Mar. 1806.
128 BL, Dropmore, Add. Mss 59260, ff. 149–59, 'Memorandum for explaining a Bill for Better Regulating the Courts of Justice in Scotland &c'; *ibid.*, Add. Mss 59261, ff. 52–3, John Clerk, solicitor general to Grenville, [18 Mar. 1807].
129 BL, Dropmore, Add. Mss 59259, ff. 16–17, Charles Hope to Grenville, 20 May 1806.
130 Phillipson, *Scottish Whigs*, p. 98–9.
131 GCA, Campbell of Succoth papers, TD219/56/1, Grenville to Ilay Campbell, lord president, 25 June 1806.
132 *Ibid.*, TD219/6/381, Lord Eldon to Ilay Campbell, 23 Feb. 1807: 'The bill seems to me to have been drawn [up] by some gentleman of the Bar in Scotland, who knew little of English law, and some gentleman of the Bar in England who, if he knew much of Scotch law, seems to have forgotten that the Court of Session had, like our Court of Chancery, an equitable jurisdiction.'
133 *Ibid.*, TD219/56/1, Robert Dundas, chief baron to Grenville, lord president, 27 Feb. 1807 (copy).
134 BL, Dropmore, Add. Mss 59260, ff. 74–80, Charles Hope to Grenville, 9 Feb. 1807.
135 Hope also pointed to the detrimental effects that Highland clanship would have on a jury system. At least one commentator argued that the Scots people were temperamentally and educationally unsuited to be jurors: NLS, Melville, Ms 12, ff. 81–96, Notes on Judicature Bill, April 1807.
136 In his own notes for a speech about the court of review, Melville noted that 'scandal has been busy in imputing other objects to this measure than have been avowed': NLS, Melville, Ms 12, ff. 147–50, notes (undated, but ?March 1807).
137 BL, Dropmore, Add. Mss 59260, ff. 83–4, Grenville to Charles Hope, 12 Feb. 1807 (copy).
138 BL, Dropmore, Add. Mss 59260, ff. 116–20, Charles Hope to Grenville, 24 Feb. 1807.
139 Phillipson, *Scottish Whigs*, p. 99; BL, Dropmore, Add. Mss 59260, ff. 172–3, 203, correspondence between Robert S. Dundas and Grenville, 5–6 Mar. 1807.
140 EUL, Laing Mss, Div. II, 500, William, Lord Craig to Robert Dundas, chief baron, (postmarked 19 Mar. 1807); NLS, Melville, Ms 12, ff. 101–2, Archibald Colquhoun, Lord Advocate to Henry Erskine, 25 Dec. 1807 (copy); Phillipson, *Scottish Whigs*, pp. 99–100.

141 NLS, Melville, Ms 12, ff. 60–5, Lord Hermand to Melville, 7 Mar. 1807, enclosing states of the faculty votes; BL, Dropmore, Add. Mss 59260, ff. 201–2, Colin Mackenzie to Lord Spencer, 6 Mar. 1807.

142 GCA, Campbell of Succoth papers, TD219/6/19, Ilay Campbell, lord president to Lord Eldon, 2 Mar. 1807; *Ibid.*, TD219/6/309, Thomas Erskine, lord chancellor to Ilay Campbell, lord president, 11 Mar. 1807. The four opposition judges were Lords Armadale, Bannatyne, Cullen and Newton.

143 *Ibid.*, TD219/6/383, Lords Dunsinnan, Woodhouselee, Craig and Meadowbank to Ilay Campbell, lord president, 19 Mar. 1807; *ibid.*, TD219/56/1, Lord Meadowbank to Ilay Campbell, lord president, 19 Mar. [1807].

144 Phillipson, *Scottish Whigs*, p. 110, discusses the split in opinions among the Whigs.

145 Matheson, *Henry Dundas*, p. 379.

146 Notes for a speech by Melville on the court of review, [? Mar. 1807] hint at the unfairness of this English intervention in Scots affairs: NLS, Melville, Ms 12, ff. 147–50.

147 NLS, Melville, Ms 5, ff. 145–6, Huntly to [Robert S. Dundas], Apr. 1807.

148 GCA, Campbell of Succoth papers, TD219/6/469, Melville to Ilay Campbell, lord president, 22 Mar. [1807].

Chapter 7: Moderates and Wild Men

1 Lockhart, J.G., *Peter's Letters to his Kinsfolk* (Edinburgh, 1819), vol. iii, p. 31.

2 Lockhart, *Peter's Letters*, vol. iii, p. 48.

3 From a letter of Leslie as recorded in *Report of the Proceedings and Debate in the General Assembly . . . Respecting the Election of Mr. Leslie* (Edinburgh, 1805), p. 16, National Library of Scotland, BCLD 2692 (8).

4 Lockhart, *Peter's Letters*, vol. iii, 37.

5 Witherspoon, J., *Ecclesiastical Characteristics, or the Arcana of Church Policy; Being an Humble Attempt to Open up the Mysteries of Moderation* (Glasgow, 1753), p. 24.

6 In the 'Select Anti-Patronage Library' series, 1842.

7 Hill, G., *A View of the Constitution of the Church of Scotland*, 2nd edition (Edinburgh, 1817), 17.

8 *Minutes of Evidence Taken Before the Select Committee on Church Patronage, Scotland*, Parliamentary Papers, 1834, vol. v, p. 252.

9 McCosh, J., *The Wheat and the Chaff Gathered into Bundles* (Dundee, 1843), p. 9.

10 Clark, I.D.L., 'From Protest to Reaction: the Moderate Regime in the Church of Scotland, 1752–1805', in Philippson, N.T. and Mitchison, R. (eds), *Scotland in the Age of Improvement* (Edinburgh 1996), pp. 221–2.

11 For a more detailed analysis of the Assemblies of this period on which the argument of much of the preceding three paragraphs is derived, see Maciver, I.F.,

'The Evangelical Party and the Eldership in General Assemblies, 1820–1843', in *Records of the Scottish Church History Society*, vol. xx, part 1 (1978), pp. 1–13.

12 NLS, Melville Papers, MS.1057, fos. 26–29, copy of a letter, Grieve to Spencer, 29 Jan. 1807.

13 [Grieve, H.], *Observations on the Overture Concerning Patronage* (Edinburgh, 1769), p. 15.

14 NLS, Lynedoch Papers, MS.16129, fos. 125–6, Inglis to General Sir Thomas Graham, 23 Oct. 1812.

15 NLS, Melville Papers, MS.352, fo. 119, D. Ritchie to Robert Dundas of Arniston, 29 Oct. 1810.

16 NLS, MS.352, fos. 5–7, Dundas to Melville, 4 July 1808.

17 Glasgow University Archives, MacFarlan Papers, DC9/43, draft letter of MacFarlan to the duke of Montrose, 7 June 1821.

18 NLS, MS.352, fos. 128–9, draft letter of Robert Dundas to Henry, Viscount Melville, 6 Mar. 1811.

19 National Archives of Scotland, Melville Castle Muniments, GD51/5/686, Melville to Buccleuch, 17 Nov. 1817.

20 NAS, GD51/5/684–5, correspondence 12–25 Jan. 1817.

21 Peel Papers, British Library, Add. Ms 40339, fo. 118, Lord Advocate Sir William Rae to Henry Hobhouse, Home Office, 18 Jan. 1824.

22 BL, Add. Ms 40339, fo. 143, Sir Robert Peel to Sir William Rae, 10 July 1824.

23 NLS, Minto Papers, MS.11805, fos. 149–50, draft letter of Minto to Lansdowne, 10 Jan. 1828.

24 For a comment on the late conversion of Inglis to 'liberality', see Cockburn, H., *Memorials of His Time* (Edinburgh, 1874), p. 200.

25 NLS, NLS, MS.11, fos. 158–160, Hope to Melville, 5 June 1824.

26 So acknowledged in the *Church Review*, i (1836), p. 451.

27 See McCosh's calculation (*The Wheat and the Chaff*, table, p. 109) that, in 1843, 59 Moderate ministers had been ordained before 1800, 75 pre-1810 and 100 pre-1820. The comparable statistics he gave for the collectively much more youthful Free Church Evangelicals were 12, 27 and 59 respectively.

28 NLS, MS.14838, fos. 77–78, Cook to Melville, 12 Jan. 1839.

29 MacFarlan's evidence to Select Committee on Patronage, PP, 1834, v, pp. 265–9.

30 NLS, MS.14838, fo. 78.

31 For analysis of party alignments of the contemporary press see generally Cowan, R.M.W., *The Newspaper in Scotland: A Study of its First Expansion, 1815–1860* (Glasgow, 1946).

32 NAS, Dalhousie Muniments, GD45/14/524, Rev. Dr W. Muir to the 10th earl of Dalhousie, 19 June 1840.

33 McCosh, *The Wheat and the Chaff*, p. 9.

34 For Aberdeen see generally Maclaren, A.A., *Religion and Social Class: The Disruption Years in Aberdeen* (London, 1974).
35 *The Witness*, 25 April 1840.
36 *The Witness*, 25 Jan. 1840.
37 NLS, Rutherfurd Papers, MS.9687, fos. 175–176, Lord Cockburn to Rutherfurd, 3 Mar. 1840.
38 *Scotsman*, 26 May and 6 June 1840.
39 Edinburgh University New College Library Extracts from Journal Letters of William to Anne Muir, neé Dirom, 1835–64, MS. MUI 2, 264-5 (22 April 1843).
40 Brown, S.J., *Thomas Chalmers and the Godly Commonwealth* (Oxford,1982), 328–9.
41 NLS, MS.11774, fos. 40–41, 44–45, Russell to 2nd earl of Minto, 30 May, 13 July 1843.
42 Ward, J.T., *Sir James Graham* (London, 1967), pp.165–7, 198–200.
43 NLS, Melville Papers, MS.14838, fos. 81–82, Graham to Melville, 21 April 1842.
44 Ward, *Sir James Graham*, p. 202.
45 Guthrie, D.K. and C.J. (eds), *Autobiography and Memoir of Thomas Guthrie* (London, 1876), vol. ii, pp. 46–8.
46 NLS, Wilson Papers, MS. 14220, fo. 26, Rev. William to Eliza Wilson, 23 Nov. 1842.
47 McCosh, *The Wheat and the Chaff*, p. 12.
48 EUNCL, Muir Journal Letters, MS. MUI 2, 163 (18 Feb. 1840).
49 See generally, *The Wheat and the Chaff*, pp. 17–107.
50 NAS,GD45/14/584, Muir to Dalhousie, 17 June 1843.
51 NAS, GD/45/14/584, Muir to Dalhousie, I July 1843.
52 EUNCL, MS. MUI 2, 274 (5 July 1843).
53 NLS, MS.11808, fo.181, Lord Murray to 2nd earl of Minto, 25 June 1843.
54 EUNCL, MS. MUI 2, 278–9 (10 Aug. 1843).
55 Bute Muniments, Mount Stewart, Isle of Bute, Papers of John 2nd Marquess (High Commissionership and Church Affairs, 1834–46), bundle 25/92, notes of Bute on voting in the Established Church General Assembly, May 1846.
56 Cockburn, *Memorials*, p. 204.

Chapter 8: The Scottish Young Conservatives

1 E.g., Mitchell, J., *Conservatives and the Union* (Edinburgh, 1990), pp. 34–7, 43–5, 58–68; Seawright, D., An *Important Matter of Principle. The Decline of the Scottish Conservative and Unionist Party* (Aldershot, 1999), Chapters 3–5, 9; McCrone, D., *Understanding Scotland. The Sociology of a Stateless Nation* (London, 1992), Chapter 6; Finlay, R.J., 'Unionism and the Dependency Culture: Politics and

State Intervention in Scotland, 1918–1997', in Macdonald, C.M.M. (ed.), *Unionist Scotland, 1800–1997* (Edinburgh, 1998), pp. 100–16; Mitchell, J., 'Contemporary Unionism', *ibid.*, pp. 117–39.

2 Ramsden, J., *The Age of Churchill and Eden, 1940–1957* (London, 1995), Chapter 3, is the most recent study; but see Johnston, J., 'Did Organisation Really Matter? Party Organisation and the Conservative Electoral Recovery, 1945–59', *20th Century British History*, 14 (2003), pp. 391–412.

3 Cf. Ward, J.T., *The First Century. A History of Scottish Tory Organisation, 1882–1982* (Edinburgh, 1982), pp. 37–43. But see Seawright, *Important Matter of Principle,* Chapter 1, for a discussion of Scottish structural reforms introduced in the 1960s.

4 Ramsden, *Churchill & Eden*, pp. 118–9; Layton-Henry, Z., 'The Young Conservatives, 1945–70', *Journal of Contemporary History*, 8 (1973), pp. 143–56; Ramsden, J., *The Winds of Change: Macmillan and Heath, 1957–74* (London, 1996), pp. 93–4.

5 Initially called the Junior Unionists, they became the Young Unionists in the mid-1950s, and in the 1960s changed to the Young Conservatives. For simplicity's sake, the last title has been used throughout.

6 Kilmarnock had been held by Labour only in 1923–4 and 1929–31, and since 1945.

7 Strawhorn, J. and Boyd, W. (eds), *The Third Statistical Account of Scotland: Ayrshire* (Edinburgh, 1951), pp. 264–74, 290–2, 304–6, 390–3, 400–2, 410–11, 478–9, 609, 615–17, 624.

8 Strawhorn, J., *A History of Irvine Royal Burgh and New Town* (Edinburgh, 1985), pp. 216–7; Opher, P., *Cumbernauld and East Kilbride* (Oxford, 1980), pp. 66ff.

9 Levitt, I., 'New Towns, New Scotland, New Ideology', *Scottish Historical Review*, 76 (1997), pp. 222–38.

10 NLS, S[cottish] C[onservative &] U[nionist] A[ssociation] MSS, Acc. 11386/82, unidentified press cutting, 20 Feb. 1961. The speaker was William Van Straubenzee.

11 NLS, C[entral] A[yrshire] C[onservative &] U[nionist] A[ssociation] MSS, Acc. 9079/35, *Central Ayrshire Unionist Newsletter*, 2 (*c.*1958–9).

12 Originally called the Junior Imperialist league, the title varied over its thirty years' existence, but Junior Unionists was the most commonly used term.

13 NLS, SCUA MSS, Acc. 10424/27(v), SCUA W[estern] D[ivisional] C[ouncil], *Annual Report* 1929–30, pp. 17–18; 10424/27/vi, SCUA E[astern] D[ivisional] C[ouncil], *Annual Report*, 1931–2; 10424/27/vii, SCUA EDC *Annual Reports*,1935–6, 1936–7; 0424/27/vi, SCUA EDC *Annual Reports*, 1933–4, 1934–5; 10424 /27/vii, SCUA EDC *Annual Reports*, 1935–6, 1936–7; 10424/27/viii, SCUA EDC *Annual Report*, 1938–9; 10424/27/vi, SCUA WDC, *Annual Report*, 1936–7.

14 NLS, SCUA MSS, Acc. 10424/64, SCUA Cen[tral] Coun[cil] Min[ute]s, 21 Mar. 1945, 7 June 1946; cf. Acc.10424/27, SCUA WDC, *Annual Report*, 1945.
15 NLS, SCUA MSS, Acc. 11368/6, S[cottish] J[unior] U[nionists] Cent[ral] Coun[cil] Min[ute]s, 17 Apr. 1948.
16 NLS, CACUA MSS, Acc. 9079/2, Ex[ecutive] Comm[ittee] Min[utes], 7 Dec. 1950, 1 Feb. 1951.
17 *Ibid.*, 1 Feb. 1951.
18 *Ibid.*, 7 May, 29 Oct 1953, cf. 10 Sep. 1953.
19 NLS, CACUA MSS, Acc. 9079/3, Ex Comm Mins, 3 Nov. 1955.
20 *Ibid.*, Ex Comm Mins, 2 Dec. 1954, 3 Nov. 1955, 4 Oct. 1956; 9079/17, Kilwinning J[unior] U[nionists] Min[utes], 29 Mar. 1956.
21 *Ibid.*, 19 Feb. 1959, 26 May 1960, 2 June 1961.
22 *Ibid.*, 24 Feb. 1965; 9079/12, 10 Sep. 1965.
23 *Ibid.*, 14 Nov. 1968, 22 Sep. 1970; Acc. 9079/12, C[entral] A[yrshire] Y[oung] C[onservatives] Coun[cil] Min[ute]s, 9 Sep. 1970, 16 Nov. 1971, 3 Nov. 1972.
24 NLS, CACUA MSS, Acc. 9079/4, Ex Comm Mins, 26 Feb., 8 Sep. 1976; 9079/12, CAYC Coun Mins, 28 Sep. 1976.
25 NLS, CACUA MSS, Acc. 9079/12, Eglinton Y[oung] C[onservatives] Min[ute]s, 6 Oct. 1976; 9079/12, Constituency Agent to Mrs D.C. Wells, 29 Nov. 1977.
26 NLS, CACUA MSS, Acc. 9079/4, Ex Comm Mins, 7 Nov. 1978, 25 June, 25 Sep., 11 Dec.1979.
27 Based on percentages in 1951 of 16–34-year-olds and those over 35 in the total Scottish population – namely, 28 per cent and 47 per cent respectively.
28 NLS, CACUA MSS, Acc. 9079/17, Kilwinning JU Mins, 31 Mar. 1955; 9079/14, Eglinton YC draft Annual Report, 1975; 9079/13, Eglinton YC Mins, 4 Sep. 1975.
29 NLS, SCUA MSS, Acc. 10424/27/ix, SCUA WDC, *Annual Reports*, 1951, 1953, 1961; *Scotsman*, 25 Sep. 1960.
30 CACUA MSS, Acc. 9079/12, CA YC Coun Mins, 31 Oct. 1976.
31 NLS, SCUA MSS, Acc. 11386/6, SJU Cen Coun Mins, 16 Sep. 1950, gives 5,000 members in the eastern division, suggesting 11,000 overall; *Scotsman*, 25 Sep. 1960; *Daily Record*, 21 Mar. 1962.
32 NLS, CACUA MSS, Acc. 9079/33, unidentified press cutting, 1 Dec. 1956.
33 NLS, SCUA MSS, Acc. 10424/27(v), SCUA WDC, *Annual Reports*, 1928–9, 1929–30; Acc. 11368/48, S[cottish] J[unior] U[nionists] W[estern] A[rea] Comm[ittee] Min[utes], 13 Sep. 1950.
34 NLS, SCUA MSS, Acc. 11368/6, SJU Cen Coun Mins, 31 Mar. 1953, 12 Jan. 1957. Acc. 11368/4, SCUA Cen Coun Mins, 20 Jul. 1961, claims 3,200 recruits, but figures in the *Daily Record*, 21 Mar. 1962, indicate a membership total only 1,500 above 6,500 for late 1960, as reported in the *Scotsman*, 25 Sep. 1960.

35 NLS, SCUA MSS, Acc. 11368/4, SCUA Cen Coun Mins, , 12 June 1954; Acc. 11368/19, Glas[gow] Y[oung] C[onservatives] Reg[ional] Comm[ittee] Min[ute]s, 15 Jan.1968.
36 NLS, SCUA MSS, Acc. 11368/48, SJU WA Comm Mins, 14 Oct. 1953.
37 NLS, SCUA MSS, Acc. 11368/7(i), SYU Cen Coun Mins, 5 Oct. 1963; 11368/19, Glas Reg YC Comm Mins, 17 Oct. 1966; 11368/17, SW Reg YC Comm Mins, 14 Sep. 1967.
38 NLS, SCUA MSS, Acc. 10424/97, SCUA WDC O[rganising] S[ecretaries] J[oint] M[eeting] Min[ute]s, 30 Jan. 1952, 25 Mar. 1954.
39 NLS, SCUA MSS, Acc. 11368/39, SCUA WDC Mins, 30 Apr. 1957; Acc. 10424/98, SCUA WDC OSJM Mins, 31 Jan. 1963; Acc. 11368/7(i), SYU Cen Coun Mins, 3 Nov. 1964.
40 NLS, CACUA MSS, Acc. 9079/10, Kilwinning JU Mins, 5 Dec. 1949, 20 Sep. 1951.
41 NLS, CACUA MSS, Acc. 9079/17, Kilwinning YU Mins, 26 Mar. 1959, 7 Apr. 1960; 9079/4, Exec Comm Mins, 22 Sep. 1970; 9079/14, Remarks on one of the two 1974 elections.
42 NLS, CACUA MSS, Acc. 9079/10, Kilwinning JU Mins, 3 Jan. 1950, 16 Apr., 4 Sep. 1953; 9079/20, Kilwinning JU, 'Survey of 1953–4'.
43 NLS, CACUA MSS, Acc. 9079/10, Kilwinning JU Mins, 20 Sep. 1951.
44 E.g., *ibid.*, 27 Mar. 1952; NLS, SCUA MSS, Acc. 11368/85, Eglinton YC syllabus, 1966–67.
45 NLS, CACUA MSS, Acc. 9079/35, *Central Ayrshire Newsletter*, Autumn 1969.
46 NLS, CACUA MSS, Acc. 9079/23 & 30 both contain copies of undated letters to this effect.
47 *Ibid.*, 13 Dec. 1973.
48 NLS, CACUA MSS, Acc. 9079/13, Eglinton YC Mins, 5 Apr. 1973.
49 NLS, CACUA MSS, Acc. 9079/10, Kilwinning JU Mins, 5 Nov. 1949, 24 Aug. 1950; cf., e.g., 9079/20, Kilwinning JU Mins, 16 Apr. [1953].
50 NLS, SCUA MSS, Acc. 11368/83, unidentified press cutting, 26 May 1961.
51 NLS, SCUA MSS, Acc. 11386/85 for 1966–7 ; CACUA MSS, Acc. 9079/13, Eglinton YC Mins, 7 June 1972.
52 NLS, CACUA MSS, Acc. 9079/12, CA YC Coun Mins, 9 Sep. 1970.
53 *Ibid.*, 31 Oct. 1972, 6 Oct. 1976.
54 NLS, SCUA MSS, Acc. 11386/6, SJU Cen Coun Mins, 11 Mar. 1950; 10424/27/ix, SCUA WDC *Annual Report*, 1959; 10424/97, WDC JOSM Mins, 28 May 1959.
55 NLS, SCUA MSS, Acc. 11368/48, SJU WA Comm Mins, 11 Apr. 1951 and 1955; Acc.10424/98, SCUA WDC JOSM Mins, 28 Mar. 1963; Acc. 11368/7(i), SYC Cen Coun Mins, 3 June 1967; 11368/37, SW Reg YC Comm Mins, 1 Feb. 1968.

56 NLS, SCUA MSS, Acc. 11368/6, SJU Cen Coun Mins, 10 Sep. 1955.
57 NLS, SCUA MSS, Acc. 11368/37, S[outh] W[est] Y[oung] C[onservatives] Reg[ional] Comm[ittee] Min[ute]s, 11 May, 6 Nov. 1965, 28 Aug. 1968.
58 NLS, SCUA MSS, Acc. 11368/19, Glas YC Reg Ex Mins, 8 Feb., 18 Mar. 1968.
59 NLS, SCUA MSS, Acc. 11368/6, SYU Cen Coun Mins, 23 Apr. 1949, 29 Apr. 1958; 11368/7(i), 3 June 1967, 21 Apr. 1964.
60 NLS, SCUA MSS, Acc. 11368/6, SJU Cen Coun Mins, 23 Apr. 1949; 11368/48, SJU WAComm, *Annual Report*, 1954, SJU WA Comm Mins, 14 Oct. 1953; 11368/6, SJU Cen Coun Mins, 11 Mar. 1950; 11368/48, S[cottish] Y[oung] U[nionists] W[estern] A[rea] Comm[ittee] Min[utes], 13 Feb. 1957.
61 NLS, SCUA MSS, Acc. 11368/19, Glas YC Reg Ex Mins, 12 Dec. 1966, 26 Feb. 1968.
62 E.g., NLS, SCUA MSS, Acc. 10424/97 & 98, SCUA WDC OSJM Mins, 28 Jan. 1954; 31 Jan. 1963, 26 Nov. 1964.
63 NLS, CACUA MSS, Acc. 9079/11, Ayrshire Y[oung] U[nionists] Fed[eration] Comm[ittee] Min[utes], 31 Jan. 1961, 23 Jan. 1962; SCUA MSS, Acc. 11368/37, SW Reg YC Comm Mins, 6 Apr., 11 May, 6 Nov. 1965, 9 Feb. 1967, and cf. 28 Aug. 1968.
64 NLS, SCUA MSS, Acc. 10424/97, SCUA WDC JOSM Mins, 28 Jan. 1960; Acc. 11368/37, SW Reg YC Comm Mins, 23 Nov. 1967.
65 NLS, SCUA MSS, Acc. 10424/98, SCUA WDC OSJM Mins, 29 Oct. 1964.
66 NLS, SCUA MSS, Acc. 10424/27/ix, SCUA WDC, *Annual Report*, 1950; Acc. 11368/6, SYU Cen Coun Mins, 18 May, 7 Sep. 1957; Acc. 10424/27/ix, SCUA WDC *Annual Report* 1959; 11368/7(i), SYC Cen Coun Mins, 18 Dec. 1965.
67 NLS, SCUA MSS, Acc. 11368/48, SJU WA Comm Mins, 10 Nov. 1954.
68 NLS, SCUA MSS, Acc. 10424/98, SCUA WDC JOSM Mins, 28 Mar. 1963.
69 NLS, SCUA MSS, Acc 11368/7(i), SYU Cen Coun Mins, 12 Jan. 1965.
70 NLS, SCUA MSS, Acc. 11368/85.
71 NLS, SCUA MSS, Acc. 11368/37, SW Reg Coun Mins, 6 Nov. 1965, 27 Aug. 1966.
72 NLS, SCUA MSS, Acc. 11368/7(i), SYU Cen Coun Mins, 21 Jan. 1964.
73 NLS, CACUA MSS, Acc. 9079/11, Ayrshire YU Fed Comm Mins, 10 Dec. 1963.
74 NLS, SCUA MSS, Acc. 11368/9, Glas Reg YC Comm Mins, 30 Mar. 1965.
75 NLS, SCUA MSS, Acc. 11368/37, SW Reg YC Comm Mins, 25 May 1967.
76 NLS, SCUA MSS, Acc. 10424/97, SCUA WDC JOSM Mins, 28 Jan. 1954.
77 NLS, SCUA MSS, Acc. 10424/98, SCUA WDC JOSM Mins, 31 Jan. 1963.

78 NLS, CACUA MSS, Acc. 9079/3, Ex Comm Mins, 4 Oct. 1956.
79 NLS, SCUA MSS, Acc. 10424/97, WDC OSJM Mins, 25 Mar. 1954
80 This aspect is fully discussed in Hutchison, I.G.C., 'The Decline of the Conservative Party in Scotland in the Second Half of the 20th Century: A Local Case Study', forthcoming.
81 NLS, SCUA MSS, Acc. 11368/39, SCUA WDC Mins, 24 June 1960.
82 Ramsden, *Churchill & Eden*, pp. 113–5, 128–31, 134–7; *Winds of Change*, pp. 75–6.
83 Cf. Smyth, J.J., 'Resisting Labour: Unionists, Liberals and Moderates in Glasgow between the Wars', *Historical Journal*, 46 (2003), pp. 375–401; Ramsden, *Winds of Change*, p. 268.
84 Ramsden, *Winds of Change*, pp. 405–6; Ward, *First Century*, p. 41.
85 NLS, SCUA MSS, Acc. 11368/48, SJU WA Comm., 'Convenor's Notes for Speech', stamped 1955.
86 NLS, CACUA MSS, Acc. 9079/3, Ex Comm Mins, 29 Nov. 1956.
87 NLS, CACUA MSS, Acc. 9079/15, Kilwinning JU Mins, 30 Sep. [1954].
88 NLS, CACUA MSS, Acc. 9079/1, CACUA AGMs in 1961, 1975–6.
89 NLS, CACUA MSS, Acc. 9079/12, CA YC Coun Mins, 28 Sep. 1976.
90 NLS, SCUA MSS, Acc. 10424/64, SCUA Cen Coun Mins, 7 June 1946.
91 NLS, SCUA MSS, Acc 11368/48, SJU WA Comm., 'Convenor's Notes for Speech', stamped '1955'.
92 NLS, SCUA MSS, Acc. 10424/97, SCUA WDC OSJM Mins., 29 Nov. 1956; 11368/6, SJU Cen Coun, 21 June 1958; 11368/39; SCUA WDC Mins, 29 Mar. 1960; Acc. 10424/98, SCUA WDC JOSM Mins, 31 Jan. 1963.
93 NLS, CACUA MSS, Acc. 9079/2, Ex Comm Mins, 25 Sep. 1952.
94 NLS, CACUA MSS, Acc. 9079/13, Eglinton YC Comm Mins, 7 Oct. 1970, 29 Feb.1972.
95 NLS, CACUA MSS, Acc. 9079/12, C[entral] A[yrshire] Y[oung] C[onservatives] Ex[ecutive] Comm[ittee] Min[ute]s, 9 Sep. 1970.
96 NLS, CACUA MSS, Acc. 9079/5, Women's Section Minutes, 19 Mar. 1951.
97 NLS, SCUA MSS, Acc. 10424/98, SCUA WDC OSJM Mins., 29 Oct. 1964, 28 Mar. 1963; Acc. 11368/7(i), SYC Cen Comm Mins, 12 Jan. 1965.
98 NLS, SCUA MSS, Acc. 11368/6, SYU Cen Coun Mins, 19 May 1956. After just over two years, these events were dropped because of lack of support: *ibid.*, 12 Jan. 1957.
99 NLS, SCUA MSS, Acc. 11368/6, SJU Cen Coun Mins, 14 Dec. 1959.
100 NLS, SCUA MSS, Acc. 11368/7(1), S[cottish] Y[oung] C[onservatives] Cen[tral] Coun[cil] Min[ute]s, 3 June 1967; 11368/37, 23 Nov., 9 Dec. 1967.
101 NLS, SCUA MSS, Acc. 11368/19, Glas YC Reg Ex Comm Mins, 7 Nov. 1966.

Chapter 9: Thatcherism, Civil Society and Home Rule

1 Quoted in the *Scotsman*, 14 May 1999.

2 Hutchison, I.G.C., *Scottish Politics in the Twentieth Century* (Basingstoke, 2001), p. xii. For those who suggest that Scottish home rule was a dominant feature of Scottish political life see Reid, J.M., *Scotland's Past and Present* (Oxford, 1959); Paton, H.J., *The Claim of Scotland* (London, 1968) and Marr, A., *The Battle for Scotland* (London, 1992).

3 Brady, C. (ed.), *Interpreting Irish History: The Debate on Historical Revisionism* (Dublin, 1994).

4 See Peden, G.C., 'The Managed Economy: Scotland 1919–2000' in Devine, T.M., Lee, C. and Peden, George C. (eds), *The Transformation of Scotland: The Economy Since 1700* (Edinburgh, 2005).

5 McCrone, David, *Understanding Scotland: The Sociology of a Nation*, 2nd edn (London, 1991).

6 Midgley, Mary, *Myths We Live By* (London, 2003).

7 In particular, the account of Canon Kenyon Wright, *The People Say Yes* (Glasgow, 1997).

8 To varying degrees, the following have tended to use civil society as a means of explaining anti-Conservatism in late twentieth century Scotland: McCrone, *Understanding Scotland*; Paterson, L., *The Autonomy of Modern Scotland* (Edinburgh, 1997); Brown, Alice, McCrone, David and Paterson, Lindsay, *Politics and Society in Scotland*, 2nd edn (London, 1988); while it does not figure much in the account of Denver, David, Mitchell, James, Pattie, Charles and Bochel, Hugh, *Scotland Decides: The Devolution Issue and the Scottish Referendum* (London, 2000).

9 Edwards, Owen Dudley, et al., *Claim of Right for Scotland* (Edinburgh, 1989).

10 Although the *Scotsman* backed a 'yes-yes' vote in the referendum, see the misgivings of the editor in chief, Andrew Neil, on 11 Sep. 1997.

11 A good example of the way in which a Whig interpretation of the movement can be constructed, albeit not the author's intention, is Paterson, Lindsay, *A Diverse Assembly: The Debate on a Scottish Parliament* (Edinburgh, 1989).

12 Brown, Gordon, 'Introduction' in Brown, Gordon and Cook, Robin (eds), *Scotland: The Real Divide. Poverty and Deprivation in Scotland* (Edinburgh, 1983), p. 10.

13 McLevy, Harry, 'Scotland's Industrial Armies', *Radical Scotland* (Dec./Jan. 1985), 11.

14 McIlvanney, William, 'Stands Scotland Where it Did?', *Radical Scotland* (Dec./Jan. 1988), p. 20.

15 *Manpower Services Commission Report* (1986).

16 See the conclusions of Tom Devine in the new edition of *Scottish Nation* (London, 2006).

17 McCrone, *Understanding Scotland.*
18 *Radical Scotland*, 29 (Oct./Nov. 1987), p.6.
19 Lee, Clive, *Scotland and the United Kingdom: the Economy and the Union in the Twentieth Century* (Manchester, 1995), 61.
20 Gray, Doreen, *Marxism Today* (July 1987).
21 Lindsay, Isobel in Devine, T.M. (ed.), *Scottish Emigration and Scottish Society* (Edinburgh, 1992).
22 Scottish Executive, *Scottish Economic Statistics*, 'Economic Activity by Gender, Scotland 1985–2000' (HMSO Edinburgh, 2001) p. 102.
23 *Ibid.*, 'Changes in Housing Tenure, Scotland 1979–1998', p. 133.
24 *Ibid.*, 'New Dwellings Completed by Tenure, Scotland 1949–1999', p. 129.
25 *Ibid.*, 'Changes in Housing Tenure', p. 133.
26 *Ibid.*, 'New Dwellings Completed by Tenure', p. 129.
27 *Ibid.*, 'Changes in Housing Tenure', p. 133.
28 McCrone, D., 'Opinion Polls in Scotland: June 1990–June 1991' in Paterson, Lindsay and McCrone, David (eds), *The Scottish Government Yearbook 1992* (Edinburgh, 1992), pp. 224–36.
29 Midwinter, Arthur, *The Politics of Local Spending* (Edinburgh, 1984), 95–9.
30 Midwinter, Arthur, Keating, Michael and Mitchell, James, *Politics and Public Policy in Scotland* (Basingstoke, 1991), p. 174.
31 *Scottish Economic Statistics*, 'Employment Rates, Scotland and the UK, 1960–2000', p. 97.
32 *Ibid.*, 'Average Earnings of Employees: Scotland and Great Britain', p. 99.
33 Whiteley, P., Seyd, P. and Richardson, J., *True Blues: The Politics of Conservative Party Membership* (Oxford, 1994).
34 Chris Harvie made this point when doing the *Scotland 2000* programme for the BBC in 1987, when a System Three poll found that 38 per cent of respondents stated that friends and family were their most trusted guides as to political decision making, *Radical Scotland*, 26 (April/May 1987) p. 6.
35 Fairley, John, 'Action for Jobs', *Radical Scotland*, 26 (April/May 1987), pp. 10–13.
36 The opinion poll surveys in the *Scottish Government Yearbook conducted by Mori* tended to concentrate on constitutional issues, but an opinion poll conducted by System Three for the BBC *Scotland 2000* series in 1987 showed that 58 per cent of those polled placed unemployment at the top of the agenda.
37 Grimes, Alister, 'Pensioners in Poverty' in Brown and Cook (eds), *Scotland: The Real Divide*, p. 136–45.
38 Spending on health and social work increased in the Scottish Office budget from 27 per cent of the total to 33 per cent of the total between 1980 and 1988. Midwinter, Keating and Mitchell, *Politics and Public Policy*, p. 113.
39 Breitenbach, Esther, 'The Impact of Thatcherism on Women in Scotland',

in Brown, Alice and McCrone, David (eds), *The Scottish Government Yearbook 1989* (Edinburgh, 1989), p. 182.

40 Information taken from General Register Office statistics, available online at http://www.scotland.gov.uk/Publications/2004/03/19144/35014.

41 Yelloly, Margaret, 'Social Work in Scotland: Problems and Prospects' in Brown and McCrone (eds.), *Scottish Government Yearbook 1989*, pp. 266–84.

42 Finlay, Richard, *Modern Scotland, 1914–2000* (London, 2004), p. 349.

43 Payne, Peter, 'The Economy' in Devine, T.M. and Finlay, R.J. (eds), *Scotland in the Twentieth Century* (Edinburgh, 1996), pp. 13–46.

44 Smail, Robin, *STUC Review*, 42 (1989).

45 *Radical Scotland*, 39 (June/July 1989), p. 16.

46 Bernard Ponsonby reviewing Gordon Brown's 'Where There is Greed', *Radical Scotland*, 39 (June/July 1989), p. 38.

47 *Radical Scotland*, 40 (Aug./Sep. 1989), pp. 16–18.

48 Ross, Jim, 'Grasping the Doomsday Nettle – Methodically', *Radical Scotland*, 30 (Dec./Jan 1988), p. 7.

49 Kellas, James, 'The Scottish Constitutional Convention', in Paterson and McCrone (eds), *The Scottish Government Yearbook 1992*, pp. 50–9.

50 See *Radical Scotland*, 38 (April/May 1989), pp. 10–11; and 39 (June/July 1989), pp. 24–5.

51 Denver, et al., *Scotland Decides*, p. 169.

52 *Ibid.*, p. 204.

Index

Note: SCJ is an abbreviation for Scottish College of Justice, whose members took judicial titles when they became members of the Court of Session.